LOVE
OUT LOUD

LOVE OUT LOUD

365 DEVOTIONS FOR LOVING GOD, LOVING YOURSELF, AND LOVING OTHERS

JOYCE MEYER

Faith
Words

NEW YORK   BOSTON   NASHVILLE

Unless otherwise indicated, Scriptures are taken from the Amplified® Bible. Copyright © 1954, 1962, 1965, 1987 by The Lockman Foundation. Used by permission.
Scriptures noted KJV are taken from the King James Version of the Bible.
Scriptures noted The Message are taken from The Message. Copyright © 1993, 1994, 1995, 1996, 2000, 2001, 2002. Used by permission of NavPress Publishing Group.
Scriptures noted NIV are taken from the HOLY BIBLE: NEW INTERNATIONAL VERSION®. Copyright © 1973, 1978, 1984 by International Bible Society. Used by permission of Zondervan Publishing House. All rights reserved.
Scriptures noted NKJV are taken from the NEW KING JAMES VERSION. Copyright © 1979, 1980, 1982, Thomas Nelson, Inc., Publishers.

FaithWords
Hachette Book Group
237 Park Avenue
New York, NY 10017

www.faithwords.com

Printed in the United States of America

First Edition: November 2011
10 9 8 7 6 5 4 3 2 1

FaithWords is a division of Hachette Book Group, Inc.
The FaithWords name and logo are trademarks of Hachette Book Group, Inc.

The publisher is not responsible for websites (or their content) that are not owned by the publisher.

Library of Congress Cataloging-in-Publication Data

Meyer, Joyce.
    Love out loud : 365 devotions for loving god, loving yourself, and loving others / Joyce Meyer. — 1st ed.
    p. cm.
    Includes bibliographical references and index.
    ISBN 978-0-446-53847-3 (regular edition : alk. paper) — ISBN 978-1-4555-0736-8 (large print edition : alk. paper) 1. Love—Religious aspects—Christianity—Prayers and devotions. 2. Devotional calendars. I. Title.
    BV4639.M424 2011
    241'.677—dc23
                                                                    2011029881

Introduction

In *Love Out Loud,* I am asking you to concentrate for one whole year on what is most important to God, and it is love! Loving God, loving yourself, and loving others. I am urging you to make this the main focus of your life and do it loud; be bold about it, pursue it, and seek it eagerly. Learn everything you can about what genuine love is. God is love, and we can never know true love apart from Him. He wants to pour His love into you until you are completely whole and secure in Him.

Whether our pain is spiritual, emotional, mental, or physical, God's unconditional love is the healing ointment we need. Everyone in the world is searching for unconditional love and acceptance. Sadly, many spend their entire lives looking in all the wrong places, and their pain multiplies instead of diminishes.

God so loved the world that He gave His only begotten Son, so that whoever believes in Him might not perish, but have everlasting life (see John 3:16). Believing in Jesus as your Savior is the beginning of love received, and without it we can never value and properly love ourselves. If we can believe that God who is perfect loves us, then we can love ourselves, and if we can do that, then we can love others.

God's desire has always been that we freely receive from Him and freely give out to others. We can never buy the love of God with our own good works or perfection, but we can look to Jesus, the Perfect One, who took our sins upon Himself and died so that we might be free. Love is the greatest thing in the world and must be our focus in life.

Most of us have wondered at some time, "How do I love God? What can I do to show love for Him?" Jesus told Peter three times that if he loved Him, he should help other people (see John 21:15–17). God's plan is so simple that we often miss it as we look for something more complex as the answer to life's pain and problems. He said to receive and give love, to abide (live, dwell, and remain) in it, and make the pursuit of it your lifetime goal. As we do this God is pleased, we have more joy than we can imagine, and we are a success because we live to help others.

I tried selfishness and self-centeredness for many years, and I can assure you that it doesn't work. It will never give the satisfaction in life that you seek. Deposit yourself with God, trust Him to meet all your needs, and get busy loving out loud. The spiritual law that rules God's Kingdom is that *"we reap what we sow."* Give and it shall be given unto you, good measure, pressed down, shaken together and running over will it be given back to you (Luke 6:38 paraphrased). After wasting much of my life pursuing what did not really matter, I learned to pursue what matters most, and it is love!

Now faith, hope, and love abide, but the greatest of these is love!
1 CORINTHIANS 13:13 ESV

LOVE
OUT LOUD

Love Perfected

No man has at any time (yet) seen God. But if we love one another,
God abides (lives and remains) in us and His love (that love which
is essentially His) is brought to completion (to its full maturity, runs
its full course, is perfected) in us!   1 JOHN 4:12

Do you know that love is intended to flow to us and then through us?
It begins with God's love for us and is brought to completion when we
learn to love one another. Being able to love is a process that I believe
God has put in place, and it involves four steps. First, God gives His
love to you. Next, you accept and receive that love. Third, you love
God in return. And fourth, you allow God's love to flow through you to
other people. Without all four steps, love is incomplete, so let's look at
each one of them a bit more closely.

The first step is God's love for you. It all starts with Him, and it
begins with the fact that He loves you unconditionally.

The second step is for you to respond to God's love. The only proper
response is to receive God's love, knowing it's something He freely
gives, not something you can earn or otherwise secure for yourself. His
love is in you, it is yours, and you will learn that loving yourself properly is God's will.

The third step is to give your love to God. This includes worshipping Him with your life, spending time in His presence, studying and
honoring His Word, praying, praising Him, and expressing gratitude
to Him. Of course, the ultimate way we show God that we love Him,
according to His Word, is to obey Him (see John 14:15).

The fourth step in love being perfected in you is to let it flow through
your life to the people around you. Throughout this book, there are
lots of ideas about ways you can do that. Plus, the spirit of God will
lead you and prompt you to do things that will demonstrate love to the
people around you.

Love God Today: Receive God's unconditional love, love yourself, love God, and let love flow through you to other people.

Seek God's Presence

I drove away from my mind everything capable of spoiling the sense of the presence of God...I just make it my business to persevere in His holy presence.   BROTHER LAWRENCE

One of the most important lessons we can learn is to seek God's face (who He is) and not just His hand (what He can do for us). Learning this is vital to our strength as believers and to our love walk with God.

This was a major lesson for me. I had to learn to enjoy God's presence, not focus on what He was doing or not doing for me. Making this transition took a while. But what an awesome difference it made in my spiritual life! Previously, I had always felt that something was missing in my walk with the Lord. I found it all in His presence, not in His "presents."

The Lord was doing a lot for me, yet I was still dissatisfied. God had established a relationship with me by doing things for me. Now it was time to take a step of maturity by seeking to do His will, not just seeking Him for what He could do for me. I was enjoying God's provision, but I had not learned simply to enjoy His presence.

I went through a time of testing in which I had to seek the Lord simply for Himself and not for anything He might give me. He once challenged me not to ask Him for one earthly thing again until He told me I could do so. Since that time my prayer life has been different. I do ask God for things I desire, but I spend much more time praising and thanking Him, loving and adoring Him, sitting in His presence and enjoying Him, than I ever do making personal requests. He knows the desires of our hearts, and as we delight ourselves in Him, He will give them to us, just as He promised in His Word.

Love God Today: "Lord, I will seek Your presence above everything else."

What God Wants

He has shown you, O man, what is good; and what does the Lord
require of you but to do justly, to love mercy, and to walk humbly
with your God?   MICAH 6:8 NKJV

Do you know what God really wants from you? We might think God requires us to do a lot of church work, read the Bible through in a year, or do a certain number of good deeds. Although all these things have their place, we may do them and still miss what God considers to be important.

God's requirements have a lot to do with how we treat people. According to today's Scripture, we are to do what is just, love mercy and kindness, and walk humbly with our God.

We should treat people justly and work to see that justice is done in their lives. Many people have been terribly mistreated and abused, and we have the opportunity to help them enjoy what Jesus died for them to have. We can help restore them to the knowledge of God and His love for them, as well as bring practical help.

God also requires us to love mercy. People do not need to be pressured to perform perfectly; they need to be loved and accepted. God is merciful and kind toward us, and He expects us to give to others what we have received from Him.

Finally, God wants humility. We should never view ourselves as better than other people.

Strive to give God what He truly requires, which is to do what is just, to love mercy and kindness, and to walk humbly with Him.

———————————

Love God Today: "Lord, help me to love mercy, to do justly,
and to walk humbly with You."

Come As You Are

It is through Him that we have received grace...And this includes you, called of Jesus Christ and invited [as you are] to belong to Him.

ROMANS 1:5, 6

Not long ago I read today's Scripture and thought about how marvelous it is and what a message of acceptance it brings. It made me think of the fact that when we are invited to a party, one of the first questions we ask is, "How should I dress?" Most of us like it best when we feel we can go "as we are." We like it when we can relax and be ourselves.

God will work in you by His Holy Spirit and help you become all you need to be, but you can come to Him just as you are. You don't have to stand far off and only hear the music of the party; you are invited to attend.

You have joy and peace today. You are redeemed, accepted, and made right with God because of the way He sees you in Christ. You are already loved and accepted by Him. Not "you will be someday."

You are destined to be molded into the image of Christ, and nothing can stop that from happening if you will simply cooperate with the Holy Spirit and spend time with God. You don't have to clean up your act first. You can come as you are, and God will make you what you ought to be.

There are stories all over the world of people who came to know God when they were in all kinds of bondage. Some were alcoholics; some were prostitutes; some couldn't keep their anger under control; and some were deeply wounded because of the pain of their past. These people are now completely transformed because they were willing to go to God as they were.

When people will come as they are, God will work miracles.

———————

Love Yourself Today: You don't have to wait for *anything*; you can go to God just as you are.

Turn Your Possibilities into "Positivelies"

For I know the thoughts and plans that I have for you, says the Lord,
thoughts and plans for welfare and peace and not for evil, to give you
hope in your final outcome.   JEREMIAH 29:11

According to our verse for today, God has a plan for each of us, a plan that should give us great hope for our futures. The Bible says it's a good plan that will bring us "welfare and peace," not a plan for evil. God's good plan is His destiny for our lives. It's what He wants for us; it reflects His heart and desires for us. However, His plan for us is a possibility, not a "positively."

God's wonderful plan for us cannot and will not come to pass if we refuse to cooperate with Him. He will not force "welfare and peace" on us; He wants us to find them as we choose to follow Him. We have to participate in God's plan for it to come true. God is not likely to do anything in our lives without our cooperation.

We need to cooperate with God. Every day we ought to grow. Every day we ought to discover something. Every day we ought to be a bit further along than we were the day before. We should be "lifetime learners."

We must understand that no one else can develop our potential for us. We must each discover our own God-given gifts and talents, and then put ourselves to the task of developing those gifts and abilities to their fullest extent.

God has a plan for each of us. It is a good plan, an uncommon plan, a great plan; it is not an average, mediocre plan. I encourage you to seek that plan and cooperate with God so that it will be wonderfully fulfilled in your life.

———————

Love Yourself Today: "Lord, I commit today to cooperate with the good plans You have for my life."

Give the Gift of Freedom

Then you recently turned and did what was right in My
sight—every man proclaiming liberty to his neighbor; and you made
a covenant before Me in the house which is called by My name.

JEREMIAH 34:15 NKJV

Have you ever experienced the wonderful feeling of being set free from something? Maybe someone has paid a debt for you or a boss has said, "Take the day off with pay." Whether it happens on a large scale or a small scale, being set free from an obligation or a burden is a great feeling.

In today's Scripture, the Bible says we can "proclaim liberty" to others. I encourage you to give the gift of freedom to others. People will love you for it, and it is a way you can show love to them. Obviously, this does not mean letting others do whatever they want to do. But it does mean that you stop trying to control people and situations.

For years I tried desperately to control and remold my husband and children, until I finally realized that my efforts were acts of selfishness, not love. I told myself that I simply wanted God's best for them; however, I had decided what His best was and was trying to force it on them.

When we give God complete control, our joy increases and we can enter His rest.

Make sure the atmosphere around you is free and relaxed. When people make mistakes, do not make them feel rejected, but go the extra mile to make them feel forgiven, accepted—and free. Treat others the way you want to be treated.

———————

Love Others Today: Relax. Loosen up a bit. Proclaim liberty, and give everyone around you the gift of freedom.

Be Friendly

Practice hospitality to one another (those of the household of faith).
[Be hospitable, be a lover of strangers, with brotherly affection for
the unknown guests, the foreigners, the poor, and all others who
come your way who are of Christ's body.] . . .   1 PETER 4:9

I encourage you to show love for others by simply being friendly. Some people go through life with a lot on their minds—and they can appear to be rather unfriendly, intense, or even rude. I know; I'm one of those people, and maybe you are, too. You aren't unfriendly; you're simply focused on other things and not always mindful to smile and greet people when you see them.

Relationships—casual ones, intimate ones, and all the ones in between—are a large part of life. In fact, the Bible is a book about relationships: our relationships with God, with ourselves, and with others. As I've studied the Bible, one of the lessons I've learned is to take the time to smile at people, ask how they are, and find something friendly to say to them.

If we're too busy to be friendly, then we are out of balance and headed for relational disaster. But being appropriately warm and open toward others can put people at ease and is often the first step toward a good relationship.

It's easy to wonder how we will feel if we smile at people and they don't smile back; we don't want to be rejected or ignored. Most of us spend more time in life trying to avoid rejection than we do trying to develop good, healthy relationships. When this happens, we are missing the opportunity to touch people with the love of God through a smile or friendly word. When we give our smiles or a happy hello, we can make someone else smile, and that is one of the best gifts we can give.

***

Love Others Today: "Lord, please help me be kind and friendly to everyone I meet as a way of showing Your love to them."

A Sermon Walking

Then Jesus answered and said to them, "Most assuredly, I say to you, the Son can do nothing of Himself, but what He sees the Father do; for whatever He does, the Son also does in like manner."

JOHN 5:19 NKJV

I once read a story in a church newsletter that I want to share with you.

In 1949, *Time* magazine called him "one of the most extraordinary men of modern times." He won the Nobel Peace Prize. One afternoon, reporters and city officials gathered at a Chicago railroad station to greet him. As passengers disembarked the train, among them was this giant of a man—six-foot-four with a bushy mustache and thick, unruly hair. Cameras flashed. City officials approached him with hands outstretched.

The man greeted them politely and then, looking over their heads, asked to be excused for a moment. He quickly walked through the crowd until he reached the side of an elderly woman who was struggling with two large suitcases. He picked up the bags with a smile and escorted the woman to a bus. After helping her aboard, he wished her a safe journey. As he returned to the greeting party he apologized: "Sorry to have kept you waiting."

The man was Dr. Albert Schweitzer, the famous missionary doctor who spent his life helping the poor in Africa. In response to Schweitzer's action, one member of the reception committee said, "That's the first time I ever saw a sermon walking."

You and I have many opportunities each week to be "sermons walking." All we have to do is look to Jesus as our example. According to today's Scripture, Jesus only did what He saw the Father doing. If we will follow Jesus' example, we can also be like sermons walking.

Love Others Today: Take every chance you get to be a sermon walking today.

You're Invited

The next day Jesus desired and decided to go into Galilee; and He
found Philip and said to him, Join Me as My attendant and follow Me.
                                                        JOHN 1:43

When Jesus invited people to become His disciples and follow Him,
I think He was basically asking them if they wanted to join His party. I
realize that He was talking about His group, but I think traveling with
Jesus was probably a lot of fun as well as a lot of hard work. Repeatedly
throughout the Gospels we see that Jesus invited people to leave their
lifestyles and join His party; He is still issuing that invitation today.

Living for God, serving Him and others, can be so much fun if we
approach it with the mind of Christ. It comes down to our attitude.
My favorite image of Jesus is of Him laughing. Jesus' mission could not
have been any more serious, and yet I am positive that He laughed with
His disciples, made jokes about their goofy ways, delighted in food,
and was fun to be with. When we receive Jesus Christ as our Savior, we
are not going to a funeral; we are joining His party!

I speak a lot on spiritual maturity, dying to selfishness, taking up
our cross, and living holy lives, and I am continually amazed at how
much people laugh while I do it. Somehow the Holy Spirit brings the
teaching out of me in a way that makes people laugh while they are
being corrected. God is amazing! People tell me all the time how funny
I am, and yet I speak a very straightforward, hard-hitting message that
is quite serious. I have joined Jesus' party.

Love God Today: Have you joined Jesus' party? Are you
enjoying your life and having a good time as you follow Him?
You're invited!

What Do You Want?

. . . Show me now Your way, that I may know You [progressively become more deeply and intimately acquainted with You, perceiving and recognizing and understanding more strongly and clearly] . . . And [Lord, do] consider that this nation is Your people.

EXODUS 33:13

I believe there are two things that reveal more about your character and your relationship with God than anything else. One is the way you treat other people; the other is the desires of your heart, meaning the things you want most in life.

Several times in Scripture, people ask God to give them the desires of their hearts. God gave Moses the opportunity to ask for his most fervent desires in Exodus 33. Moses' response was that he wanted to become more and more "deeply and intimately acquainted" with God and that God would "consider" His people, the nation Moses was responsible for leading.

Think about this. Moses had witnessed breathtaking, historic miracles. He was there when God parted the Red Sea and brought water from a rock. But Moses didn't ask to see greater miracles; what he wanted most of all was to know God better.

Part of learning to love anyone is getting to know that person. The same is true with God. The more we become acquainted with Him, the more intimate relationship with Him we can enjoy. This happens as we hunger for His presence, seek His truth through His Word, show love to others, and spend time with Him every day.

Love God Today: Do you hunger more than anything else to know God more intimately? God has no favorites, but He does have intimates. Are you one?

On the Way to Where You're Going

But the path of the [uncompromisingly] just and righteous is like the light of dawn, that shines more and more (brighter and clearer) until [it reaches its full strength and glory in] the perfect day [to be prepared].   PROVERBS 4:18

You cannot give away something you don't have. And unless we possess love for ourselves, we can never progress in the will of God, which is to love other people.

When I became active in church life and started hearing sermons about loving other people, I really tried to do so but always seemed to fail. This concerned, confused, and discouraged me until God showed me that I could not love others until I actually embraced His love for me and loved myself. Loving yourself with the love God pours out is what it means to *receive* God's love.

We all need to accept ourselves, knowing that although we are not where we need to be, we are making progress. Jesus died for us because we have weaknesses and imperfections, and we don't have to reject ourselves because of them. God wants us to love ourselves and enjoy ourselves while we are letting Him work in us.

We have been trained to dislike ourselves as long as we have imperfections. In the world, a striving for perfection always exists. But in God's Kingdom, this is not the case. We need to have a perfect heart toward God and start enjoying Him and ourselves right where we are on the way to where we're going.

———————————

Love Yourself Today: You aren't where you're going to be, but you aren't where you used to be. God is moving you forward every day—enjoy the journey!

Take Care of Your Body

Do you not know that your body is the temple (the very sanctuary)
of the Holy Spirit Who lives within you, Whom you have received [as
a Gift] from God?   1 CORINTHIANS 6:19

I want to ask you today the same question Paul asked the believers in Corinth centuries ago: Do you know that your body is the temple of the Holy Spirit? You are the home of God! Are you loving yourself, God, and others by caring for your physical body, treating it well, and using it for God's purposes?

Some Christians focus only on the spiritual side of life and they fail to properly care for their bodies. Other people have such low self-esteem or a shame-based nature that they don't feel their bodies are worth caring for. But God's plan for us involves maintaining spiritual, emotional, *and* physical health. He wants us strong in every way! He wants us to feel good physically so we can serve Him and others, and be able to enjoy the life He has provided for us.

No matter what shape you are in physically, it's never too late to improve and do some repair or maintenance on your temple. You can start by learning the basic principles of good nutrition, drink lots of water, employ stress management, exercise, and rest. Laughter is also important. It has been scientifically proven to improve your health. It's amazing how much better you can feel if you will begin to make positive changes in these areas. Give it a try; I promise, you'll be glad you did.

———————

Love Yourself Today: Do you need to learn how to make good food choices or get out and exercise? Whatever you do, just get started on a new path of health and wellness!

What to Do When People Make Mistakes

*Therefore encourage (admonish, exhort) one another and edify
(strengthen and build up) one another, just as you are doing.*
1 THESSALONIANS 5:11

I want you to know about a great gift you can give other people. It's permission to not be perfect! I enjoy being around people who do not pressure me to be perfect. God loves us unconditionally, and that means He accepts us the way we are and then helps us to be all we can be. The world is filled with pressure to perform and excel, but when people fall short, they need a word of kindness that lets them know they are still accepted and valuable.

When you are with people who make mistakes, immediately try to remind them of their strengths or of something amazing you have seen them do recently. We should not take anything that people do well for granted. The devil works overtime trying to make people feel like a failure, and we should work equally hard to make them feel like a success.

Bearing with one another's weaknesses is just one simple way of showing love. The apostle Paul had taught people to encourage and build up others, and he frequently reminded them to keep doing it, just as he did in our verse for today. The Holy Spirit lives in us and walks alongside us in life. He urges us to become all we can be. When we make mistakes, He does not condemn us; He urges us forward.

Lack of encouragement causes depression, despair, and it prevents people from reaching their potential in life. We all need to be encouraged. Remember, simple encouragement is one of the primary ways we can spread love to everyone we meet.

Love Others Today: Make a deliberate decision to be kind and encouraging when people make mistakes.

It Takes a Team

Two are better than one, because they have a good [more satisfying]
reward for their labor; for if they fall the one will lift up his fellow.
ECCLESIASTES 4:9, 10

In 1867, John Roebling had a vision and a passion to do something experts said couldn't be done: build a bridge from Manhattan to Brooklyn, in New York City. No one believed it could be done, but Roebling and his son Washington, a young engineer, persevered.

The Roeblings hired their crew and finally got to work on John's dream. Only a few months into the project, a worksite accident took John's life. But the project continued, with Washington as its leader.

Three years later, Washington was severely injured. He was unable to talk, walk, or even move most of his body. But his mind was sharp, and his dream of building the bridge still burned in his heart.

Washington had two things in his favor: one finger that still worked and a wife who loved him. Roebling and his wife figured out a communication system in which he tapped on her arm. For *eleven years,* Washington tapped out messages and instructions for the bridge, until it was finally complete.

Washington Roebling needed a dependable team of people to achieve his dream. He needed his father, his crew, and his wife. We need other people too; we can love, support, help, and encourage them, and they can do the same for us.

Love Others Today: Who do you need on your team in life? Who needs you on their team?

The Name Above All Names

Therefore God also has highly exalted Him and given Him the name
which is above every name, that at the name of Jesus every knee
should bow, of those in heaven, and of those on earth, and of those
under the earth.   PHILIPPIANS 2:9, 10 NKJV

There is unbelievable power in the name of Jesus! His name is higher than any other name; it is mightier than any other name; and it is the only name that will ultimately command obedience from all people and all principalities.

If we really understand what Paul is trying to communicate in today's Scripture, we will begin to see the incredible power that is available to us in Jesus' name. What does it mean for His name to be above every name? It means the name of Jesus is the name above the name of cancer. It is the name above the name of poverty. It is the name above the name of drug addiction. It is the name above the name of divorce. Whatever name we can think of, the name of Jesus is above that name—and we have been given His name because He has given His life for us. We do not have to be defeated by anything that comes our way as long as we know the power that is available to us in Jesus' name.

I encourage you to keep the power of Jesus' name in mind when you pray and all throughout the day. When you feel weary, stop for a moment and simply speak the name of Jesus out loud, and it will make you feel better. Remember that using His name is a privilege that comes from your relationship with Him. As you continue to grow in intimacy with Him, His name will become more and more precious to you.

Love God Today: "Thank You, Jesus, that Your name is more powerful than any other name!"

God's Delivering Power

Now when Daniel knew that the writing was signed, he went into his house, and his windows being open in his chamber toward Jerusalem, he got down upon his knees three times a day and prayed and gave thanks before his God, as he had done previously.   DANIEL 6:10

Notice in today's Scripture that Daniel got on his knees to pray and thank God three times a day. He had a habit of prayer and thanksgiving. When we get on our knees before the Lord, we humble ourselves and say with our actions, "Lord, I reverence and honor You. I am nothing without You. I need You and I humble myself in Your presence."

Daniel was delivered from a den of hungry lions. His enemies threw him into the lions' den because they were jealous of him, a foreigner who rose to a high position in their country's government. When they conspired to hurt him, they knew he was a righteous man and they could not accuse him of wrongdoing. So they asked the king to issue a decree stating that anyone who did not worship the local gods or the king would be thrown into the lions' den.

Daniel was not afraid. He refused to compromise his worship. He kept up his habit of praying and praising his God three times a day. He did get thrown into the lions' den, but God shut the mouths of the lions and Daniel emerged unharmed.

We can never underestimate the power of worshipping God. Like Daniel, our prayer and worship needs to be a habit and we need to keep doing it, no matter what anyone says. When enemies or circumstances rise against us, we can count on God to hear our prayers, receive our worship, and deliver us.

Love God Today: When something or someone comes against you, remember what Daniel did. Worship God in the midst of it, and He will deliver you.

Make Time, Take Time

Don't pray when you feel like it. Have an appointment with the Lord and keep it.   CORRIE TEN BOOM

When we love someone, we want to spend time with that person. Particularly when we are *in* love, we are happy to change our schedules so we can be with the person who has captured our heart. One way we express our love for God is to prioritize spending time with Him. I like to think of it as keeping a daily appointment with Him, an appointment that is more important than anything else I have to do that day.

If I had a dear friend who lived in another city and wanted to come to my house for a visit, I would be delighted to schedule time with that person. I certainly would not accept an invitation to do anything else during that appointment, because I would be so excited to be with my friend. Time spent together would be vital for our ongoing, growing relationship.

Sometimes, we may become slack in keeping our appointments with God because we know that He will always be there for us. We may skip or reschedule our time with Him in order to do something else that seems urgent. But if we spent more "priority moments" with God, we might not have so many "urgent" situations.

A commitment to spend time with God is as serious a commitment as any we will ever make.

If you struggle to keep your appointments with God, I encourage you to be disciplined and diligent about them. With persistence, you will reach the point where you so enjoy fellowship with Him that you don't want to live a single day without time spent sharing your love for Him and receiving His love for you.

———————————

Love God Today: Does your daily routine include time for you to be with God? Do you need to make any adjustments in your schedule in order to prioritize Him?

God Is Pleased and Delighted with You

He brought me forth also into a large place; He was delivering me because He was pleased with me and delighted in me.

PSALM 18:19

Have you ever taken time to think about what you think about yourself? God thinks you are special, and He celebrates you all the time. He doesn't mention your past sins, and He rejoices over you with singing (see Zeph. 3:17).

According to Scripture, King David, who wrote our verse for today, was far from perfect, but he believed God was pleased with him. David made the same statement again in 2 Samuel 22:20. He really knew God's pleasure and delight in him.

I hope you also know how pleased and delighted God is with you. Can you imagine walking around your house or driving around in your car singing, "God is pleased with me and He delights in me!" Many people would not have that kind of confidence, but we should. We should believe what God says in His Word about how He feels toward us. If you have the courage to begin speaking over yourself that God is pleased and delights in you, you may feel embarrassed at first, but soon you will begin to walk in new levels of confidence, power, peace, and joy.

God may not be pleased with all our behavior, but He is pleased with us if we love Him and want to make progress. When we make positive confessions like the ones I'm suggesting today, we are agreeing with God's Word.

Love Yourself Today: God is not mad at you, and He loves you. He's smiling over you and singing over you because He is pleased and delighted with you.

Celebrate Ordinary Life

Behold, what I have seen to be good and fitting is for one to eat and
drink, and to find enjoyment in all the labor in which he labors
under the sun all the days which God gives him—for this is his
[allotted] part.   ECCLESIASTES 5:18

Every day is not Christmas or your birthday or even a holiday at school
or work. In fact, most days are ordinary; they don't have anything special about them unless we make them special. Too many ordinary days,
especially if stress is "ordinary" for you, can lead to fatigue, lack of joy,
resentment, or even bitterness. The way to avoid these things is to take
time to celebrate and do things you enjoy—for no particular reason.
Do them to celebrate life and to keep yourself in a good frame of mind.

The first thing your brain may say to you when you decide to have a
little celebration in the middle of a mundane day is, *You don't have time*
to do that. But I am telling you that you need to take the time. If you do,
your remaining tasks will go more smoothly and joyfully. If you don't,
then you are probably headed for some version of sinking emotions—
discouragement, anger, resentment, or self-pity. When you start to feel
down, just take the time to do something "up" that lifts your mood and
helps you feel better about life in general.

Perhaps we could enjoy everyday life more if we learned to celebrate
the ordinary. Eat a cookie (not a dozen), go to lunch with a good friend,
sit in the sunshine, go for a walk. Take the time to do whatever is special to you in the midst of your ordinary, everyday activities.

No day needs to be ordinary if we realize the gift God is giving us
when He gives us another day.

———————————

Love Yourself Today: I invite you to find a creative reason to
celebrate and a creative way to do it.

It Doesn't Take Much

. . . You shall love your neighbor as yourself . . .   LEVITICUS 19:18

One of the many reasons I love God's Word is that it is full of little things we can do to bless, encourage, and strengthen one another— things that don't take much time or cost much money. Here are some of the acts of kindness the Bible says we can and should do for one another:

* Watch over one another
* Pray for one another
* Look for kindnesses we can express to others
* Be friendly and hospitable
* Be patient with one another
* Bear with others' faults and weaknesses
* Give others the benefit of the doubt
* Encourage one another
* Be loyal to one another
* Be happy for people when they are blessed
* Keep people's secrets and don't tell their faults
* Believe the best of one another

The ideas listed here are relatively simple things we all can do if we are willing. We don't have to make special plans for most of them, but can do them throughout the day as we have opportunities.

Love Others Today: In what simple ways can you express love to others by the end of the day?

Help People Help Themselves

Then all those virgins got up and put their own lamps in order. And the foolish said to the wise, Give us some of your oil, for our lamps are going out. But the wise replied, There will not be enough for us and for you; go instead to the dealers and buy for yourselves.

MATTHEW 25:7–9

Look at the life of a truly committed, dedicated Christian, and then look at the life of an excuse waiting to happen—someone who grumbles, complains, and feels sorry for himself or herself. Compare the fruit of these two people and you'll soon see what works in life and what doesn't.

People who never want to do anything extra in life can be very frustrating. They can be especially taxing when they go through hard times and then want to borrow from you the "extra oil" that you have worked for or obeyed God to have in your life.

There are times we need to graciously accommodate people when they make requests of us. There are also times we need to say, basically, "Sorry, you'll have to get your own oil."

We don't always help people by doing everything for them. When you really love someone, it can be difficult not to meet all their needs, but if they are not doing their part to help themselves, the most helpful thing you can do may be to require that they handle a situation on their own.

Love Others Today: Ask God to help you say "no" when you need to. Don't do what is easiest for you, but always do what is best for the other person.

Uniquely Gifted to Help

Do not neglect the gift which is in you, [that special inward endowment] . . .   1 TIMOTHY 4:14

Helen Keller achieved amazing goals despite being unable to see or hear. At nineteen months of age, an illness caused her to go completely blind and completely deaf.

Helen's parents sought help for her in Boston at Perkins School for the Blind.

The Perkins School assigned a tutor named Anne Sullivan to work with the child. Helen was terribly frustrated and often became resistant and violently angry. Many teachers would have lost their patience, but Anne Sullivan kept her composure and persisted in her efforts to teach Helen. Eventually, Helen learned to read Braille, to write, and even to speak.

Helen also decided she wanted to attend college. Anne Sullivan helped her prepare and gain acceptance to Radcliffe College, associated with Harvard University. With Sullivan's help, she graduated with honors, having mastered several languages, four years later.

While in college, Helen started a writing career that would last more than fifty years. She went on to receive many awards, including the Presidential Medal of Freedom.

A vital key to her success was the fact that Anne Sullivan believed in her. Her patience, wisdom, and teaching ability combined to make her a uniquely gifted teacher for Helen.

Love Others Today: God has uniquely gifted you to help someone. Be available as God opens doors for you to do so.

Enjoy the Party

On the third day there was a wedding at Cana of Galilee, and the
mother of Jesus was there. Jesus also was invited with His disciples
to the wedding.   JOHN 2:1, 2

The first recorded miracle Jesus performed was done at a party, a wedding to be specific. I think that's worth remembering.

Jesus was invited to a wedding, and while He was there the hosts ran out of wine. Jesus turned some water into wine so the party could continue as planned. No matter what your particular doctrine is about wine, the fact remains that Jesus made it for the party, so don't get so caught up in the wine that you miss the point. Jesus attended the party; He had nothing against the party; and He wanted people to enjoy the party. God wants us to enjoy life!

I mention this because I believe that many religious people could not have a good time at a party if their lives depended on it. They would probably find something wrong with the music and the way people dressed. Religious people often do not seem to know how to have a really good time, but people who have a genuine relationship with Jesus can somehow enjoy everything.

I know the Bible says we are to be serious minded, sober, disciplined, prudent, and diligent. This is true, but it is equally true that we need to celebrate and enjoy our lives. Are you enjoying your life? If not, then start doing so today!

Love Yourself Today: Next time you get invited to do something fun, go and have a good time.

Stay Calm

Fear not; stand still (firm, confident, undismayed) and see the
salvation of the Lord which He will work for you today . . . The Lord
will fight for you, and you shall hold your peace and remain at rest.
EXODUS 14:13, 14

When troubled times come our way, one of our biggest challenges is to stay calm. Our natural tendencies are to fear, to worry, and to try to do something to fix the situation or solve the problem. But we must learn to get our emotions under control so we can think clearly, act wisely, and pray in faith.

Moses often had to help the Israelites calm down. When Pharaoh's army was gaining ground on them, they kept running, but knew they were headed straight into the Red Sea. Death seemed certain! Exodus tells us the people were frightened and angry with Moses, and they decided they would have been better off as slaves to the Egyptians than trying to outrun Pharaoh's forces.

Moses was saying in today's Scripture, "Stop it! I know the situation looks hopeless, but don't be afraid. Just be still for a minute and watch what God is going to do for you."

Before Pharaoh's army reached the Israelites, God rolled back the waters of the Red Sea so His people could cross over on dry land. When they were all on the other side, the sea closed again and Pharaoh's fighters drowned. This same miracle-working God is on your side today. He still fights for His people. Your job, if you belong to Him, is simply to "hold your peace and remain at rest."

Love God Today: "Lord, I will not fear. I will stand still, stay calm, and watch what You will do on my behalf."

Reward Yourself

Look to yourselves, that we do not lose those things we worked for,
but that we may receive a full reward.   2 JOHN 1:8 NKJV

How can you motivate yourself to do the things you know you need to do? Is it better to reward yourself for doing well and making progress, or to punish yourself when you make mistakes or do not reach your expectations? I believe that rewarding ourselves for a job well done is always better than punishment.

I set some goals for myself at the gym this year. I wanted to move up in the amount of weight I can bench-press, and I also wanted to be able to do lunges in such a manner that my knee touches the floor during the exercise. If you aren't familiar with these exercises, let me just say that they both mean pain!

I reached my goal on the bench press within a month of setting it, but it took longer to reach my goal with the lunges. Suppose I decided to punish myself for not reaching a goal by denying myself the privilege of eating dessert for two weeks, but I did nothing to reward myself for the other goal I did reach. Experience says I would begin to connect the lunges with punishment and would more than likely begin to dread and despise them. I might even lower my goal so I could remove the punishment.

I find that rewarding myself even in small ways motivates me and gives me something to look forward to while I am doing the job that needs to be done. When I reach those goals I stop and do something I enjoy. I encourage you to motivate and reward yourself too.

———————————

Love Yourself Today: Reward yourself as you work toward your goals.

Hope for the Future

Before I formed you in the womb I knew [and] approved of you [as My chosen instrument], and before you were born I separated and set you apart, consecrating you; [and] I appointed you as a prophet to the nations.   JEREMIAH 1:5

Over the years, I have come to believe that people either look forward to the future with enthusiasm and confidence, or they are concerned or fearful about it. But God takes a positive view of the future, and we need to agree with Him. He loves us unconditionally, has had good plans for our lives since before we were born, and we can trust that He is leading us into good things in the days to come.

God had a great plan for Jeremiah before he was even born. He also has a great plan for your life; He's had it since before you drew your first breath. He did not wait until He saw what you looked like, or until you began to develop talents and abilities to assign you a purpose in life. No, your purpose was decided in heaven before you were born.

I really want you to understand and believe the truth that God has a great future for you. He has a more awesome plan for your life than you could ever imagine simply because He loves you.

I challenge you today to believe God's Word about your life. If you have ever doubted that He has a purpose for your life, it's time to change your mind. If you have ever wondered whether He has good plans for you, it's time to believe it with all your heart. I guarantee you: You have a great future ahead. All you have to do is believe it and embrace it.

———————————

Love Yourself Today: "Lord, thank You for having such a great plan for my life. Help me to embrace it with all my heart!"

Everybody, Somebody, Anybody, Nobody

If anyone knows the good they ought to do and doesn't do it, it is sin for them.   JAMES 4:17 NIV

Years ago I heard a story about four people named Everybody, Somebody, Anybody, and Nobody. There was an important job to be done, and Everybody was sure Somebody would do it. Anybody could have done it, but Nobody did it. Somebody got angry about that because it was Everybody's job. Everybody thought Anybody could do it, but Nobody realized that Everybody wouldn't do it. In the end, Everybody blamed Somebody when Nobody did what Anybody could have done.

I once read about a shocking incident that shows the principles of this story at work—tragically—in real life. In 1964 Catherine Genovese was stabbed to death over a period of thirty-five minutes while thirty-eight neighbors watched. Their reaction was described as cold and uncaring, a result of urban apathy and alienation. Later, research by Latane and Darley revealed that no one had helped simply because there were so many observers. The observers looked to one another for guidance on what to do. Since no one was doing anything, they determined that no one should do anything.

We are affected by the actions of people around us. We look to one another for direction, often without even knowing it. Most people will agree with the majority even if they really don't agree.

If, as Christians, we want to demonstrate love to the world around us, we must become examples to others instead of merely following the crowd.

———————

Love Others Today: When you have the ability to help someone, don't assume somebody else will do it. Do it yourself.

Love on Wheels

*He who oppresses the poor reproaches His Maker, but he who
honors Him has mercy on the needy.*   PROVERBS 14:31 NKJV

I once met a ten-year-old girl named Gchi. When we met, she had lived
in a trash dump in Cambodia for six years; many other children had
lived there much longer. Gchi's parents could no longer support her, so
they asked her older sister to take her, and the only way the two could
survive was to live and work in the trash dump. Gchi spends seven
days a week digging through the trash with a metal pick or with her
hands, looking for food to eat or for pieces of plastic or glass she can
sell to get money for food.

This is the *city trash dump,* and every night the garbage trucks back
up to the pile of trash to dump the remains of other people's lives,
which they have gathered around the city. The children work at night,
in the dark, wearing helmets with lights on them because the best garbage is found when it first arrives.

When I shared this story with people, many wanted to help. We
began to plan, work, and raise money. After about a year and a lot of
effort, we managed to turn two large buses into mobile restaurants,
showers, and schoolrooms. They pull up to the trash dump; the children get onto the bus, get a shower, sit down to a nice meal, and even
receive some lessons in reading and math to help prepare them for a
better future. Of course, we share God's love with them, but we don't
merely *tell* them they are loved, we *show* them by meeting practical
needs in their lives.

Love Others Today: How can you meet practical needs for
needy children in your community or around the world?

God Is in the Details

And I will ask the Father, and He will give you another Comforter (Counselor, Helper, Intercessor, Advocate, Strengthener, and Standby), that He may remain with you forever.   JOHN 14:16

The Lord cares about every tiny detail of your life. People who don't believe this truth have a difficult time experiencing real intimacy with Him. You can and should talk to Him about everything. Nothing is too big and nothing is too small. He will help you put in your contact lens or drive in snow. He said, "I am with you always" (Matt. 28:20 NIV), and He is always ready to help, strengthen, encourage, or comfort you.

The Holy Spirit is called "The Helper." He is also referred to as "The Standby." I love that He is standing by me at all times, waiting to assist me with whatever I need. But He is a gentleman and won't push His way into our lives. We open the door for Him to work simply by asking, which is prayer.

God is love, and when we dwell in His love, enjoying and being aware of it, we dwell in God. To *dwell* means, "to live and remain in." "Dwelling" is not an occasional visit, but a permanent, fixed situation. I don't say, "I visit my house." I say, "I live in my house." God wants us to say the same about Him and His love for us. His love is where we live. God is with us at all times, watching over us, keeping us safe, overseeing every detail of our lives. And the Holy Spirit is standing by to help you!

Love God Today: Whatever you need today—a parking place, help navigating a tough situation at work—know that God cares about the little things and the details of your life, and He wants you to depend on Him.

Signs That God Is Working

The path of the righteous is like the first gleam of dawn, shining ever brighter till the full light of day.   PROVERBS 4:18 NIV

One thing that excites God is to see us making progress in life. And our progress should cause us to be excited, too. I spent way too many years mourning over my faults and weaknesses. I was taught to grieve over my sin, but nobody in the church world ever told me to celebrate my progress. If you have missed this important lesson like I did, then today I am telling you to celebrate, celebrate, and then celebrate your progress some more.

I am not where I want to be in terms of holy behavior, but thank God I am not where I used to be. I have made a lot of progress in the years I have had a serious relationship with God. God has changed me so much that truly I am a new creature just as His Word promises in 2 Corinthians 5:17. My husband probably thinks he has been married to several women during his journey with me, because I certainly am not like the one he started with!

Today's Scripture says that the path of the righteous grows brighter and brighter every day. If you can look back and say, "I've improved over the last year. My behavior is a little bit better" then you can celebrate! If you feel you have made no progress at all, then the devil is probably lying to you. I believe you want to improve, and the truth is that anyone who wants to improve will improve.

Love God Today: Your path is growing brighter and clearer every day, and celebrating your progress is one way of saying, "Thank You, God."

Praying with Focus

Let your eyes look right on [with fixed purpose], and let your gaze
be straight before you. Consider well the path of your feet, and let all
your ways be established and ordered aright. Turn not aside to the
right hand or to the left...   PROVERBS 4:25–27

When we talk with God in prayer, we want to know He will answer. But sometimes we feel we're getting no response at all. One reason for this could be that we do not stay focused when we pray. We often find ourselves distracted by the many pressures or activities of life. We end up not concentrating on talking to God, not really paying attention to Him—and that's not a good way to have a prayer answered!

One of the best stories I know about focus has to do with taming lions. When a lion trainer goes into a cage with a lion, he takes three things with him—a whip, a stun gun, and a stool with three or four legs on it. He holds the stool with the legs pointing toward the lion. Why? Because a lion cannot focus on more than one thing at a time. When the lion sees more than one leg on the stool, he actually "freezes" and cannot move to attack the trainer. I believe we are like the lions and can be paralyzed, in a way, when too much comes at us at one time. When we cannot focus, we are not effective or productive.

If we want our prayers answered, we need to learn to stay focused not only in prayer, but also in life. Staying focused on what we are doing gives us added power. We need to know what God has called us to do, prioritize that, focus on that, pray about that, and watch as God answers our prayers and does great things through us.

———————————

Love God Today: Focused prayer is powerful prayer! A focused life is a powerful life!

A New Attitude Toward Yourself

Who gave Himself on our behalf that He might redeem us (purchase our freedom) from all iniquity and purify for Himself a people [to be peculiarly His own, people who are] eager and enthusiastic about [living a life that is good and filled with] beneficial deeds.

TITUS 2:14

In today's verse Paul writes that Jesus gave His life so that we could be people who are "eager and enthusiastic about living a life that is good" and a life that is full of actions that benefit others.

We are not to spend our lives moping around, thinking about all our faults and failures so much that we lose our hope and zeal for living.

God is not honored when people have bad attitudes toward themselves; in fact, that is downright insulting to Him. If you loved and valued a group of people so much that you were willing to die for them so they could enjoy their lives, how would you feel if they refused your gift? God wants you to enjoy your life and enjoy yourself.

Paul knew he was not perfect, but he pressed on to lay hold of the quality of life Jesus wanted him to have. Paul knew that he did not deserve it, but for Jesus' sake he was determined to have it. Likewise, we do not deserve "the good life," but Jesus died to give it to us, so we honor Him when we receive it with eagerness and enthusiasm.

If you struggle with negative attitudes that hold you back from the good things of God in your life, I urge you to make a change today.

––––––––––––

Love Yourself Today: Choose a new attitude toward yourself. Paul had to make that choice; I had to make it; and you have to make it, too, if you want to love yourself and glorify God with your life.

Trade Reasoning for Trust

God has wisely kept us in the dark concerning future events and reserved for Himself the knowledge of them, that He may train us up in a dependence upon Himself.   MATTHEW HENRY

One activity that takes lots of energy, yet is entirely fruitless, is called "reasoning." When we reason, we try to figure things out with our minds, and ask questions such as: "Why, God, why? When, God, when? What about this? What about that?" We can trade in all of these questions that torment us for a simple trust in God's goodness and wisdom.

God wants us to trust Him. There will always be situations in which we say, "I don't understand." We may not understand why God didn't keep us from losing our job or heal someone we prayed for. When we do not understand things, we must resist the temptation to try to figure them out.

Reasoning not only frustrates us, it also leads to confusion. The more we try to figure things out, the more confused we become. Years ago, the Lord impressed these words upon me: "You cannot be confused if you will stop trying to figure things out." That's clear. If we will simply stop our minds from rotating around and around a situation and rest in Him, confusion will cease.

The Holy Spirit is our counselor and our guide. He will show us what we need to know. We simply need to stop trying to figure out everything and learn to trust Him.

Love God Today: "Lord, help me trust You enough to be peaceful even when there are things I don't understand."

The Best Time to Give

In my affliction and trouble I have provided for the house of the Lord...   1 CHRONICLES 22:14

God said that David was a man after His own heart—one who would do all of His will and carry out His program fully (see Acts 13:22). David was a giving man, and he gave generously toward the building of God's house. Even in his own times of trouble and affliction, he continued to give generously.

Sometimes when we are struggling, we are tempted to stop giving to others. Our thoughts turn toward ourselves and we do not feel like being a blessing to others; we want someone to comfort us. But when we are hurting, we should behave as we would if we were not hurting. We should keep all our commitments, including our financial commitments to the work of God.

We all go through difficult seasons of testing, and our behavior during those times clearly reveals our level of spiritual maturity. Mature Christians do what is right because it is right—and they never quit. They do not change when their circumstances change.

People who are givers look for opportunities to give to others; they do not look for reasons to get out of giving. I believe that seeds sown during hard times are more powerful than any other kind. God appreciates our faithfulness.

If I am hurting because of a trial I am going through and I feel tempted not to give because of my personal pain, I purposely give a little extra, just to let the enemy know where I stand. When Jesus died for us He was hurting, yet He still gave His best. Let's always go the extra mile and never compromise on our commitments.

Love Others Today: Do not be an emotional giver; choose to be a person who does what is right on purpose, no matter how you feel.

Don't Forget Your Own Flesh and Blood

Is it not to divide your bread with the hungry and bring the homeless poor into your house—when you see the naked, that you cover him, and that you hide not yourself from [the needs of] your own flesh and blood?   ISAIAH 58:7

Some people become so involved in ministry that they overlook their own family members and friends, but the Lord makes clear in today's Scripture that we are not to neglect one in order to attend to the other.

In this verse, God tells us that we are not only to meet the needs of those around us in the world (the poor, needy, and disadvantaged), but that we are also to meet the needs of our families.

I have a widowed aunt to whom I minister quite often. I once thought I was too busy to help her, but God showed me that she is my "flesh and blood." She is part of my family, and I am responsible to minister to her needs just as I am responsible to minister to thousands of people in many locations. If I ignore my responsibilities toward my relatives, I will pay the price of losing an aspect of God's anointing in other areas of my life.

Isaiah 58:7 says that we must not only feed the hungry and clothe the naked, but that we also must not hide ourselves from the needs of our own flesh and blood. *After* we have done these things, then Isaiah 58:8 will work for us: our light shall break forth like the morning, our healing (our restoration and the power of a new life) will spring forth speedily, our righteousness (our rightness, our justice, and our right relationship with God) will go before us (conducting us to peace and prosperity) and God's glory will guard us from behind.

Love Others Today: "Lord, help me be a blessing to all people, including my family."

What's in a Name? Everything!

*...Jesus is the Christ...you may have life through (in) His name
[through Who He is].*   JOHN 20:31

The name of Jesus represents everything that He is—all His righteousness, perfection, grace, and love. There is no power in your name or my
name, but there is awesome power in the name of Jesus. It represents
everything about who He is.

Let's think about this in practical terms. My name has not always
been Joyce Meyer. I did not take Dave's last name until I married him.
Nothing of his belonged to me until we entered into the legal covenant of marriage. When we married, I did not have much money; in
fact, I was in debt. Dave did have money, so when I married him, I
had money, too, and was able to pay off my bills. I did not have access
to anything of Dave's until I married him and took his name. When I
became Mrs. Dave Meyer, everything he had became mine.

We cannot "date" Jesus and expect to enjoy the privileges that come
with true commitment. By that, I mean that we cannot just spend time
with Him occasionally and try to keep up a relationship only because
of the blessings He offers us. We can only enjoy the full privileges of
a relationship with Him when our hearts are truly committed. God
knows whether we are "dating" or whether we have given ourselves to
Him in total commitment. When we are joined to Him in committed
relationship, we can be confident that He will give to us everything His
name affords—and we can enjoy it.

Love God Today: Are you in a committed relationship with
Jesus? Then everything His name represents belongs to you.

Don't Keep Records

. . . Love . . . is not touchy or fretful or resentful; it takes no account of the evil done to it [it pays no attention to a suffered wrong].

1 CORINTHIANS 13:5

Love forgives; it does not hold a grudge. It is not touchy, easily offended, nor is it fretful or resentful. Some people get their feelings hurt about everything. It is very difficult to be in a relationship with people like this. We have many opportunities every day to get offended; each time we must make a choice. If we choose to live by our feelings, we will never succeed in this all-important facet of love.

If we don't forgive quickly, but instead keep records of how others have hurt us, sooner or later the list will get so long that we can no longer be in relationship with these people. That kind of resentment is a part of what causes many divorces. If we can learn this important facet of love and abide by it, we'll save ourselves—and others—tremendous pain and damage to our relationships.

By keeping records of things that others have done to offend us, we fill ourselves up with poison. Bitterness makes our life attitude, words and thoughts bitter. Drop it, leave it and let it go, is what the Amplified Bible says we are to do with offenses (Mark 11:25). It is important to forgive quickly. The quicker we do it, the easier it is.

Let's begin to behave as if we believe the Bible. In it, God tells us over and over again what to do about those who offend us: love them, pray for them, bless them.

Love Others Today: Sow mercy, and you will reap mercy. So start sowing forgiveness. You may need some yourself someday.

Be Comfortable with God

So the LORD spoke to Moses face to face, as a man speaks to his friend...   EXODUS 33:11 NKJV

God wants you to be comfortable in your love relationship with Him. He wants you to approach Him freely and talk to Him as easily and naturally as you talk to your friends. If you are approaching God trying to sound eloquent, then *stop it* and be yourself. If you use funny expressions in everyday conversation, it is not necessary to abandon your unique expressions when you talk to God. He has a sense of humor, too, you know! Talking to God should be a natural extension of your personal communication style. It should be comfortable and enjoyable for you, and it needs to come from the heart.

I used to worry about how I sounded when I prayed, but I no longer worry about that anymore; I simply tell the Lord what is on my heart—and I tell it the way it is—plain, simple, and straightforward. That is the way I talk to my husband, my children, and people I work with; so that is the way I talk to God. I am not trying to impress Him; I am trying to share my heart with Him—and I can do that best when I am simply being myself. God made us the way we are, so we need to approach Him without pretense and without thinking we have to sound a certain way in order for Him to hear us. As long as we are sincere, He will hear. Even if what is on our hearts cannot be articulated, He still hears and understands what it is. Sometimes we hurt too badly to pray and all we can do is sigh or groan—and God understands even that.

Love God Today: When you spend time with God, just be yourself and be comfortable in His presence.

Give Your Soul a Break

Find rest, O my soul, in God alone; my hope comes from him.
PSALM 62:5 NIV

When you take a vacation, do you give your soul a break, just as you give your body some rest, recreation, and refreshment?

Your soul is comprised of your mind, will, and emotions, and it is a very important part of your entire being. You are a spiritual being, and you live in a physical body. But if you don't understand your soul's needs, you will not be a whole, healthy individual.

When we are weary, exhausted in strength, endurance, and vigor, we need help. We need to be refreshed not only physically, but mentally and emotionally as well. Being weary is not something to be ashamed of; it's simply a sign that we need a break.

You can take a vacation thinking you need a physical rest, but if you don't let your soul rest at the same time, you will return home just as exhausted as you were when you left. Lying on the beach worrying does not equal a day of vacation. If you take a day off and spend it trying to deal with personal problems, traffic, high prices, and rude people—you'd have been better off at work!

Learning to let our souls rest is vitally important. Jesus said in Matthew 11:28–30 that if we are overburdened, weary, and worn out, we should spend time with Him and see how He handled life. He promises to give us rest. The Amplified Bible's translation of these verses indicates that the type of rest He is talking about is recreation, refreshment, and blessed quiet for our souls. Jesus is really offering us a vacation for our souls, our inner lives.

Love Yourself Today: Permit your entire being to take a vacation. Get plenty of rest physically. Rest your mind, quiet your emotions, and let your will be in total agreement with God's.

Defeating Discouragement

Why are you cast down, O my inner self? And why should you moan over me and be disquieted within me? Hope in God and wait expectantly for Him, for I shall yet praise Him, my Help and my God.
PSALM 42:5

In today's verse, the psalmist is clearly discouraged. Discouragement destroys hope, so naturally the enemy tries hard to discourage us. Without hope we give up, which is exactly what the devil wants us to do.

The Bible repeatedly tells us not to be discouraged or dismayed. God knows that we will not be strong or victorious if we lose our courage, and He wants us to be *en*couraged, not *dis*couraged.

When discouragement tries to overtake you, the first thing to do is to examine your thought life. What kinds of thoughts have you been thinking? Have they sounded something like this? *I am not going to make it; this is too hard. I always fail; I may as well give up. God probably doesn't answer my prayers because He is so disappointed in the way I act.*

If these examples represent your thoughts, no wonder you despair! You become what you think. Think discouraging thoughts, and you will get discouraged. Change your thinking and be set free!

Love Yourself Today: Instead of thinking negatively, think more like this: *Well, things are going a little slowly, but, thank God, I am making some progress. I am sure glad I'm on the right path. I had a rough day yesterday. I chose wrong thinking all day long. Father, forgive me, and help me to keep on keeping on. This is a new day. You love me, Lord. Your mercy is new every morning. I refuse to be discouraged. Father, You sent Jesus to die for me. I'll be fine—today will be a great day. I ask You to help me choose right thoughts today.*

Learn to Bear the Yoke

*Take My yoke upon you and learn of Me, for I am gentle (meek)
and humble (lowly) in heart, and you will find rest (relief and ease
and refreshment and recreation and blessed quiet) for your souls.*
                                                    MATTHEW 11:29

A yoke is a device that couples two things together, such as the pairing
of oxen used to pull a plow for farming. A yoke is also used to balance
a load. The word *yoke* is used metaphorically in the Bible as a reference
to submission to authority. If we stay yoked (very close) to Jesus and
submit to His authority, He will help us carry and balance the loads we
have in life.

We must be willing to take up Jesus' yoke in every area. For example, we may wish we could get away from a person or situation, and
yet we feel we are where God wants us. This is an opportunity to take
Jesus' yoke and learn how He wants us to respond. It is an opportunity
to grow spiritually.

God puts different people together and wants us to learn how to
love one another and get along peacefully. When we are with other
people, especially our opposites, this gives us an opportunity to learn
the nature of Christ, and treat people the way He would treat them. If
we struggle against it, we will have no rest. But, if we say to God, "I am
willing to take my place; I am willing to obey; I am willing to bloom
where I am planted, I am willing to love all kinds of people with Your
love," then we will find rest and joy.

Love Others Today: "Lord, help me to remember to love
everyone unconditionally, just as You have loved me."

Love People, Use Things

But if anyone has this world's goods (resources for sustaining life) and sees his brother and fellow believer in need, yet closes his heart of compassion against him, how can the love of God live and remain in him? Little children, let us not love [merely] in theory or in speech but in deed and in truth (in practice and sincerity).   1 JOHN 3:17, 18

Many people love things and use people to get them. God intends for us to love people and use things to bless them. Sharing our possessions with others is one way to move love from something we think about and talk about doing to actually doing it.

God has given us a heart of compassion, but today's Scripture teaches us that we are the ones who can choose to open or close it. God won't force us to be compassionate, but as believers in Jesus Christ, God gives us His Spirit and puts a new heart (and mind) in us. There is something deep in every believer that wants to help others; however, selfishness can cause us to become oblivious to the needs around us.

People are hurting everywhere. Some are poor; others are sick or lonely. A simple act of kindness like giving a small gift or a compliment can make them feel loved and special.

People can get caught in the trap of striving to have more things, which often produces few or no results. We should strive to excel in giving. If we do so, we will find that God makes sure we have enough to meet our own needs plus plenty to give away (see 2 Corinthians 9:8).

Love Others Today: "Lord, help me to remember to love people, not things."

Make Adjustments for the Sake of Others

I have [in short] become all things to all men, that I might by all means (at all costs and in any and every way) save some [by winning them to faith in Jesus Christ].   1 CORINTHIANS 9:22

Paul said that although he was free in every way from anyone's control, he made himself a servant to everyone (see 1 Cor. 9:19–23). In today's Scripture passage, Paul says that he became as a Jew to the Jews, and to the weak he became weak. In other words, he adjusted himself to be whatever people needed him to be.

Paul did whatever it took to win people to Christ and show love to them. He was highly educated, but I am sure that when he was with people who were not educated, he did not make a display of how educated he was. In fact, the following statement shows his humility and determination never to make others feel belittled. He wrote: "For I resolved to know nothing... among you except Jesus Christ... and Him crucified" (1 Cor. 2:2).

When Paul was with people, he chose to listen to them and take time to genuinely learn about them. I believe this is something we all need to do, and I know this enhances relationships in amazing ways. We should get to know people: find out what they like and dislike, want or don't want, what they need and what their dreams are for the future. If they are weak in an area where we are strong, we should make sure we don't boast of our abilities.

Love Others Today: What kinds of adjustments do you need to make in your life for the sake of having a positive, godly influence on someone?

God's Love Gives Us Confidence

In this [union and communion with Him] love is brought to completion and attains perfection with us, that we may have confidence for the day of judgment [with assurance and boldness to face Him], because as He is, so are we in this world.   1 JOHN 4:17

To be bold actually means to be courageous in the presence of fear. To be confident does not mean we never feel fear; it simply means that no matter how we feel, we magnify God above all else and step out in faith to do whatever He asks us to do.

We never have to be afraid of God. We should have reverential fear, meaning a respectful awe, of Him, but He does not want us to lack confidence when we face Him. The Bible tells us to come "fearlessly and confidently and boldly" to the throne of grace and make our requests known (Heb. 4:16). We cannot operate in boldness and fear at the same time. We may "feel" fear, but we must not bow down or give in to it; we can approach God with confidence.

In our society today we have an epidemic of insecurity. The world is full of people who lack confidence. Our confidence is to be placed in Christ alone and in His love for us. We are to put no confidence in the flesh, but to be bold and courageous in Christ. Begin to believe today that from now on you will step out in faith to do whatever He asks you to do. Don't draw back in fear and timidity, but go all the way through to the finish of each task.

Love God Today: "Father, deliver me from insecurity and a lack of confidence. Help me be bold and courageous."

Confidence Brings Comfort

You will show me the path of life; in Your presence is fullness of
joy...   PSALM 16:11

Being confident in God's love enables us to be comfortable in His presence. Yet many people are tense and uptight most of the time. They are
nervous and sometimes even afraid to meet new people, begin tasks, or
have to make decisions. Some people are often tense or anxious when
they attempt to meet with God in prayer and fellowship. They are afraid
they won't pray properly, long enough, with the right posture, or with
enough eloquence.

I was always uncomfortable in my earthly father's presence. He was
mean and abusive, and my discomfort was understandable. But I am
grateful to have learned that I don't ever need to be uncomfortable in
my heavenly Father's presence. He loves us at all times and is always
glad to spend time with us; He's happy when we want to be with Him,
and He delights in hearing our prayers and answering them. He doesn't
expect us to be perfect or our prayers to be perfect. So we need to accept
our imperfections and work on our weaknesses while allowing God to
love us as we are. If any one of us could be perfect in our behavior, we
would not need Jesus and His death would have been in vain. He paid
for all our imperfections and makes a way for us to be comfortable in
God's presence. Because of what Jesus did, we can relax in God and be
confident in His love.

Love God Today: "I thank You, Lord, that I can relax in life,
living free from the tyranny of anxiety, nervousness, or fear.
I am confident in You and comfortable in Your presence!"

Make the Most of Every Day

*The kingdom of God is like a man who scatters seed upon the
ground, and then continues sleeping and rising night and day while
the seed sprouts and grows and increases—he knows not how.*

MARK 4:26, 27

Today's Scripture teaches us that a seed's growth and nourishment
takes place while the seed is underground. The same principle applies
to our lives. Most of life involves getting up in the morning, going to
bed at night, and doing what we need to do in the interim. When everything is "business as usual," that's where we develop the ability to
enjoy everyday life.

Sometimes people think enjoying life means celebrating special
occasions or getting raises and promotions. The truth is that life is
not one big party, and we cannot sit around waiting for the next exciting event. We do need to celebrate life's big, exciting occasions, but in
between them, we must be able to find joy in going to work, cleaning
house, raising children, and dealing with grouchy neighbors.

One key to enjoying each day of our lives is to understand that most
of life consists of a routine, unremarkable series of events that take
place day after day. So if we are really going to enjoy every day, we must
learn to embrace the ordinary—to delight in little things, and to find
pleasure in situations other people might overlook. And as we enjoy life
moment by moment, day by day, week after week and year after year,
we find that all of life has become rich, deep, and satisfying.

Love Yourself Today: "God, help me to enjoy ordinary days!"

What Do You See?

Write the vision and make it plain...   HABAKKUK 2:2 NKJV

Do you have a vision for your life? If you can envision great things for yourself, you can experience that vision as reality. Before a woman can give birth she must be able to conceive. Can you mentally conceive that God has something great in mind for you?

One excellent way to develop and pursue your vision for your life is to see it in your imagination and talk about it as if it already existed (see Rom. 4:17). See yourself the way God's Word says that you can be. See yourself doing great things and having your needs met.

If you have never been a disciplined person but you would like to be, stop saying, "I'm just not disciplined," and begin saying, "I am a disciplined person." If you'd like to be more creative, say, "I have lots of creative abilities and I enjoy using them."

Write down your goals. Describe your ideal self's activities, appearance, values, goals, and so on. Make it concrete, so it feels as real as possible. Writing down your goals helps bring them into the real world and make them solid. Keep your vision and a list of your goals handy so you can consult it periodically and check your progress.

Make sure your goals align with God's Word and have the right focus. Your list of goals can serve as steppingstones on your way to becoming the person God wants you to be.

———————

Love Yourself Today: Have a vision for your life that agrees with God's Word, and don't ever give up until you see it come to pass.

Keep Your Promises

Let your Yes be simply Yes, and your No be simply No...
MATTHEW 5:37

In 1867, a little girl named Marie was born in Poland to a pianist and a professor. Early in life, the child demonstrated an interest in education and a remarkable ability to learn.

After she excelled all the way through secondary school, she wanted to continue her education, but her father could not afford to do so because he lost much of his money in an unwise investment. With her dreams for further study crushed, Marie took a job as a teacher and soon thereafter, as a governess.

Marie and her sister, Bronia decided to help each other. Marie agreed to finance Bronia's continuing education with her earnings from her governess job. When Bronia completed her studies, she would pay for Marie to attend university. Both sisters kept their word to each other.

In 1891, Marie began her studies at the world-famous Sorbonne in France. She lived in a tiny, cramped dormitory and survived primarily on bread, butter, and tea. She married a physics professor in 1895, and the two of them dedicated their lives to science. She was Marie Curie. In 1911, she won a Nobel Prize for chemistry.

Marie Curie could never have made her groundbreaking contributions to the human race without the promise she and her sister made to each other. Because both of them kept their word, they were each able to fulfill their dreams.

Love Others Today: When you make a promise to someone, keep it. God always keeps His word, and we should keep ours.

Prayer Instead of Judgment

There are many in the world who are dying for a piece of bread, but there are many more dying for a little love.

MOTHER TERESA OF CALCUTTA

God often allows us to see or know things about people specifically for the purpose of praying for them, but we often judge and criticize instead of praying.

Years ago, I saw two women leaving a donut shop. They were both at least 100 pounds overweight, and they were each carrying an entire box of donuts. I could sense in my heart that they had serious problems with their emotions and were eating to comfort themselves. Perhaps they had been abused or had endured a lifetime of emotional pain and rejection. When we encounter people, we never know what they have been through or what they are currently suffering.

Although I was tempted to criticize them, the Holy Spirit prompted me to pray instead. I simply prayed, "God, help those two women lose weight. And help them know that You are the answer to their problems. Send someone into their lives who can speak the words they need to hear. Amen."

There have been times in my life when I needed to lose weight and hoped someone was praying for me. I would much rather have people's prayers than their judgment.

Too often people see situations such as the one I just described and think, *That's terrible. The last thing those women need is a donut!* Many of us are quick to judge others and jump to conclusions about them. We need to discipline our minds to refrain from judgment; we need to view people through the lens of compassion and do the one thing that can make a difference: pray!

Love Others Today: "Lord, help me to see others in a loving way and not make quick, unkind judgments."

Hopeless?

Love never fails...   1 CORINTHIANS 13:8

Is there someone in your life you find difficult to love? Maybe you have tried and tried to help the person, and nothing seems to work. I want to share a story with you.

Before Dave and I married, he asked God to send him someone he could help. When God sent him me, he got more than he bargained for! I had serious, serious problems. I am sure many men would have given up. But Dave continued to pray and seek God for ways to help me, even when I acted as though I did not want help. At times, he even wept because he did not know what to do. He has even shared that he often went for drives in the car to pray and cry, and returned home trusting that God would change me.

I am so thankful today that God was faithful to Dave and to me. He has brought healing, deliverance, and wholeness to me. He had to teach me to think differently, to trust people, to allow myself to be loved, and to love others.

Our journey was not easy, but Dave refused to give up on me, and we both refused to give up on God. Though our early years were difficult, we have had many years of happiness and we look forward to many more.

Love never fails. Don't give up on people, but keep walking in love and seeking God, and you may see the situation turn around completely!

Love Others Today: If you have a difficult person in your life, don't give up. Each time they come to mind say out loud, "I believe that God is working."

Let God Interrupt You

And who knows but that you have come to the kingdom for such a
time as this and for this very occasion?   ESTHER 4:14

Have you ever noticed that the men and women we read about in the Bible and consider "great" were all people who allowed God to interrupt their lives and were willing to make tremendous sacrifices for Him?

Joseph saved a nation from starvation, but not before God dramatically removed him from his comfortable home where he was his father's favorite and allowed him to be imprisoned for many years. Joseph probably wasn't planning a life of hardship and rejection, but God took him through those things in order to position him to be in the right place at the right time. But Joseph could only know that after the fact.

Esther was a young maiden who undoubtedly had plans for her future when suddenly, without warning, she was asked to enter the king's harem and gain favor with him so she could reveal the plan of wicked Haman, who intended to slaughter the Jews. She was asked to do things that left her frightened for her life, but her wise uncle knew that God had brought her to this point in her life and allowed everything she had endured in the past to prepare her for a moment of greatness.

These people had plans, but they let God interrupt them and they followed Him instead. If you will decide that you don't mind having God interrupt your life, He can prepare you, too, for moments of greatness and use you in awesome ways.

Love God Today: "Lord, interrupt my life for Your purposes at any time and in any way You see fit."

Show God You're Serious

So we fasted and besought our God for this, and He heard our
entreaty.   EZRA 8:23

In today's Scripture we read that Ezra proclaimed a fast to show his desperation to God when the Israelites required protection and needed to know what to do. Fasting is still powerful and relevant today. It causes us to deny ourselves and focus on God. Missing a few meals and taking that time to seek God is not a bad idea; if you can't fast food, you might fast television or some form of entertainment. Spend the time you would normally give to these things with God.

Ezra and the Israelites sought God. When we seek God we pursue, crave, and go after God with all our might.

We need to seek God all the time, not only during times of difficulty or desperation. I believe the reason so many people have problems so often is that they only turn to God when all else has failed. I have wondered if they would spend any time with Him at all if He were to remove their problems. If we will seek God as though we are always desperate for Him, we won't find ourselves so "desperate" in reality on a regular basis.

Make a habit of spending time with God, and in moments when you're facing a critical situation, consider some kind of fast and concentrated prayer to demonstrate to Him that you are willing to sacrifice your own desires in order to seek His direction, help, and strength.

———————

Love God Today: What can you sacrifice for a while in order to *seriously* seek God and spend time in His presence?

Step Out, Find Out

. . . Launch out into the deep and let down your nets for a catch.
LUKE 5:4 NKJV

The only way we ever fulfill God's plan for our lives and live life to the fullest is to take many, many steps of faith. Stepping into the unknown can leave us feeling a bit frightened and insecure. Because of these fearful feelings, many people never *step out,* therefore, they never *find out* what they are capable of.

Prompt obedience to the will of God is vital for the growth of God's Kingdom as well as for us personally. We must learn to follow the leading of the Holy Spirit.

Many people miss the will of God for their lives because they "would rather be safe than sorry." Had I tried to be safe, I never would have sown the seeds of obedience that have produced good fruit for God's Kingdom and my own personal life.

We need to be discerning and led by the Spirit, not by our own thoughts or emotions or by other people's advice. When we decide to step out, we should do all we can to make sure we are obeying God's voice and responding in faith to Him.

When Dave and I step out to do something we believe God is leading us to do, we do so little by little, watching to see how God responds. If He blesses our actions, then we know that we are in His will and we take another step. Don't be afraid to "step out," because it is the only way you will "find out" what God wants you to do.

————————

Love Yourself Today: What has God put on your heart, and what small step can you take in that direction?

Sit Down

But God, who is rich in mercy, because of His great love with which He loved us, even when we were dead in trespasses, made us alive together with Christ (by grace you have been saved), and raised us up together, and made us sit together in the heavenly places in Christ Jesus.   EPHESIANS 2:4–6 NKJV

Today's Scripture says that we are seated in heavenly places with Christ Jesus.

I read past that passage one day, and the Holy Spirit stopped me. I just felt that I had missed something so I went back and read it again: "God...seated us with Him in the heavenly places in Christ Jesus." I still didn't get it. So I went back and read it once more, and finally, I got it! We are seated. We are *seated*.

After His resurrection and ascension, Jesus is often depicted as being seated at the right hand of the Father.

Do you know what people do when they sit? They rest. To be seated in heavenly places with Jesus is to enter an "inner rest."

Sometimes when you start to get nervous and upset, anxious or worried, tell yourself, "Sit down." That does not mean just your physical body; it also means your soul—your mind, will, and emotions. It is important to let your entire being rest and just wait on God. Wait expectantly for God to do what you cannot do. Don't worry, get frustrated, or become fearful while you rest. We often feel that we should always be "doing" something. The promise of God's peace is not made to those who work, struggle, and strive in their own strength, but to those who enter God's rest.

———————

Love Yourself Today: "Lord, teach me how to sit down in Your holy rest."

Become an Aggressive Encourager

So let us then definitely aim for and eagerly pursue what makes for harmony and for mutual upbuilding (edification and development) of one another.   ROMANS 14:19

One of the easiest ways to express love to others is to help them feel valuable. Mother Teresa of Calcutta ministered in the midst of appalling poverty, hunger, and disease, yet she said, "Being unwanted, unloved, uncared for, forgotten by everybody...is a much greater hunger...than the person who has nothing to eat."

I've discovered that most people we meet do not have a sense of their infinite value as children of God. The thought that God loves them and sees them as precious has never entered their minds. I think the devil works very hard to make people feel devalued and worthless, but we can neutralize his lies by building people up and encouraging them. One way to do this is with a sincere compliment.

A compliment does not have to be something major. Little remarks such as, "That color really looks good on you"; "I like your hair that way"; or "I'm glad you are my friend" are very effective and meaningful.

Most people are quick to compare themselves with others, which means they often fail to see their own abilities and worth. Making another person feel valuable doesn't have to be time consuming. Let's train ourselves to be aggressive encouragers. Find some way to encourage every person you come in contact with throughout your day. Making people feel valuable won't cost any money, but it gives them something worth more than anything money can buy.

———————————

Love Others Today: When you are with another person, make them feel better before you leave their presence.

Take Time to Listen

Understand [this], my beloved brethren. Let every man be quick to hear... slow to speak...   JAMES 1:19

A friend of mine lives in a large city where homelessness is a huge problem. One winter night she was coming home from work and walked by a man asking for money. It was cold and dark, and she was anxious to get home. Not wanting to pull out her wallet in a less than safe situation, she reached deep into her purse fishing for change. As her fingers searched in vain, the man started telling her that his coat had been stolen in the homeless shelter where he'd stayed the night before. Still trying to come up with a couple of quarters, she nodded and said, "That's too bad." When she finally found the money, she dropped it into the man's cup. He smiled and said, "Thank you for talking with me." My friend realized that what meant the most to that man was the fact that someone had heard him and responded.

We have a team of people from our ministry who try to help people living in the tunnels under the downtown bridge. They have found that each of these people has a story. Something tragic happened to them that resulted in their present circumstance. They appreciate the sandwiches and clean clothes, but mostly they appreciate someone caring enough to actually talk with them long enough to learn about them.

Let me encourage you to take time to listen.

———————————

Love Others Today: Do you know someone who simply needs a person to talk to? Be the one who will listen.

When You Pray

And when you pray, do not heap up phrases (multiply words,
repeating the same ones over and over) as the Gentiles do, for they
think they will be heard for their much speaking.   MATTHEW 6:7

Jesus knew the power of a short, simple prayer and spoke the words of
today's Scripture when He taught on prayer during the Sermon on the
Mount.

At times we are led by the Holy Spirit to pray for long periods of
time, but it is the sincerity of our prayers that is important, not their
length. If God always wanted our prayers to be long and drawn out, I
really believe He would have put only long, drawn-out prayers throughout the Bible. Many of the examples of prayer in Scripture are short and
concise. The enemy is the one who tells us that our prayers are never
long enough. It is fine with God for us to pray using only a few words.

In fact, all the way through the Bible are some incredibly brief, but
awesomely powerful, prayers, just a few of which are listed below.

- Moses cried out for his sister: "Please heal her, O God, I pray!"
  (Num. 12:13 NKJV).
- The Psalmist pleaded: "Have mercy and be gracious unto me,
  O Lord, for I am in trouble" (Ps. 31:9).
- Elijah prayed: "O Lord my God, I pray, let this child's soul come
  back to him" (1 Kings 17:21 NKJV).
- Jesus said: "Father, forgive them, for they do not know what
  they do" (Luke 23:34 NKJV).

———————

Love God Today: Remember what Jesus said: "...Do not heap
up phrases..." Short prayers are powerful!

Don't Be Afraid to Be YOU!

He fashions their hearts individually; He considers all their works.
PSALM 33:15 NKJV

God created everything about you to be unique, and He wants you to build an honest relationship with Him based on who you really are, not who you *think* you should be or who other people say you should be.

We relate to God as individuals. When we talk to God, we are not supposed to check our individuality at the door of the prayer closet. We need to go before Him just the way we are and give Him the pleasure of enjoying the company of the "original" He has made each one of us to be. God enjoys meeting us where we are, developing a personal relationship with us and helping us grow to become everything He wants us to be.

Our verse for today teaches us that God has fashioned our hearts individually. As we develop our individual styles of communication with God, we can learn from people who may be more experienced than we are, but we need to be careful not to make them our standard.

Most people are afraid to not be like everyone else; many are more comfortable following specified rules than daring to follow the Spirit's leading. When we follow man-made rules, we please people, but when we step out and follow God's Spirit, we please Him. So remember, come as you are!

Love God Today: Don't think your relationship with God has to look like someone else's. He made you to be unique, and He wants to relate to you just the way you are.

God Can Use Us All!

But God has chosen the foolish things of the world to put to shame the wise, and God has chosen the weak things of the world to put to shame the things which are mighty.   1 CORINTHIANS 1:27 NKJV

Today's Scripture says God purposely chooses the weak and foolish things of the world. The King James Version says He does this to "confound" the wise, which means to astound them. He wants those who are wise in their own eyes to look at people God is using and say, "What? He's using *you*?" God wants to astound them!

Why do you think Jesus chose the disciples He chose? Had He been looking for natural talent or human perfection, He probably wouldn't have picked tax collectors and fishermen.

God chooses the weak and foolish things of the world on purpose, so people will look at them and say, "It has to be God." He wants people to look at us and know He is the one behind our success.

Years ago, I read this statement: "God leaves glaring imperfections in some of His choicest saints, on purpose, just to keep them in a position where He can use them." Think about that! How proud and haughty do you think we would be if we could get through even a day without making a mistake? We would become arrogant, and that would prevent God from using us. He delights to use humble men and women who realize their complete dependence on Him.

This is great news! If you aren't perfect, then you're in perfect position for God to use you.

———————————

Love God Today: "Lord, I admit that I am flawed and imperfect. I pray that people will be amazed at the way You can use me."

God Will Meet You Where You Are

And God heard the voice of the youth, and the angel of God called
to Hagar out of heaven and said to her, What troubles you, Hagar?
Fear not, for God has heard the voice of the youth where he is.

GENESIS 21:17

Throughout the Bible, when people were in trouble, God met them where they were and helped them. Thank God He doesn't wait for us to manage to make our way to Him; He comes to us!

In today's Scripture, "the youth" whose voice God hears "where he is" is Ishmael, who was banished to the desert with his mother, Hagar. Ishmael could definitely be considered a "mistake." He was born because God promised a child to an elderly couple named Abraham and Sarai, but when the promise wasn't fulfilled quickly, Sarai asked Abraham to sleep with Hagar, her servant. When he did, Ishmael was conceived. This story is found in Genesis 16–18; practically everyone in it made some kind of mistake. But God forgave them and He never stopped working with them. He is faithful, even when we are not.

God often makes miracles out of mistakes. I suffered sexual abuse as a child, and that was definitely a mistake; it should never have happened. However, God has taken that mistake and made a ministry out of it. God met me where I was, accepted me, loved me, and healed me. He will do the same for you. Your mistakes are not a problem for God if you are willing to trust Him to work something good out of them.

Loving Yourself Today: "Thank You, God, for meeting me where I am and for redeeming every mistake."

Establish Boundaries

*The lot for the tribe of Judah according to its families reached
southward to the boundary of Edom, to the Wilderness of Zin at its
most southern part. And their south boundary was from the end of
the Salt [Dead] Sea . . .*   JOSHUA 15:1, 2

The Old Testament includes many verses that delineate boundaries
of land given to various groups of people. This tells me that territorial
boundaries are important to God, and I believe relational boundaries
are equally important.

Just as people build fences around their property to keep intruders
out, one way we can love ourselves is to establish limits to what we
allow other people to do to us. We can think of these as invisible lines
that keep us healthy, safe, and protected from being used and abused.

If you had a fence around your yard and looked out one day to see
your neighbors lounging on your patio furniture, you would probably
inform them that they need your permission to relax in your yard. The
same principle applies to your life. You need to lovingly let people know
you expect them to respect your personal limits.

Unfortunately, some people will take advantage of us if we let them;
that is just human nature. It is impossible for others to take advantage
of us unless we allow them to do so. We need to take responsibility for
ourselves and make sure we don't let others treat us inappropriately.

It is never good for you or the other people in your life if you allow
them to take advantage of you. Healthy relationships must have boundaries.

Love Yourself Today: "Lord, help me to establish and enforce
good, healthy boundaries in my life."

Start a Blessing Box

Give generously to them and do so without a grudging heart; then because of this the Lord your God will bless you in all your work and in everything you put your hand to.   DEUTERONOMY 15:15 NIV

Here's an idea: Get yourself a big box and start going through your possessions, asking God to show you what you have that you can use to bless others. Fill it up with things that are nice but that you no longer need.

Look in cabinets, drawers, closets, the basement, and the garage. You will fill up your box quickly. Don't keep something for years in case you ever need it—if you're anything like me, by the time you need it, you will have forgotten that you have it and go buy another one anyway.

Take the clutter that is frustrating you and turn it into blessings. Keep the box in a handy place and start asking God to show you who needs to be blessed.

One woman I know, who is a radical giver, got all the things together she wanted to use to bless people and displayed them on her kitchen table. She invited several friends over and told them to take anything they wanted from the table. She urged them to keep on taking until everything was gone.

I encourage you to be a giver and look for ways in which you can use what you have to be a blessing to others.

———————————

Love Others Today: I challenge you to start a blessing box before you go to bed tonight. Even if you only put one or two things in it, get it started.

Love Through the Little Things

He who has a generous eye will be blessed, for he gives of his bread to the poor.   PROVERBS 22:9 NKJV

What we do for others does not always need to be a big thing. It is often little acts of kindness that mean the most. If we always do just a little more than we have to, we will end up being a blessing to many. If you have eaten at a restaurant and your meal is eight dollars and you pay with a ten-dollar bill, you can leave a one-dollar tip, or you could do a little extra and tell the waiter to keep it all. It is only a dollar, but it is a way of doing a little something extra.

If we treat other people with generosity, we will find our own blessings increasing. We will have more joy, and God will bring a harvest of good things in our own lives. Don't be the kind of person who only does what they have to, but always go the extra mile. One day I was checking out at a bookstore and my change was a little over a dollar. I noticed a collection box at the register asking people to give their change to help hungry children. My first thought was, "I don't have to do that, I give all the time." But my second thought was, "I don't have to, but I am going to, just to go the extra mile." It isn't difficult to figure out which of my thoughts was from God and which one was just my own mind.

I gave the change and of course I never missed it, but my small extra gift was enough to feed a child for an entire day in a third world country like India or Africa. What seems like a small thing to us is often huge to someone else. Do all you can, as often as you can, for as many people as you can. It is the way God wants us to live.

Love Others Today: What kinds of little things can you do to show love toward others before you go to bed tonight?

Serve the Lord

*Choose for yourselves this day whom you will serve . . . but as for me
and my house, we will serve the Lord.*   JOSHUA 24:15

In Jesus' day, many leaders who were believers in Jesus would not confess their faith to others. They feared they would be expelled from the synagogue if they went public with their belief in Him (see John 12:42, 43). They were hindered from a relationship with Jesus because they cared too much about other people's approval. They wanted a relationship with the Lord, but they wanted the approval of their peers more.

Joshua, on the other hand, was bold about his belief in God, declaring that, "as for me and my house, we will serve the Lord." Be like Joshua, and determine that you and your household will serve the Lord. Whether other people agree or not, serving and following God is the only way to live a fulfilling, victorious life.

The leaders of Jesus' day who knew He was real believed in Him, but their love of people's approval would not permit them to have a true relationship with Him. I wonder how their lives turned out. What did they miss because they said *yes* to people and *no* to God?

We need to realize that not everyone is going to like us. If we live our lives worrying about what other people think, we will never take risks or stretch ourselves into new realms.

Jesus died to give you the freedom to follow the leading of the Holy Spirit for you as an individual. As you follow Him, I guarantee that He will lead you into a rewarding life.

––––––––––––

Love God Today: Like Joshua, make a deliberate, personal decision to serve the Lord and boldly declare: "As for me and my house, we will serve the Lord."

Walk This Way

And your ears will hear a word behind you, saying, This is the way; walk in it, when you turn to the right hand and when you turn to the left.

ISAIAH 30:21

No matter what has happened to you in your lifetime—even if you have been abandoned by your spouse or abused by your parents or hurt by your children or others—if you will stay on the path on which God leads you and be willing to leave your past behind, you will find peace, joy, and fulfillment. As you walk through this process, you can find comfort in God's promise from today's Scripture to guide you.

Jesus is the Way, and He has shown us the way in which we are to walk. The Lord has sent His Holy Spirit to lead and guide us in the way we are to go, the narrow way that leads to life, not the broad way that leads to destruction (see Matt. 7:14).

God says that as long as the earth remains, there will be "seedtime and harvest" (Gen. 8:22). We might paraphrase it this way: "As long as the earth remains, there will be *seed, time,* and *harvest.*" When we walk in God's path, we must be patient like the farmer who plants and expectantly waits for the harvest. He looks forward to the harvest, but he knows that time will elapse between seed planting and reaping. He does not allow that God-ordained process to frustrate him. Don't let it frustrate you, either.

Today's Scripture promises that God will lead us in the way that we should go. Don't be afraid, continue doing what is right, and you will live a blessed, joyful life.

Love God Today: Listen for God's voice, and keep walking on the path that leads to life and blessing.

Don't Run

Oh, that I had wings like a dove! I would fly away and be at rest.
PSALM 55:6

David prayed that he could fly away from trouble and be at rest, but running from trouble is not the answer. We must face our enemies and defeat them in God's power, just as David defeated Goliath. God has given us a "going through" power. He has given us a spirit not of fear, but of a calm, well-balanced, disciplined mind (see 2 Tim. 1:7). God's will is for us to confront challenges head-on, knowing the battle is not ours, but God's!

God can't help people who run. He gives us power and wisdom to deal with situations, not to try to escape them. Avoidance is not a godly trait.

Elijah tried to run and hide, but God made him go back and continue the work he'd been called to do. After God gave him some food and some rest, He confronted him about his attitude. He asked why he was hiding. Elijah answered with a bitter attitude. He said that he alone was left to serve God and people were seeking to kill him. He told God that all the Israelites had forsaken His covenant, and once again, Elijah was filled with self-pity as he told God that only he was being faithful. God told Elijah that He had seven thousand prophets left who had not bowed their knees to Baal; He also told him to get back to work. Sometimes we want to run away from responsibility, but as we can see with Elijah, God will not allow us to do that because escape is never the answer to life's challenges.

Love God Today: Face up to your challenges and responsibilities, knowing that God will give you power and wisdom to deal with them.

Peace, Peace . . . Wonderful Peace

Therefore love truth and peace.   ZECHARIAH 8:19 NKJV

Are you at peace today?

Nothing is worth anything if you don't have peace. Money is no good if you don't have peace. You absolutely cannot put a price on the value of peace.

Many people spend their lives trying to climb the ladder of success, and every time they go up one more rung, because of the pressure, they lose more of their peace, joy, and time to spend with their family. Their whole life is consumed with the pressure and stress of trying to keep that job. But we are never truly successful unless we have peace.

Some even work several jobs to acquire what the world dangles in front of them, saying, "You must have this to be truly happy." They get those "things," but they still don't have any peace.

Romans 14:17 tells us, "The kingdom of God is not meat and drink"—it is not things that money or worldly power can secure—but it is "righteousness, peace, and joy in the Holy Ghost" (KJV). The kingdom of God is in knowing who we are in Christ and having "the peace of God, which surpasses all understanding" (Phil. 4:7 NKJV).

God has no objection to our having nice things. He wants us to have our needs met abundantly and be in a position to bless other people. Never doubt that God wants to bless you, but don't seek to own or do anything that you cannot do with peace.

―――――――――――――

Love Yourself Today: "Lord, I would rather have peace than anything this world has to offer."

Develop Your Abilities

There are diversities of gifts, but the same Spirit.
1 CORINTHIANS 12:4 KJV

God has given us different natural gifts to help us fulfill His call on our lives. And we will find that exercising these gifts is fulfilling. However, if we waste our time trying to exercise gifts we don't have, we will be very frustrated. I think we have all had the experience of looking at what someone else can do and wishing we could do it.

Have you wasted your time trying to be like someone else instead of being the best you can at being yourself? I did that for a long time and I was always frustrated. God will never help you be anyone other than your unique self.

God puts gifts in us for others to enjoy and benefit from, and He puts gifts in them for us to enjoy and benefit from. However, if we are jealous of what they can do, we lose the enjoyment of what He has placed in them. I used to wish with all my heart that I could sing like one of the girls who traveled with us, and God taught me that I needed to enjoy her gift, not want it for myself.

Be satisfied and content with the gifts God has given you, and enjoy all the gifts He has placed in other people. Love yourself, and enjoy yourself, and never feel the need to compare yourself with others or compete with them.

If we are dissatisfied with the gifts God gave us, we won't give ourselves completely over to developing them. Forget about what you can't do and focus on what you can do. When you do this your joy will increase and you will be fulfilled and satisfied.

Love Yourself Today: Thank God for the gifts He has given you, and let yourself be blessed by the gifts He's given others.

The Secret of True Success

This Book of the Law shall not depart out of your mouth, but you shall meditate on it day and night... for then you shall make your way prosperous, and then you shall deal wisely and have good success.

JOSHUA 1:8

What comes to your mind when you hear the word *success*? Do you think of money or the things money can buy? Do you think of a powerful position in a corporate setting? Do you think of being well liked and influential among your friends and associates?

There was a time in my life when I thought success meant being a popular and powerful minister. I spent hours praying for my ministry to grow and appear "successful" to others. Over time, though, I came to realize that true power and success are found in love. I no longer want people to be impressed by me or by my ministry; I want them to think of me as someone who loves them, and I want them to be hungry and thirsty for God when they are with me. Now I spend my time praying to love as best I can.

Chances are, you have a certain standard of success, and maybe you strive to reach that standard. Maybe you have an ideal or a goal that represents success that may actually leave your heart empty if you attain it. The Bible speaks of success in terms of obeying God's Word, and throughout His Word, He urges us to love one another.

I want to encourage you to change the way you view success and see it in terms of love. Being able to love others is the essence of success; if you can do this, you can call yourself a success in life.

Love Others Today: "Lord, give me creative ideas that will demonstrate love in powerful, personal ways to everyone I meet. Let me understand and experience true success in life, which can only be found in love."

The Power of Forgiveness

If You, Lord, should keep account of and treat [us according to our] sins, O Lord, who could stand? But there is forgiveness with You [just what man needs], that You may be reverently feared and worshipped.   PSALM 130:3, 4

One morning in 1987, a man took his twenty-year-old daughter to a parade in a town in Northern Ireland.

As the father and daughter stood beside a brick wall waiting for the parade to march in front of them, a terrorist's bomb exploded behind them, instantly killing several people and leaving the two of them crushed under a pile of bricks. Unable to move, the father soon felt his daughter take hold of his hand.

Over the screaming voices around them, the father asked his daughter, "Are you all right?"

"Yes," she said.

At one point, the daughter said to her father, "Daddy, I love you very much."

She never said another word; she died of brain and spinal injuries about four hours later in a local emergency room.

That night, the father granted an interview to a reporter. When asked how he felt about the people who planted the bomb, he replied, "I bear them no ill will. Bitter talk is not going to bring my daughter back to life. I shall pray every night that God will forgive them."

Months later, people asked the father how he could forgive such a brutal act. He said, "My daughter's last words to me—words of love—had put me on a plane of love. I received God's grace, through the strength of His love for me, to forgive."

Love Others Today: You can receive God's grace, through the strength of His love, to forgive.

The Trademark of a Disciple

By this shall all [men] know that you are My disciples, if you love one another [if you keep on showing love among yourselves].

JOHN 13:35

Jesus says that there is one way people will know whether we belong to Him or not, and that is our love for one another. I like to say that love is the trademark, the distinguishing sign or characteristic, of a Christian. It's what sets us apart from the rest of the world.

Before you buy something, do you read labels or look for certain trademarks (brand names) that have a reputation for being good? That is what people should be able to do with us because we are disciples of Jesus Christ. They should be able to look at us and say, "This is good. This is a person of quality!" People should be able to identify us not only by our talk, but also by our walk.

The world is looking for something to believe in, something real, something tangible. They are looking for love, and God is love (see 1 John 4:8). Those of us who are Christians need to show them Jesus, and we do that not by merely wearing Christian jewelry or putting bumper stickers with Christian messages on our cars, but by walking in His love and demonstrating that love to others.

Many people have gone to church looking for God and instead been met with the rules and regulations of religion, and not even so much as a friendly smile. They left without encountering God.

Countless people are hungry for God, and God needs us to be His ambassadors, representing Him in every way, starting with His trademark characteristic, which is love.

———————————

Love Others Today: Are you expressing love to everyone you meet? This is the way the world will know you are a Christian.

The Secret of a Deeper Life

When He had stopped speaking, He said to Simon (Peter), Put out into the deep [water], and lower your nets for a haul.   LUKE 5:4

In *Celebration of Discipline,* Richard Foster teaches about the importance of inner disciplines, which can also be called spiritual disciplines. Without inner discipline, we will never have the outer disciplines we need. For example, if we don't discipline ourselves to study God's Word, then how can we know anything about what is right and wrong, wise or foolish?

In today's Scripture, we see that Jesus challenged the disciples to come out into the deep to find what they truly desired. In order to live a deeper life we must learn to discipline our thoughts, attitudes, and emotions. We must learn the disciplines of prayer, worship, Bible study, meditation, fasting, giving, serving, submission, solitude, and other things. Only those who practice the art of discipline can live the deeper life in God.

Spiritual disciplines are intended for ordinary human beings and not just for "spiritual giants" or those who hold some type of ministry position. They are for people who go to work every day, clean house, cut grass, and buy groceries. They are for boys and girls, married people and unmarried people. Don't be deceived into thinking you are not one of the elite called to develop a deep spiritual life. Jesus calls us all in the same way He called Peter, to come out into the deep.

Love God Today: "Lord, help me to develop the disciplines I need to cultivate a deeper spiritual life."

Thank God

I will praise You, O Lord, with my whole heart; I will tell of all Your marvelous works.   PSALM 9:1 NKJV

Throughout the Bible we see people celebrating progress and victory in a variety of ways. One way was to specifically take the time to give an offering to God and to thank Him.

Noah had been in the ark one year and ten days when God told him it was time to go forth and begin a new life. I cannot even imagine how happy he and his family were to see dry ground. The first thing Noah did was build an altar to the Lord and sacrifice various animals to Him. God was pleased, and He pronounced a blessing on Noah and his sons (see Gen. 9:1).

Abram (later renamed Abraham) regularly built altars to God and sacrificed, giving praise and thanks to God for his progress as he journeyed through the land.

We would quickly add a lot of celebration to our lives if we would take time to give thanks and perhaps some other type of offering when God does amazing things for us. An attitude of gratitude shows a lot about the character of a person. We should never have an attitude of entitlement, but we should have one that says, "I know I don't deserve God's goodness, but I am sure grateful for it."

———————————

Love God Today: "God, I never want to take Your goodness for granted, so please help me celebrate all You have done, are doing, and will do in my life."

Cross the Finish Line

But we do [strongly and earnestly] desire for each of you to show the same diligence and sincerity [all the way through] in realizing and enjoying the full assurance and development of [your] hope until the end.

HEBREWS 6:11

Beginning something is easy, but finishing takes courage. In the early stages of something new, we get all excited about it. We have a lot of emotions to support us. When the emotions wear off and all that's left is a lot of hard work and the need for patience, that's when we find out who really has what it takes to reach the goal and truly succeed.

In God's mind we aren't successful if we abandon what He's called us to do. He wants us to finish and do it with joy!

If you have been tempted to give up—don't. If you don't finish the thing you're currently involved in, you will face the same challenges with the next endeavor.

Some people spend their entire lives starting all kinds of new things and never finishing any of them. This happens for various reasons. Sometimes people lose interest or get distracted. Sometimes they aren't willing to press through obstacles that arise as they move toward their goal.

God doesn't promise that finishing everything we start will be easy. In fact, most of the time things don't go smoothly because we need to learn the lessons that come from resolving problems. But we cannot let ourselves quit; we must rely on God's grace and keep moving toward the finish line until we cross it in victory.

———————————

Love Yourself Today: Is there any unfinished business in your life? I encourage you to set goals for finishing and be diligent to reach them.

Your Thoughts Will Lead You

*All the days of the desponding and afflicted are made evil [by
anxious thoughts and forebodings], but he who has a glad heart has
a continual feast [regardless of circumstances].*   PROVERBS 15:15

I like to say, "Where the mind goes, the man follows." In other words,
positive thoughts are precursors to a positive life. On the other hand,
anxious thoughts and negative expectations set us up for miserable
lives.

Many people think they cannot control their thoughts, but they
can. Like anything else, it takes practice. What you think is up to you.
You can choose your own thoughts and should do so carefully, since
thoughts have a lot of creative power in your life. If you don't reject bad
thoughts, you will ultimately turn those thoughts into bad words and
actions that are not pleasing to God.

When our lives don't go well, we tend to blame our problems. But
most of the time, it's not the problems causing the trouble; it's the way
we *think* about the problems. One person, when faced with difficulty,
might think, *This is terrible! I will never get through this! My life is ruined!*
Another person, faced with exactly the same hardship, might choose to
think, *This is a challenge, but God promises to fight for me, and He will win
this battle.* Which of the two people do you think would come through
the difficulty in better shape?

Learning how to think correctly is mandatory for every aspect of
health. I urge you to make a priority of learning to think upbeat, healthy
thoughts that agree with God's Word. Don't let negative thoughts lead
you into an unhappy life; choose positive thoughts that will strengthen
and encourage you, and lead to a life of joy, peace, and victory.

———————

Love Yourself Today: In what ways do you need to change
your thoughts about yourself and your life?

Patience, Patience

Patience is the companion of wisdom.   ST. AUGUSTINE

One of the greatest ways to show love to others is to be patient with them. Sometimes we talk about being patient in very general terms, so today I want to call your attention to some specific everyday life situations in which you can express love through being patient.

Be patient with people's different opinions.

We all have people in our lives who have personalities that are hard for us to handle. That's an opportunity to exercise patience.

Be patient when someone tells you a story for the third time, even though you mentioned in the beginning, "Yes, you told me that last week."

Be patient when people interrupt you.

Be patient when people call you before you're really awake and say, "Oh. You're not up yet? I've been up for a couple of hours."

Be patient when people goof around and act silly when you're trying to be serious.

Be patient when people push in front of you in line or take a parking space when you've been waiting for it with your blinker on.

Be patient when a clerk has to change the receipt tape in the cash register before she can complete your purchase.

There are lots and lots of ways to demonstrate patience with others. When you do, you are showing them love.

———————————

Love Others Today: Help me, God, to be patient with others in every possible way.

God Looks Inside

Let not yours be the [merely] external adorning with [elaborate]
interweaving and knotting of the hair, the wearing of jewelry, or
changes of clothes; but let it be the inward adorning and beauty of
the hidden person of the heart, with the incorruptible and unfading
charm of a gentle and peaceful spirit, which [is not anxious or
wrought up, but] is very precious in the sight of God.

1 PETER 3:3, 4

Sometimes we are more concerned with outward things than we should be and are not nearly concerned enough about our inner life. If we paraphrase today's Scripture, we could say, "God may like your outfit, but He is not nearly as concerned about your outer appearance as He is with the inner condition of your heart."

It is very important that we live our lives with godly character and the inner qualities that matter to God. Most people spend a lot of time getting dressed each morning and making sure they look just right, and that is a good trait. But, we should first and foremost spend time making sure we are right in our thoughts and attitudes, because we cannot have good behavior unless we begin with a right heart attitude.

Take some time each morning to "set your mind" in the right direction. Confess any sin you have committed, forgive anyone you have anything against, and cast all your care on God concerning situations that are bothering you. With your mind set in the right direction, you will be able to be a good example to others throughout the day.

Loving Others Today: "Lord, help me develop such inner strength and peace that I can handle every situation in a way that represents You well to others."

Praise God on Your Way to Victory!

When Gideon heard the telling of the dream and its interpretation,
he worshipped and returned to the camp of Israel and said, Arise,
for the Lord has given into your hand the host of Midian.

JUDGES 7:15

Gideon was a shy, inexperienced man whom God called to lead troops into battle. Not only that, but he had far fewer men than he thought he needed in order to win the battle. God said to Gideon, "Arise, go down against their camp, for I have given it into your hand." As soon as Gideon received this personal word from God, he began to talk about the battle before him as though it were already won (see Judges 7:14, 15).

In contrast, we read in Exodus 15:1 that the Israelites sang a song after they passed through the Red Sea and their enemies had been drowned: "For He has triumphed gloriously; the horse and his rider . . . has He thrown into the sea." However, they sang this song of victory on the wrong side of the river. They were all excited; they were singing and dancing about the greatness of God *after* they had seen the manifestation of His power. They sang the right song at the wrong time. It would have been so much better if they had sung their victory song *before* they crossed the river.

All Gideon needed was to hear from God that he would win—and then he started worshipping. Learning to worship God before the battle gets His attention, demonstrates our faith and inspires us to boldly enter any challenge we face.

Love God Today: Whatever battles you're facing, praise God ahead of time for your victory.

On Slippery Slopes

The Lord God is my Strength, my personal bravery, and my
invincible army; He makes my feet like hinds' feet and will make
me to walk [not to stand still in terror, but to walk] and make
[spiritual] progress upon my high places [of trouble, suffering, or
responsibility]!   HABAKKUK 3:19

In Habakkuk 3, people were going through a time when everything
in their lives seemed to be going wrong. You may be thinking, *I can*
relate! Perhaps you are having problems in several areas: with your
children, in your marriage, at work, or with your finances. Maybe you
have health concerns. We all go through seasons when we seem to have
more trouble than usual, and these struggles in your life can be the
"high places" mentioned in today's Scripture—places of trouble and
suffering.

God says He will give us "hinds' feet" for the high places in our
lives. A hind is a mountain goat that can leap about freely on rocky, pre-
carious slopes. These animals can navigate what others cannot because
of the way God has designed them.

Be encouraged today because God has designed you to leap over
your troubles, too—not in your own abilities, but because He is your
strength. He will sustain you and provide a way out of the challenges
for you.

Depression, despair, and discouragement are from the enemy and
they will weaken you. Even if you cannot find something to rejoice
over, you can rejoice in your relationship with the Lord. When you love
God and trust in Him, He enables you to keep on walking forward.

———————————

Love God Today: "Thank You, Lord, for giving me 'hinds' feet'
when I'm on slippery slopes."

Where Is God?

*[After all] what kind of glory [is there in it] if, when you do wrong
and are punished for it, you take it patiently? But if you bear
patiently with suffering [which results] when you do right and that is
undeserved, it is acceptable and pleasing to God.*   1 PETER 2:20

Suffering is one of the most difficult things to understand in life and
in Christianity. We know that God is good, and we know that He sees
everything and is all-powerful, but why does He allow us to suffer,
especially unjustly?

God does not delight in our suffering, but He is honored and
pleased when we endure it with a good attitude, according to our Scripture for today. Trust requires unanswered questions. If we knew all the
answers, faith would not even be necessary. We must remember that
even Jesus suffered unjustly.

Some people become angry with God when tragedy or extreme difficulty comes their way. After a man watched his only son die of cancer,
he bitterly asked God, "Where were You when my son died?"

God replied, "The same place I was when Mine died."

God gave His only Son and allowed Him to go through unspeakable
suffering He did not deserve, and He did it for us.

The true test of faith is how we behave during trials and tribulations.

Love God Today: Suffering can make you bitter or better; the
decision is yours.

You Are What You Think

For the rest, brethren, whatever is true, whatever is worthy of
reverence and is honorable and seemly, whatever is just, whatever
is pure, whatever is lovely and lovable, whatever is kind and
winsome and gracious, if there is any virtue and excellence, if there
is anything worthy of praise, think on and weigh and take account
of these things [fix your minds on them].   PHILIPPIANS 4:8

We are what we think. What we think about truly determines our character, our emotions, our attitudes, and our decisions. Our thinking has a direct impact on our lives.

For example, if we think unkind thoughts, we become unkind. If we think loving thoughts, we become loving. If we think angry thoughts about a person, we often do not treat him in a loving way. The same principle applies to circumstances and situations. If we think things will go well, that's often the way we experience them. I am not saying that we can control everything that happens to us with our thinking, but if we think right, it can sure improve the quality of our journey.

Today's Scripture is so important because it tells us exactly the kinds of things we need to think about. The verse encourages us to think in the most positive ways and to "fix [our] minds" on the virtues it mentions. This means we are not to allow our minds to be easily distracted from them.

God wants us to discipline ourselves to think right thoughts—He knows that right thinking is one of the best ways we can love ourselves and other people.

———————

Love Yourself Today: Think happy thoughts and be a happy person!

God Gives Second Chances

I will restore or replace for you the years that the locust has eaten...

JOEL 2:25

The way to overcome the results of a series of bad choices is through a series of right choices. The only way to walk out of trouble is to do the opposite of whatever you did to get into trouble—one choice at a time. Maybe the current circumstances of your life are direct results of a series of bad choices you have made.

You cannot make a series of bad choices that result in significant problems and then make one good choice and expect the results of all those bad choices to go away. You did not get into deep trouble through one bad choice; you got into trouble through a *series* of bad choices. If you really want your life to change for the better, you will need to make one good choice after another, over a period of time, just as consistently as you made the negative choices that produced negative results.

No matter what kind of difficulty you find yourself in, you can still have a blessed life. You may have suffered some losses, perhaps you lost some things you will never get back. You cannot do anything about what is behind you, but you can do a great deal what about lies ahead of you. I believe if you are really faithful to God, He will even give you better things than you previously had. You are never hopeless with God! God is a redeemer; He causes bad things to work for your good; and He will always give you another chance.

Love Yourself Today: "Thank You, Lord, for giving me second chances again and again!"

Show and Tell

*And Moses was learned in all the wisdom of the Egyptians, and
was mighty in words and deeds.*   ACTS 7:22 NKJV

I heard a story about a man who went to Russia with good intentions
of telling people about the love of Jesus Christ. During his visit, many
people were starving. When he found a line of people waiting hope-
fully to get bread for the day, he approached them with Gospel tracts
in hand and began to walk the line telling them that Jesus loves them
and handing each of them a tract with the salvation message on it. One
woman looked into his eyes and said bitterly, "Your words are nice, but
they don't fill my empty stomach."

I have learned that some people are hurting too badly to be open to
the good news that God loves them; they must *experience* it. And one of
the best ways for that to happen is for us to meet their practical needs.
In other words, we need to *show* them they are loved in addition to telling them.

Many people around you are in need of practical help, and there are
many simple ways you can bless them. Consider contributing to a local
charity, volunteering your time at a feeding program, or taking someone who doesn't have transportation somewhere he or she needs to go.
Rake leaves or change lightbulbs for an elderly person in your neighborhood, or fix a meal for a busy young family. These things will require
some time, energy, and perhaps some money, but helping others not
only helps them, it blesses you!

—————————————

Love Others Today: What ways can you think of to show
God's love in practical ways to people around you?

Just for Today

If you can't feed a hundred people, then just feed one.
MOTHER TERESA OF CALCUTTA

I don't have to tell you that the world is full of problems. Hunger, disease, poverty, the oppression of women, and the exploitation of children are taking place in every country on earth right this minute. Heartbreaking stories are unfolding while you and I drink our morning coffee. I've seen so much of the world's anguish in my ministry travels, and it is truly overwhelming. I have also committed to do whatever I can do to relieve suffering and make the world a better place in any way I can. I challenge you today to do the same.

You may be thinking, *Joyce, what I can do won't even make a dent in the problems we have in the world.* I know how you feel, because I once felt the same way. But if we all think that way, nobody will do anything and nothing will change. Although our individual efforts may not solve the problems, together we can make a major difference. God won't hold us accountable for what we could not do, but He will hold us accountable for the things we could have done.

I realize that you can't do everything; I don't question that at all. You must say no to some things or your life will be filled with stress. I think the question each of us must answer is, "What am I doing to make someone else's life better?" And perhaps a better question is, "What have I done *today* to make someone else's life better?"

Nothing good ever happens accidentally. If we want to make the world a better place, each of us must say: Change begins with me!

Loving Others Today: Go ahead and say it: "Change begins with me!"

Doing vs. Being

O God, You are my God, earnestly will I seek You...
PSALM 63:1

For decades, Billy Graham led crusades all over the world, and his ministry was the vehicle through which countless thousands of people came to know Jesus as Lord and Savior. But at age ninety-two, when asked what he would do differently if he could live his life over again, he said, "I would spend more time in meditation and prayer and just telling the Lord how much I love Him and adore Him..." If anyone can claim great "spiritual accomplishments," Billy Graham could do so, but he knows the secret each of us must learn: What we do *for* God is not nearly as important as the time we spend simply *being with* God. Certainly, serving God is important and God blesses us when we do things in His name. But we cannot allow ourselves to become unbalanced in Christian service and neglect our personal, one-on-one time with Him nor can we let ourselves believe that serving God takes the place of intimate relationship with Him.

When we have been in God's presence, people notice. We are more joyful and more pleasant; we are more peaceful; we're easier to get along with and more gracious toward others. As with any friend, the more time we spend with God, the more like Him we become.

The more we become like God, the better we are able to love—because He *is* love—and the more sensitive we become to the love He wants to pour out to us and to others through us.

Love God Today: "Dear Lord, help me to remember that the time I spend *being with You* is more important than the things I do *for* You."

Doctor's Orders

He who gives to the poor will not want, but he who hides his eyes
[from their want] will have many a curse.   PROVERBS 28:27

A well-known psychiatrist named Dr. Karl Menninger presented many
lectures on mental health. At the end of one of them, he took questions
from the audience and someone asked, "What would you advise a person to do if he or she felt a nervous breakdown coming on?"

To the audience's surprise, Dr. Menninger responded, "Lock up
your house, go across the railroad tracks, find somebody in need, and
help that person."

Whether he knew it or not, the brilliant psychiatrist gave advice
that comes straight from God's Word. Today's Scripture says those who
give to the poor "will not want." Another way to express the point this
verse makes is to say that when we are generous, we will have no lack.
Certainly, part of having "no lack" includes having peace of mind and
mental well-being. Dr. Menninger prescribed the same remedy that the
wise writer of Proverbs suggested in today's verse and that Jesus Himself advised.

God knows the benefits of loving others. He knows that getting our
minds off ourselves is often the best thing we do for ourselves mentally.
It will stop the downward spiral of negative thoughts and turn self-
focus into "others-focus." Perhaps this is one reason God's instruction
for believers to love other people is a commandment, not a suggestion.
He requires us to do it because He knows it will not only bless the
people we help; it will be good for us, too.

———————————

Love Others Today: Next time you feel depressed, anxious, or
fearful, think about Dr. Menninger's advice. Get up and go do
something for someone in need.

Faith That Works

Faith goes up the stairs that love has built.
CHARLES SPURGEON

Many of us have been taught that faith is the pinnacle of all Christian virtues, that developing strong faith should be at the top of our spiritual to-do lists. Certainly, faith is vital to a strong, fruitful life as a believer. In fact, without faith, we cannot please God (see Heb. 11:6). But as important as faith is, 1 Corinthians 13:2 says that we can have enough faith to move mountains but amount to nothing if we don't have love.

"Faith works by love." In other words, love provides the energy for our faith. Knowing God's love for us as individuals and learning to allow His love to flow through us to others is the power behind our faith. Just as a car needs gasoline in order to move, our faith needs love in order to take us where we need to go.

Many people think faith alone is sufficient, but let me ask this: How can we place our faith in God unless we are convinced that He loves us? The assurance of His love empowers us to trust Him and place all our confidence and expectation in Him. In the same way, how can we ask God to help us if we are mistreating others? Loving God gives us confidence to trust He will do the things He has promised us. Similarly, our personal love walk enables us to receive from Him what we ask and believe for when we pray (see 1 John 3:18–23).

———————————

Love God Today: Remember: Faith works by love.

Untangle Yourself!

No soldier when in service gets entangled in the enterprises of
[civilian] life; his aim is to satisfy and please the one who enlisted
him.   2 TIMOTHY 2:4

Do you ever find yourself struggling to do something God has called you to do because you're busy with other things? In today's verse, Paul tells Timothy that a good soldier avoids getting entangled in things that won't please the person who enlisted him. In other words, a good soldier keeps his priorities in order and pleases God by refusing to do things that could distract him.

If you want to fulfill God's purpose for your life, you'll have to learn how to stay away from the entanglements of the world. This may mean saying no to an opportunity you'd like but really don't have time for. It could mean exercising good boundaries and not getting too wrapped up in other people's problems; there is a difference between godly involvement and entanglement. At times, it may even mean being less focused on your own problems, because they certainly can distract us from God's will and purpose for our lives.

When God calls you to do something, He will also raise up others to do the things that you don't need to be doing. Trust Him to do this, and don't let yourself get entangled in them.

———————————

Love Yourself Today: Focus on your true priorities.

Let God Do the Healing

O Lord my God, I cried to You and You have healed me.
PSALM 30:2

James A. Garfield became president of the United States in 1880 and was shot in the back six months later, in July 1881.

After the shooting, a doctor tried to remove the bullet, but couldn't. In the following weeks, more doctors probed his wound to try to locate the bullet, to no avail. Eventually, Alexander Graham Bell provided an electrical device doctors thought might locate the bullet, but that didn't work. Doctors later learned that sometimes removing a bullet causes more trouble than leaving it alone.

Garfield died on September 19, 1881, not as a result of his wound, but because of infection and hemorrhage that probably developed after so much probing for the bullet. The very thing physicians thought would heal Garfield ended up killing him.

When you have a "wound" of some sort, whether it's a disappointment, a betrayal, being abandoned or rejected, or some other hurtful situation, don't keep probing it. Go to God and ask Him to heal you in the way He knows is best for you. Then take your hands off. Don't try to "fix" yourself, but do follow the Holy Spirit as He leads you into healing and wholeness.

Love Yourself Today: Is there a wound in your heart that you have probed too much? Ask God to heal it; stay sensitive to His Spirit; and let Him bring new life and strength to you.

The Golden Rule

So then, whatever you desire that others would do to and for you,
even so do also to and for them, for this is (sums up) the Law and
the Prophets.   MATTHEW 7:12

Today's Scripture is often called the "Golden Rule," meaning that if we follow this one principle, everything will work out much better.

Most people treat others the way they are being treated, but God's principle is the exact opposite. We are not to treat people the way they treat us, but as we want to be treated. This is not easy to do. In order to obey God, we must move beyond feelings and what seems fair. If people mistreat us, God tells us to forgive them, pray for, and bless them. I don't think anybody "feels" like doing that, but if you have ever tried it, you know that it releases joy in your life and gives God the opportunity to deal with the person who mistreated you.

Imagine what would happen in the world if everyone operated by the Golden Rule. Everyone would be giving instead of just taking. We would be merciful because we all want mercy. Living this way would set us free from selfish living, the root of all of our unhappiness. Jesus said that in order to follow Him we must forget about ourselves. Sadly, most of us stay busy trying to take care of ourselves and make sure nobody mistreats or takes advantage of us. We need to deposit ourselves with God, retire from self-care, and obey the Golden Rule.

Love Others Today: "Father, make me aware of other people's needs and feelings, and help me treat them the way I would like to be treated."

Love Includes Everyone

"But if you love those who love you, what credit is that to you? For even sinners love those who love them."   LUKE 6:32 NKJV

The Bible teaches us that love is the most important thing to be concerned with. It is "the main thing," and we should let the main thing be the main thing in our lives. Are you majoring in things that really don't matter and paying very little attention to walking in love? For many years that was exactly what I did, and the result was an unfulfilled, dissatisfied feeling that I couldn't get rid of no matter how I tried. I had a relationship with God; I even had a ministry to others! But I was not happy and couldn't understand why. It seemed that I had most of what I wanted in life, but joy evaded me. As I cried out to God to help me, He showed me that I had my priorities out of line. I was more concerned with how I was being treated than with how I treated others.

I believe love can be seen or not seen in how we treat people, especially people we come in contact with who don't particularly interest us or have any ability to do anything for us. According to Jesus, our love should include everybody, not just those who can pay us back. He said if you merely love those who love you, what credit do you get? Even a sinner can do that!

We don't have the power of the Holy Spirit in our lives to help us do easy things, but to do things that are hard and sacrificial. Loving some people is very hard. They don't act lovable or even seem to want to be loved. They certainly don't reciprocate any affection shown to them. But when we begin to treat others as we would like to be treated and not as they are already treating us, we are obeying a principle that releases multitudes of blessings into our lives and pleases God.

––––––––––

Love Others Today: "Help me, Lord, to love *everyone*— even those who are difficult to love."

Communicating with Your Friend

Prayer is an appeal to the friendship of God.
ANDREW MURRAY

An earthly friendship involves loving and being loved. It means knowing that someone is on your side, wanting to help you, cheering you on, and always keeping your best interest in mind. A friend is someone you want to spend time with, and someone who is dear to you. You invest time in and with that person, and share your life with him or her.

One important key to developing an intimate, loving relationship with God is learning to communicate with Him as His friend. If we do not know God as a friend, we will be reluctant to tell Him what we need or to ask Him for anything. But if we go to Him as our friend, without losing our awe of Him, the time we spend with Him will stay fresh, exciting, and intimate.

Developing your friendship with God is similar to developing a friendship with someone on earth. It takes time. You can be as close to God as you want to be; it all depends on how much time you are willing to invest in the relationship. I encourage you to get to know Him by spending time in prayer and in the Word, and by walking with Him on a regular basis so you can experience His faithfulness over time.

The difference between developing a relationship with God as a friend and building relationships with people is that with God, you end up with a friend who is perfect! Don't try to keep God in a religious compartment, because He wants to have free access to every area of your life. He wants to be your friend.

Love God Today: "Thank You, Lord, for thinking of me as Your friend and for being a perfect friend to me."

Exercise Your Authority

And He has put all things under His feet and has appointed Him
the universal and supreme Head of the church [a headship exercised
throughout the church].   EPHESIANS 1:22

From the beginning of time, God had good plans for our lives, but the devil disrupted His original plan when he tempted Adam and Eve to sin and they listened to him instead of obeying God. God had given Adam and Eve dominion over everything in the Garden, but when they disobeyed Him, they lost their authority and suddenly, Satan had the upper hand.

We must never forget that Satan is a thief and a liar. He wants us to believe his lies because that will cause us to be deceived and not to live in truth. He will tell us God doesn't love us or want the best for us. From the beginning of time he has sought to divert the good things that are ours, and he will continue to do so if we allow him to. In other words, he will stay on our property if we don't run him off!

Satan may attack us, but he does not have to defeat us. We can have dominion over his works. All we have to do is exercise the authority that belongs to us in Christ by opening our mouth in faith and saying, "No, Satan, you have no authority over me." In His love for us, God sent Jesus to earth to deliver us from the power and authority of the enemy. Jesus is Lord over all; He has put all things under His feet. Because we are "in Christ" as believers, the only place Satan has in our lives is under our feet!

Love God Today: As you think of Easter and of Jesus' sacrifice for us, thank God that He has given you authority over the devil and that you have the Power of the Holy Spirit available to help you live in victory.

Communicating with the One You Love

Prayer is the most wonderful act in the spiritual realm, as well as a most mysterious affair.   WATCHMAN NEE

When we love people, we want to communicate with them. We want to share our thoughts and feelings, and hear their thoughts and feelings in return. In terms of a relationship with God, this communication is called prayer. I suspect many people pray much more than they know and that they have more effective and successful prayer lives than they realize. They do not always recognize when they are praying because they have been taught that prayer requires a certain environment or form. But prayer is simply talking to God and listening to what He has to say. The truth is that we can pray anytime, anywhere—even just directing a thought toward God qualifies as silent prayer.

Short, simple prayers can be mighty beyond description, but that does not take away from the fact that prayer is also a grand mystery. I believe that the greatest mystery of prayer is that it joins the hearts of people on earth with the heart of God in heaven; this is part of what loving God and receiving His love for us is all about. We human beings are the only creatures in the known universe who can stand in the natural realm and touch the spiritual realm. When we pray, we connect with that spiritual realm and with the God who desires to communicate with us because He loves us!

Love God Today: Prayer is an expression of your love for God, so when you pray, be sure to spend some time simply loving God and receiving His love for you.

Getting Off to a Good Start

Then the Lord said to me, "Arise, begin your journey..."
DEUTERONOMY 10:11 NKJV

One way to love yourself is to keep your physical body in shape, and one of the best ways to do that is to be committed to some kind of exercise. I often say the toughest part of a new exercise program is getting started. Following are some extremely simple ways to begin exercise programs that stick.

1. *A Daily Walk.* Something as simple as walking thirty minutes every day is very beneficial for your health. Do what's manageable, not what leaves you gasping!
2. *Indoor Exercise.* You can exercise in the privacy of your own home using a video, or you can take an exercise class.
3. *Strength Training.* Strengthening your muscles can be done quickly and at home, without any special machines. Sit-ups, push-ups, or lifting simple weights doesn't take long or cost much, but these things are good for you!
4. *Running or Biking.* Running and biking are good options, but riding a bicycle is easier on your joints than running.
5. *Swimming.* Swimming provides a good, gentle cardiovascular workout and works many muscle groups at once.

Start slowly, do your best, and keep it up. Soon you'll find yourself in better shape!

Love Yourself Today: Take care of your physical body through regular exercise, and do something to get yourself off to a good start today.

The Secret to Success

And the Lord your God will clear out those nations before you, little by little; you may not consume them quickly, lest the beasts of the field increase among you.   DEUTERONOMY 7:22

Walking a mile takes about two thousand steps. There are no other options or shortcuts. And every one of those steps is a tiny success that brings you closer to your goal. The same is true of any other goal. When you set your sights, it's essential to break down your goals into doable steps. As today's Scripture teaches us, we make progress "little by little." If you concentrate only on your ultimate goals, it is easy to get lost halfway there.

Whether your goals are financial, health related, spiritual, family oriented, or professional, plan to achieve them by setting short-term goals that are within your reach. This way, you continually have something within reach to shoot for and won't get discouraged. Writing down your goals will give you a sense of whether or not you are on track. For example, if your ultimate fitness goal is to walk three miles a day, five days a week, you might start off with a half-mile three days a week. The next week, you might aim for a mile each of the three days, and so on, upping your accomplishments without risking failure and disappointment. Don't make light of little victories. Small successes breed large ones. Remember, you have nothing to prove to anyone but yourself. Reaching short-term realistic goals will encourage you to press on toward the big prize.

Love Yourself Today: I am going to reach my goals in life, and I will do so by setting small, achievable goals along the way.

The Power of the Blood

The blood shall be for a token or sign to you upon [the doorposts of]
the houses where you are, [that] when I see the blood, I will pass over
you . . .   EXODUS 12:13

The miraculous events of the first Passover illustrate the power of the blood. It is an amazing foreshadowing of the sacrifice of Jesus, which gives us life. In this story, an angel of death was going to pass through the land of Egypt to kill the firstborn sons in every household. But God instructed His people to apply the blood of lambs to the doorposts of their homes so the angel of death would see it and pass over their houses or families.

Today, Jesus is our Passover Lamb. He shed His blood to set us free from the curse of sin and death. I do not think we fully avail ourselves of all the benefits of the blood of Jesus. I believe that we need to be diligent to apply the blood over our lives by faith and seal the doors of our lives through which Satan can gain access to us.

The Israelites had to go to a lot of trouble to get the blood on their doorposts. They had to kill the lambs, skin them, remove the blood, and put it into containers; they had to get some hyssop (a brush-like plant), dip it in the blood, and put the blood on their doorposts. That could not have been a neat, clean endeavor! But they did it, and they did it by faith because God told them to. The Israelites had to apply the blood of the lamb physically, but we can do it by faith. Jesus is the Lamb of God, and, as believers, we can apply the power of His shed blood to our lives by simply believing in it.

Love God Today: "Thank You, Jesus, for being my Passover Lamb."

Be Good—and Do Good!

*That you may walk worthy of the Lord, fully pleasing Him, being
fruitful in every good work . . .*   COLOSSIANS 1:10 NKJV

Goodness is a fruit of the Holy Spirit, and it's based on the foundation that God is good. God instructs us to allow His goodness to flow
through us to the people around us. Learning to be good to people, no
matter how difficult it may seem, is a basic requirement of experiencing
God's goodness in our lives.

Have you ever noticed how excited we are when someone is good to
us? But when it's time for us to be the ones who do good to someone
else, we're not nearly as interested. I believe we need to be less selfish
and say, "From now on, God, every day, I'm going to be good to someone. In fact, every day, all day, I will be good to all people."

There are many ways to be good to people. People are starving for
someone—anyone—to show them the love of God. Demonstrating
love starts with a simple act of goodness.

Start by asking God to develop the fruit of goodness in you. Ask
Him to put opportunities in your path that allow you to demonstrate
goodness daily. Ask God to display His character through you; to make
someone feel better, give someone joy, make someone happy. Ask God
to use you as an instrument to bless someone. You'll be amazed at how
your life will change by simply getting your mind off yourself and your
problems. Leave your list of "I wants" in God's hands. Instead, concentrate on being a blessing wherever you go. You'll be surprised at how
many of your "I wants" will be taken care of because of your goodness
to others.

———————

Love Others Today: "Lord, take away my 'I wants' and
replace them with Your wants."

The Resurrection Side of the Cross

He is not here; He has risen, as He said [He would do]. Come, see
the place where He lay.   MATTHEW 28:6

I like to say that we need to live on the resurrection side of the cross. Jesus was crucified and raised from the dead so that we might no longer be stuck in sin, living miserable lives. Many people wear a necklace called a crucifix, which is an emblem of Jesus hanging on the cross. Often we see a crucifix with Jesus hanging on it in a church. I know this is done to remember and honor Him and I am not against it, but the truth is that He is not on the cross any longer. He is seated in heavenly places with His Father and has also lifted us above the low level of thinking and living that takes place in the world.

The apostle Paul said he was determined to know Jesus and the power of His resurrection (see Phil. 3:10). Jesus came to lift us out of the ordinary, out of negative thinking, guilt, and shame. He came to take our sin to the cross to defeat it. It has no power over us any longer because we are forgiven and the penalty for our sins has been paid.

It is good and respectful to remember that Jesus suffered a terrible death for us on the cross, but we need to also realize that He rose from the dead and made a new life available to us. We need to appreciate and be thankful for His sacrifice, but we need to live in the joy of His resurrection.

Because Jesus lives, we can love God, ourselves, and others in unselfish ways, and we can overcome every challenge that the world and the enemy present to us.

———————

Love God Today: Which side of the cross are you living on: the crucifixion side or the resurrection side?

Seriously, Don't Worry!

And which of you by being overly anxious and troubled with cares can add a cubit to his stature or a moment [unit] of time to his age?

LUKE 12:25

Don't worry. Be happy. I'm sure you've heard the saying many times. Have you noticed that it's easier said than done? I believe that to actually stop worrying requires having experience with God. I don't think there is any way a person can fully overcome habits of worry, anxiety, and fear—and develop habits of peace, rest, and hope—without years of experience trusting and receiving God's love.

This is one reason why having faith and *continuing* to have faith in the midst of trials and challenges is so important. During these hard, trying seasons, God is building in us the patience, endurance, and godly character we need in order to eventually develop joyful hope, strong love, and confident expectation in Him.

When you find yourself in the midst of a battle against our enemy, remember that every round you fight produces valuable experience and strength. Every time you endure an attack, you become stronger.

Loving God means trusting Him in every situation and refusing to allow the enemy to control you, torment you, and rob your peace through worry. It will take practice and experience with God to break this habit, but you can do it by His grace. Commit to the process of becoming a worry-free, trust-filled person who lives in the peace and joy God wants you to experience.

———————————

Love God Today: Today, refuse to worry, be anxious, or allow fear to operate in your life. Declare your trust in God in every situation.

It's All Good

We are assured and know that [God being a partner in their labor]
all things work together for and are [fitting into a plan] for good to
and for those who love God and are called according to [His] design
and purpose.   ROMANS 8:28

In 1989 I went to the doctor for a regular checkup and, much to my surprise, discovered that I had very aggressive breast cancer which required surgery immediately. During this very difficult and seemingly tragic time in my life, God clearly spoke to my heart and told me that I was not to lose sight of His love. I repeated many times each day out loud, "God loves me!" I said it purposefully and firmly.

I have been cancer free for more than twenty years, praise God!

When you face hardships, choose to rest in God and trust His promises instead of becoming fearful and taking matters into your own hands. Don't give in to the temptation to compare your problems with anyone else's, but know that you are an individual and God has a specialized plan for your life. God doesn't do bad things, but He can certainly work them out for good in our lives if we trust Him to do so.

No matter how difficult or long your trials may be, don't let them separate you from the love of God (see Rom. 8:35–39). By refusing to believe anything except the fact that God loves you and has a good plan for your life, you conquer Satan and defeat him.

Love God Today: "Even in the midst of great difficulty, Lord, I love You, and I know that You love me. I trust You to work all things out for my good."

Every Good Thing Comes from Above

Bless (affectionately, gratefully praise) the Lord... Who satisfies your mouth... with good, so that your youth, renewed, is like the eagle's.

PSALM 103:1, 5

God gave us the sense of taste and the ability to enjoy eating! He also has admonished us to care for our bodies, which He refers to as our "temple." Here are some simple keys I've learned that will help you love yourself by eating balanced meals and being healthier.

1. *Make food sacred:* Do you know that you can choose your foods and meals in ways that please and glorify God? Every time you choose good, nutritious foods, you are choosing life, which is God's gift to you.
2. *Avoid refined carbohydrates:* This will work wonders for your health. Refined carbohydrates are found in foods made with white flour (breads, crackers, pasta, cakes, cookies, etc.), potato products, and in sugar, corn syrup, and other sweeteners.
3. *Load up on fruits and vegetables:* You can't become unhealthy or gain weight by eating too many fruits or vegetables. Their water and fiber contents prevent that. Learn to choose fruits and vegetables, which are good for your body.
4. *Focus on unsaturated fats:* This means cutting down on red meats, dairy, and foods made with hydrogenated oils. Focus instead on fish, poultry, olive oil, nuts, and avocados.
5. *Balance your plate:* Make sure half of your plate contains salad or vegetables, while using one-quarter of it for meat and the remaining quarter for a starch.

Love Yourself Today: Make a decision to change one thing about your eating habits that will help you feel better and live longer.

Take Responsibility

Apply your mind to instruction and correction and your ears to words of knowledge.   PROVERBS 23:12

Many times in my meetings, someone has asked me to pray for physical healing. I do pray for people, but I also know that many times what people really need is to take personal responsibility for their health and well-being. Often, their physical problems can be solved by improving their health—eating better, exercising, drinking more water, getting enough sleep at night, or taking time for leisure, recreation, and relaxation.

Personally, I have worked hard for many years. As I grow older, I realize that I cannot do everything I could do years ago. For example, I must be careful to observe the same bedtime every night, and I must be very disciplined about eating sweets because they affect my blood sugar, which causes me to feel tired and lethargic.

I have also learned that not feeling strong and healthy has a tremendous effect on my ability to enjoy my daily life. It sends my "joy level" plummeting. Since I know these things, I am determined not to waste any more days not enjoying them. If I have to make some changes to feel better so I can enjoy myself more, then I'm willing to do so. I encourage you to do the same and to make a priority of being healthy so you can enjoy the abundant life God wants you to have.

Love Yourself Today: In what specific areas do you need to take responsibility to improve the quality of your life?

Let Love Win the War

For the weapons of our warfare are not physical [weapons of flesh and blood], but they are mighty before God for the overthrow and destruction of strongholds.   2 CORINTHIANS 10:4

We are definitely in a war. The Bible teaches us that the weapons of our warfare are not carnal, natural weapons, but ones that are mighty through God for the pulling down of strongholds. "Casting down" wrong thinking is vital to proper spiritual warfare. Selfish, self-centered, "what about me" thinking is definitely wrong thinking.

Purposely forgetting about ourselves and our problems and doing something for someone else while we are hurting is one of the most powerful things we can do to overcome evil.

When Jesus was on the cross in intense suffering, He took time to comfort the thief next to Him (Luke 23:39–43). When Stephen was being stoned, he prayed for those stoning him, asking God not to lay the sin to their charge (see Acts 7:59–60). And when Paul and Silas were in prison, they took time to minister to their jailer. Even after God sent a powerful earthquake that broke their chains and opened the door for them to come out, they remained just for the purpose of ministering to their captor. How tempting it must have been to run away quickly while the opportunity was there, how tempting to take care of themselves and not worry about anyone else. Their act of love moved the man to ask how he might be saved, and he and his entire family were born again (Acts 16:25–34).

Love Others Today: Which battles in your life need to be fought with love right now?

Speak and Act with Humility

Talk no more so very proudly; let not arrogance go forth from your mouth...   1 SAMUEL 2:3

When we can do something well, or when we reach a personal goal, we tend to feel good about those things. As long as we feel positively about ourselves in a balanced way, it's fine. When we become proud and fail to be merciful toward others who struggle with things we have mastered, it's a problem.

I am fairly disciplined in my eating habits, and I recently spent a week with someone who really struggles in that area. She mentioned several times how disciplined I am and how undisciplined she is. Each time she did so, I said, "I have areas of weakness also, and you will overcome this as you continue to pray and make an effort."

There was a time in my life when I would not have been so sensitive to my friend's feelings. I probably would have given a sermon about the dangers of overeating and poor nutrition. But I would not have succeeded in doing anything but making my friend feel guilty and condemned. I have discovered that one way to love people is to help them not to feel worse about things they already feel bad about.

Meekness and humility are two of the most beautiful aspects of love. Paul said that love is not boastful (see I Cor. 13:4). Love never wants to make people feel badly because they cannot do what we can do. Instead of bragging about our strengths, let's thank God for them and encourage those who are weak in ways we are strong.

Love Others Today: What are some things you do well? Be merciful and humble toward people who are struggling in those areas.

Your Source of Security

Let the beloved of the Lord rest secure in him, for he shields him all day long, and the one the Lord loves rests between his shoulders.

DEUTERONOMY 33:12 NIV

One way to know whether you really love yourself in a healthy, balanced way or not is to ask yourself whether you are a relatively secure person or whether you struggle with insecurity. Simply put, insecurity is a feeling that you really aren't "good enough," or needing others' approval in order to be confident. It has to do with whether your life is built on the unshakable foundation of God's love or the faulty foundation of what others think of you.

Your security does not depend on your bank account, your job, the way you look, other people's opinions of you or even the way others treat you. I know this can be tempting in today's world, but I urge you not to base your security on your educational or professional achievements, the labels inside your clothes, your car, or the house you live in. Don't base it on whether you are married or single, or whether you have children or not. Don't look for your security anywhere but in Jesus Christ and in Him alone. He is the only one whose opinion matters, and He is the only one who will love you forever and never change His thoughts toward you.

Re-read the scripture for today and be encouraged. You are the beloved of the Lord and you can rest secure in Him.

Love Yourself Today: Start working with God to develop a rock-solid sense of security. He loves you, and through Him you can do whatever you need to do in life.

Actions Speak Louder Than Words

If you [really] love Me, you will keep (obey) My commands.

JOHN 14:15

Obeying God is the way we show our love for Him. Talk is easy, but actions speak much louder than words. I believe that the more we get to know God and experience His faithfulness in our lives, the more we willingly respond with prompt obedience to Him. It's easy to sing songs about our love for God, but we must ask ourselves, "Am I being obedient to God's will?"

Everything God asks us to do is something that will ultimately work out for our benefit. When we truly believe that, it becomes much easier to obey Him promptly. God is never trying to take anything away from us unless it is something that will be harmful to us. He never asks us to obey Him in anything unless it will benefit us in the long run.

I encourage you to make a new commitment today to obey God in little things as well as big things. Brother Lawrence said that he delighted in picking up a straw from the ground for the love of God. Let's develop that kind of devotion to our Lord.

Jesus loved His heavenly Father so much that He was obedient even unto to the point of death (see Phil. 2:8). Are we willing to love Him enough to at least be obedient enough to say "no" to ourselves if that is what's necessary for us to obey Him?

The Holy Spirit is in our lives to lead and guide us into the perfect will of the Father. Let's pray for His infilling daily. He will be glad to help you do it if you'll simply ask.

———————————

Love God Today: "Lord, today I will obey You in the little things as well as the big."

Short and Sweet

Woe to you, scribes and Pharisees, hypocrites! For you...for a
pretense make long prayers...   MATTHEW 23:14 NKJV

Sometimes people think they have to spend a long time praying in order to demonstrate their love for God. But prayer does not have to be long to be powerful. The length of our prayers really makes no difference to God. All that matters is that our prayers are Spirit-led, heartfelt, and accompanied by true faith.

There is certainly nothing wrong with praying for an extended period of time. I believe we should set aside times for prolonged prayer and that our willingness or lack of willingness to spend time with God determines our level of intimacy with Him. If issues in our lives really require us to pray at great length, then we need to do that, but we do not have to pray prolonged prayers just for the sake of logging time.

I have learned that some of the most powerful, effective prayers I can pray are things like, "Thank You, Lord," or "Give me strength to keep going, Lord." And perhaps the most powerful of all: "Help!!!" See? Just a few words will connect us with heaven, and God will know how much we love Him simply because we turn our thoughts toward Him.

If you have thought your prayers had to be long in order to be effective, I hope you have now been relieved of that burden. Just one word spoken to Him in faith from a sincere heart can reach His heart and move His hand.

———————————

Love God Today: Let prayer be like breathing, easy and natural. Lift your heart to God all throughout the day.

Take More Vacations

The world is indeed a wearisome place.   WATCHMAN NEE

If I were to say to you, "Take more vacations," you might think, *I would do that if I had more money or more time off work.* But the truth is we can take vacations without money and we can use the time we do have more wisely.

For example, try taking half days off, but don't use them to run errands, unless, of course, the errands are fun ones. When you do take time off, refer to it as "vacation," not "time off," because the word *vacation* has a nice feeling and a good emotional effect.

I think we actually hesitate to say we are on vacation too often because we don't want people to think we don't work hard enough. When some people find out that I am taking some time off, I often feel I need to justify my plans by saying, "Yes, but I will be doing some work, too."

We should be able to take time off without working and not feel guilty about it. We don't always have to be working in some way to justify our existence on earth. If work isn't balanced out with rest and fun, then we become a slave to it.

Whenever possible, it's a good idea to take one or two vacations, consisting of a week or more, each year. It takes us a couple of days to unwind enough to reach the point where we can truly rest and relax. In the meantime, take one-day, half-day, or ten-minute vacations to keep your life balanced. Do things that will refresh you, and be sure to spend your time with people who will make you laugh.

———————————

Love Yourself Today: Make enough changes in your life so that when people ask you what you have been doing, you can say something besides "working."

Dream Big

Through skillful and godly Wisdom is a house (a life, a home, a family) built, and by understanding it is established [on a sound and good foundation].

PROVERBS 24:3

I hope you have a dream or vision in your heart for something greater than you are currently experiencing. Ephesians 3:20 tells us that God is able to do exceedingly abundantly above and beyond all that we can hope or ask or think. If we are not thinking, hoping, or asking Him for anything, we are cheating ourselves. We need to think big thoughts, hope for big things, and ask for big things. God wants to fill our lives with precious and pleasant things.

I always say I would rather ask God for a lot and get half of it than to ask Him for a little and get all of it. However, only an unwise person thinks, dreams, and asks for big things, but fails to realize that an enterprise is built by wise planning.

Dreams for the future are possibilities, but not "positivelies." They are possible, but they will not positively occur unless we do our part.

I believe there is enormous potential hidden in you, but like an athlete who has gold medal potential, you may have to work hard to see it become a reality. God has given you great dreams; He wants to bring them to pass. And if you will diligently do your part, He will help you and do "exceedingly abundantly" more than you could ever ask for or imagine.

––––––––––––––––

Love Yourself Today: What kinds of big thoughts, big hopes, and big things do you want in your life? What can you do now to start working toward them?

Make the World a Better Place

*Let each of you esteem and look upon and be concerned for not
[merely] his own interests, but also each for the interests of others.*

PHILIPPIANS 2:4

Do you ever look at the things that are going on in the world today
and think, *Something's got to change! Someone needs to do something!* If
so, many people would agree with you. I think we all know something
is wrong in society and that it needs to be fixed, but nobody seems to
know how to begin making changes. We often wish the world would
change without stopping to realize that nothing will change in our
world unless each one of us is willing to change.

We cannot fix what we don't understand, so our first need is to
locate the root of the problem. Why are the majority of people unhappy?
You may say, "People are sinful. That is the problem." I agree in theory,
but let's approach the problem from a practical viewpoint that we all
deal with daily. I firmly believe the root of most problems is *selfishness*.
Selfishness exists whenever a person goes against God and His ways.
Selfishness takes place when a person says, "I want what I want and I
am going to do whatever I need to do to get it."

I believe you can do something to change the world today simply by
becoming aware of selfish thoughts and actions and working to eliminate them from your life while replacing them with love.

Love Others Today: Declare war on selfishness and be a
blessing to everyone you meet.

Lay Down Your Life

No one has greater love [no one has shown stronger affection] than to lay down (give up) his own life for his friends.   JOHN 15:13

If you were to hand someone one hundred dollars, you would actually be handing them a piece of your life. You worked to earn the money you gave away. It took your time and effort, so it represents a part of you. When we think about laying our lives down for others, we need to see it in a practical way. We can over-spiritualize a thing until it has no practical value.

First John 3:16 and 17 says that if anyone has this world's goods and sees his brother in need, yet closes his heart of compassion, the love of God cannot live and remain in him. Verse 16 tells us to lay down our lives for each other, and verse 17 tells us that we are to meet needs!

We have hearts of compassion because God has given us new hearts and new spirits, which are both His. Jesus was *moved* with compassion. Compassion is quite different from pity. We can feel sorry for people and do nothing, but compassion moves us to get involved and help in some way.

When Jesus asks us to lay our lives down for others as He laid down His life for us, He is not asking to get on a cross and be crucified. He is asking us to let Him use us and flow through us. Jesus needs bodies to work through on the earth today, and the church is called the "body of Christ." We are His hands, feet, arms, eyes, mouth, and whatever He needs to accomplish His purposes through us. The only good works that will get accomplished are those we are willing to do.

———————

Love Others Today: What is the last thing that you did to help somebody?

It Is What It Is

You shall not covet your neighbor's house, your neighbor's wife, or his manservant, or his maidservant, or his ox, or his donkey, or anything that is your neighbor's.   EXODUS 20:17

Do you like your life and enjoy it? Or do you struggle with it and wish you had a different life? Do you want to look the way someone else looks, or have someone else's family or career? Wanting what others have is called "coveting" in the Bible, and God forbids it.

You are never going to have anyone else's life, so wanting it is a waste of time. You won't look like someone else, either, so you might as well learn to do the best you can with what you have to work with.

When I adopted the phrase "It is what it is" into my vocabulary, it really helped me deal with reality and not waste my time being upset about things I can't do anything about. It helps me realize I quickly need to deal with things the way they are, not the way I wish they were.

Nobody has a perfect life, and it is entirely possible that if you want someone else's life, he or she may want someone else's life, too. Unknown people want to be movie stars, and movie stars want privacy. Employees want to be the boss, while the boss often wishes he had less responsibility.

Contentment with life is not a feeling; it is a decision we must make. Contentment doesn't mean we never want to see change or improvement; it simply means we'll do the best we can with what we have and will maintain an attitude that allows us to enjoy the gift of life.

Love God Today: "Lord, I decide and declare today that I am not envious of anything that belongs to anyone else. I am content with the life You've given me, and I will make the most of it."

Live for God

Behold, I am coming soon, and I shall bring My wages and rewards with Me, to repay and render to each one just what his own actions and his own work merit.   REVELATION 22:12

Every person, with no exception, will one day stand before God and give an account of his life (see Rom. 14:12). I want to encourage you to remember Jesus will come for us when we least expect it, and then it will be too late to do all the things we intended to do but never got around to.

Salvation is a gift of God; He extends it to us because of His grace, and we receive it by faith. We do not get into heaven because of good works, but today's verse teaches us that our works will be judged and rewarded according to what we have merited.

God sees what we do in secret and will reward us openly. Everything that is now done behind closed doors will one day be brought out into the open, so we should realize that nothing can be hidden forever. A day of reckoning will come.

Some people might think, *Well, as long as I am going to heaven, that is enough.* Simply hoping to get to heaven after death is a selfish motive that produces a selfish life. We should live for God and for His glory. We should love God with all our hearts in response to His great love for us and realize that we are alive for a purpose, and part of that purpose is for God to use us to help reconcile others to Him. We are actually created for good works that God prepared for us ahead of time (Ephes. 2:10). God's desire and will is that we do those good works, but do them because He loves us, not to get Him to love us or to impress people.

Love God Today: You are created for good works, and you will never be happy unless you are doing them.

Make a Sacrifice of Praise

Through Him, therefore, let us constantly and at all times offer up to God a sacrifice of praise, which is the fruit of lips that thankfully acknowledge and confess and glorify His name.   HEBREWS 13:15

Today's Scripture encourages us to offer God "a sacrifice of praise." We often interpret this as praising God when we do not feel like praising Him, and that can certainly be a type of sacrifice. But I believe the writer is talking about praise actually being the sacrifice, not just doing it when we don't feel like it.

The Old Testament sacrificial system required the blood of animals to atone for people's sins. We, however, live in New Testament times, when we no longer need to put slain goats and bulls on an altar. Instead, the sacrifice—the offering—God wants from us today is to hear right words coming out of our mouths, rising up before His throne. Just as the smoke and the aroma of the animal sacrifices went up before His throne under the Old Covenant, the praise from our hearts rises up as a sacrifice before Him today. In Hebrews 13:15, the Lord was really saying, "The sacrifice I want now is the fruit of your lips thankfully acknowledging Me."

We need to apply this Scripture to our everyday lives, making sure that we speak God's praises every chance we get. We need to tell people about all the great things He's doing for us; we need to thank Him; we need to tell Him we love Him. In our hearts and with our mouths, we should go through our days praising Him. We need to be people of praise, acknowledging God "constantly and at all times."

———————————

Love God Today: "Lord, I will acknowledge and praise You every chance I get today."

Keys to a Healthy Self-Image

*For You did form my inward parts; You did knit me together in my
mother's womb.*   PSALM 139:13

There is considerable focus on "self-help." Many books have been written; conferences and seminars are held, and people want to get all the
self-help they can. But the truth is that we need more than self-help,
we need God's help. People want to have a more positive self-image or
better self-esteem. There is no better source of teaching on the subject
than God's Word. He has a book full of good things to say to us and
about us.

I believe that having a positive self-image is biblical. If we have a
healthy self-image and a strong sense of self-worth, we no longer need
to worry about what people think or say about us. We don't have to
be first or best. We have no need to compare ourselves with others
because we are happy being who we are.

So, what does a healthy self-image look like? It is believing with your
heart that *God created you and He loves you unconditionally.* It means
knowing that you have faults and weaknesses and wanting to improve,
but realizing God is working in your life and changing you day by day. A
healthy self-image also means that you don't focus excessively on your
weaknesses. When you have a godly self-image, you like yourself.
You may not like everything you do, but you refuse to reject yourself.
Your sense of worth is not based on how other people treat you or what
they think about you. It's rooted in the fact that God created you and
Jesus died to redeem you!

——————————

Love Yourself Today: Remind yourself today, *"I must be
valuable—Jesus died for me!"*

My Beloved Son (and Daughter)

*And all of us ... are constantly being transfigured into His very
own image in ever increasing splendor and from one degree of
glory to another ...*   2 CORINTHIANS 3:18

We all make mistakes every day of our lives. But if we love God and
want to do what is right, He keeps working with us and loving us into
wholeness. We don't have to feel rejected in the meantime. God sees
the end from the beginning. He knows where we are now and is fully
aware of every one of our faults, but He also knows where we can be if
He keeps loving us and encouraging us to go forward. God changes us
from "one degree of glory to another," according to 2 Corinthians 3:18,
but He also keeps loving, accepting, and approving of us while we are
making the journey.

The Scripture tells us that a voice came from heaven two different
times and said, "This is My beloved Son, in whom I am well pleased."
Why was this necessary? I believe that Jesus needed to hear these
words, and I believe we need to hear the same expression of love and
affirmation. Knowing that God is on our side gives us confidence. Jesus
received God's encouragement, and we need to do the same. Don't concentrate on everything that is wrong with you. That will distract you
from proper fellowship with God. Thank God for your strengths and
turn your weaknesses over to Him.

When God finished all of His creation, including man, He looked
at it and said, "It is good!" God intends to work in and through you, so
relax and believe that God approves of you!

———————————

Love Yourself Today: Say out loud, "I am God's beloved child.
He approves of me and will finish the good work He started!"

Make Yourself Happy

So then, as occasion and opportunity open up to us, let us do good [morally] to all people. . . . Be mindful to be a blessing, especially to those of the household of faith [those who belong to God's family with you, the believers].   GALATIANS 6:10

Selfish people are the unhappiest people on the face of the earth. They suppose that joy is found in owning things and getting their way, yet they are deceived and do not know the truth. Real life is not about what we own, but what we give.

Selfishness is the most natural thing in the world to the human being. We don't have to even learn it: we're born with it. Just watch how newborn babies act when you don't give them what they want when they want it. That may be acceptable for babies, but it is not appropriate for grown men and women.

Jesus teaches we must die to ourselves, to all of our own interests and plans if we intend to be His disciples and truly live. Dying to them doesn't necessarily mean we will never have them, it just means they will come in God's way and timing if they are His will. Yes, there is a wonderful life available to every person willing to follow God fully, and it is provided through Jesus Christ and released through receiving and giving love.

When we reach out in love to others joy is released in our lives. God has not called us to "in-reach"; He has called us to "out-reach." Don't wait until you feel like doing something loving; start doing it on purpose.

———————————

Love Others Today: *Reach out* today and do something for somebody else, expecting nothing in return.

Loving Others with Your Words

*Love (affection and goodwill and benevolence) edifies and builds up
and encourages one to grow [to his full stature].*

1 CORINTHIANS 8:1

Are you a part of God's construction crew, or part of Satan's destruction crew? God's Word teaches us to edify and build up people. They need to hear our words of encouragement. We all like to have people say loving things to us, so we should do for others what we want them to do for us (see Matt. 7:12). We should never fail to do something God asks us to do merely because it doesn't come easily.

Ask God to put words into your mind that you can sincerely say to people that will build them up. You may be shopping for a new dress and see a store clerk and think, *That dress she is wearing is really pretty.* Your thought won't help her, but saying it to her will. Tell people you appreciate their hard work, because you might be the only person who ever tells them.

Start your encouragement ministry with the people in your family, then move on to those at work or church, and then get radical and compliment complete strangers (use wisdom when speaking to members of the opposite sex).

If you like to set goals for yourself, why not set one in this area? Start by committing to give three compliments each day and keep increasing the number until it becomes part of who you are and not just something you try to do.

———————

Love Others Today: Don't go to bed tonight without paying someone a compliment.

The Miracle of Encouraging Words

Anxiety in a man's heart weighs it down, but an encouraging word makes it glad.   PROVERBS 12:25

One of the best encouragers I know is John Maxwell. He truly has the gift of encouraging others and is the writer of today's devotion.

"The impact of an encouraging word can be profound—nearly miraculous. A word of encouragement from a teacher to a child can change his life. A word of encouragement from a spouse can save a marriage. A word of encouragement from a leader can inspire a person to reach her potential.

"To encourage people is to help them gain courage they might not otherwise possess—courage to face the day, to do what's right, to take risks, to make a difference. And the heart of encouragement is to communicate a person's value. When we help people feel valuable, capable, and motivated, we often get to see their lives change forever. And we sometimes get to see them go on to change the world.

"If you'll just take time to encourage people, you can make a big difference in the world. You can add value to others. Everyone can become an encourager. You don't have to be rich. You don't have to be a genius, and you don't have to have it all together. You just need to care about people and be willing to get started. You don't have to do anything big or spectacular. The little things you can do every day have the potential for a much greater impact than you can imagine."

––––––––––––

Love Others Today: Do you want to make an impact in the world around you? Become an encourager!

We're Adopted

Although my father and my mother have forsaken me, yet the Lord
will take me up [adopt me as His child].   PSALM 27:10

Today's Scripture has been particularly meaningful and encouraging to me over the course of my life.

I was abused as a child. During my childhood, my mother was deeply afraid of my father, so she was unable to rescue me from the various kinds of abuse he perpetrated against me. I felt very alone, forgotten, and abandoned. I have come to understand that multitudes of people we encounter daily are just trying to survive until someone rescues them—and that someone could be you or me.

The Bible says that in God's love, "He chose us [actually picked us out for Himself as His own] in Christ before the foundation of the world" (Eph. 1:4). He planned for us to be adopted as His own children. These beautiful words brought a great deal of healing to my wounded soul. God adopts the forsaken and the lonely, and He lifts them up and gives them value.

Mother Teresa of Calcutta felt that each person she met was "Jesus in disguise." Just try to imagine how much differently we would treat people if we thought of them as she did. She realized that God loves everyone as His own sons and daughters. If someone insulted, slighted, ignored, or devalued one of my children, I would take it as a personal insult, so why is it so hard to understand that God feels the same way when one of His children is mistreated? You and I belong to Him, so we need to love ourselves appropriately and treat ourselves well. We also need to treat others as part of God's family and do what we can to build them up and add value to their lives.

———————————

Love God Today: Always be on the lookout for Jesus in disguise.

Seek the One Thing

One thing have I asked of the Lord, that will I seek, inquire for, and [insistently] require: that I may dwell in the house of the Lord [in His presence] all the days of my life, to behold and gaze upon the beauty [the sweet attractiveness and the delightful loveliness] of the Lord and to meditate, consider, and inquire in His temple.

PSALM 27:4

If you could ask for only one thing in life, what would it be? David said there was only one thing he sought after: to dwell in God's presence. Truly, to know God is the highest calling we have.

We can get so distracted with life that we neglect the most important thing—spending time with God, knowing Him, appreciating Him, seeking His wisdom.

How foolish we are to spend our lives seeking those things that cannot satisfy while we ignore God, the "One Thing" Who can give us great joy, peace, satisfaction, and contentment. The world is filled with empty people who are trying to satisfy the voids in their lives with a new car, a promotion, a relationship or some other thing. Their efforts to find fulfillment in those things never work. They never know the joy of seeking the "One Thing" they really need. Each of us has a God-shaped hole inside, and nothing can fill it except God Himself. No matter what else we try to fill it with, we will remain empty and frustrated.

If God is on your list of things to seek but not at the top, I encourage you to move everything around and put it all *after* Him. If you will put Him first in everything you do, you will be blessed beyond measure.

———————

Love God Today: "Lord, I will seek You as my One Thing above everything else. *You are my number one priority.*"

Choose to Enjoy Today

I call heaven and earth to witness this day against you that I have set before you life and death, the blessings and the curses; therefore choose life . . .   DEUTERONOMY 30:19

All it takes to begin enjoying something—anything—is a choice. It requires a deliberate decision to enjoy what you are doing. Just as you can decide to be frustrated or unhappy, you can decide to be happy.

All of us are tempted at times to complain and say we are not happy. We all have moments and seasons when we do not enjoy our lives. Sometimes you just have to make a decision and tell yourself: "This is what I need to do today so I *will* enjoy it." We must prepare ourselves mentally for what we need to do. We can perform the most common tasks for the glory of God and find joy in doing them.

If we are going to enjoy our lives, we will have to do so on purpose. If we don't do it intentionally by making a decision, we are not likely to do it at all. Wherever we are, whatever we are going through, we can say: "This is where I am; this is what's going on in my life; and I choose to make the most of it."

I believe you can enjoy almost everything about your life by making the decision to do so. Even in challenging situations, you can usually find something positive if you search for it.

––––––––––––––

Love Yourself Today: Make a choice today to enjoy every moment.

Take the Best Advice

Your word is a lamp to my feet and a light to my path.
PSALM 119:105

One way to love yourself is to live your life according to the best wisdom and advice available. The Bible contains answers to every question you could ever have and every situation you will ever face. True, it will not tell you specifically what to have for dinner or what color to paint your house, but it will impart to you principles of right living, right thinking, wisdom, and faith. It will instruct you through stories of people who lived long ago, but faced many of the same challenges and relational struggles you and I deal with today. It will encourage you to persevere, inspire you to overcome, help you make good decisions, and teach you to hear and obey God's voice.

It holds ancient truths that have stood the test of time and been proven over and over again. The words of Scripture are alive and are saturated with the power of God. They are as real and applicable today as they have ever been.

God has given us His Word as a source of strength and guidance in our everyday, ordinary lives. It gives us wisdom in areas such as managing finances, choosing friends, overseeing a household, raising children, dealing with anger and many, many more practical situations you probably face on a regular basis.

Be sure to spend time in God's Word every day. Seek His advice, then do yourself a favor and apply it to your life.

Love Yourself Today: Living by the Word is a way of loving and taking care of yourself. I encourage you to ask God to speak to you personally through His Word.

Let Me See You Smile

Greet every saint in Christ Jesus...   PHILIPPIANS 4:21 NKJV

It is amazing how a smile and a friendly greeting put people at ease. It takes more muscles to frown than it does to smile, so smile and give your face a break! You might be thinking, *Well, that is just not me. I am a serious-minded person; I am more reserved and private. I just prefer not to get involved with people that much, especially people I don't know.* If you feel that way, I understand because I was exactly the same way until I kept seeing what the Bible says about encouragement, edification, exhortation, and making people feel valuable. I finally decided that God had not called me to merely be comfortable, but to be obedient, so I started being friendly on purpose.

For years, I excused myself from being friendly by saying, "That just isn't me; I have a lot on my mind, a lot of responsibility, and I am more of a loner," but I realized that "loner" is not listed as a gift in the Bible. Thinking of ourselves as "loners" is simply an excuse to avoid the often messy business of being vulnerable. After all, we think, *How will I feel if I smile at people and they don't smile back?* I will feel rejected, and that never feels good. What if I try to make friendly conversation with a stranger while waiting at the doctor's office and it is evident he or she wants to be left alone? Suddenly I am now embarrassed and feeling odd, so rather than "chance it," I may remain uninvolved for my own protection. When this happens, we are missing the opportunity to touch people with the love of God through a smile or friendly word. When we give our smiles, we can make someone else smile, and that is one of the best gifts we can give.

The apostle Paul told those to whom he ministered to greet one another with a holy kiss (see Rom. 16:16), which was customary in their day. I am only asking for a smile!

———————————

Love Others Today: Remember to smile and be friendly today!

Speak What You Want to See

Train up a child in the way he should go [and in keeping with his individual gift or bent], and when he is old he will not depart from it.

PROVERBS 22:6

As parents, we have tremendous influence over our children, and we can make that influence extremely positive by using loving words, or we can make it negative by using derogatory words.

If a parent tells a child he is stupid and can't do anything right, he will start producing the seed that is planted in him. He will literally become what he believes himself to be based on what he has been told about himself. The biblical principle is set forth in Galatians 6:7: "For whatever a man sows, that and that only is what he will reap." We should not tell our children they are something unless we want them to become what we say they are.

I have four grown children, and I am glad that my husband and I sowed good words into their lives. We corrected them, but we were careful not to reject them. Even when we did not like the things they did, and told them so, we emphasized that our love for them was unchanging.

By the time Danny, our younger son, was born, we had a lot of God's Word in our hearts. I recall the Lord showing us never to say to Danny, "You're a bad boy!" We told him the wrong things he did were bad, but we never told him he was bad. I believe that plants an image in children that they are bad and produces an unwanted harvest of more bad behavior.

Love Others Today: Whether you have children or not, make a habit of speaking positive, life-giving words to all the people in your life.

Rejoice Anyway

Rejoice in the Lord always [delight, gladden yourselves in Him];
again I say, Rejoice!   PHILIPPIANS 4:4

Many times, when people have problems or challenges, they focus so intensely on finding a solution that they do not relax or enjoy life until the problems are solved. I want to encourage you not to put off "joy" any longer, because joy will help you get through the crisis you are going through. We can rejoice in spite of and in the midst of our problems!

The apostle Paul knew that joy gives us strength. He had plenty of reasons to be afraid, discouraged, and depressed! Paul could have decided to live his life in "survival mode," but he *chose* to be joyful. We need to make the same choice Paul did—to rejoice always, even in difficult situations. This is one way we demonstrate our trust in God and prove our love for Him.

Jesus said in John 17:13: "...I say these things while I am still in the world, so that My joy may be made full and complete and perfect in them [that they may experience My delight fulfilled in them, that My enjoyment may be perfected in their own souls, that they may have My gladness within them, filling their hearts]."

What a Scripture! Jesus wants His joy to be made full in us; He wants us to experience His delight. That's what I'm praying for you today—that the joy of the Lord would fill your heart and be your strength. Don't let circumstances or situations steal your joy, but love God (and do yourself a favor, too) by being joyful.

Love God Today: "Lord, I pray that no matter what difficulties or problems I face today, I will choose to rejoice anyway!"

No "Ifs"

*For I am persuaded beyond doubt (am sure) that neither death
nor life, nor angels nor principalities, nor things impending and
threatening . . . nor anything else in all creation will be able to
separate us from the love of God which is in Christ Jesus our Lord.*

ROMANS 8:38–39

To fully understand all the different facets of love, we must talk about
the two kinds of love: the God-kind of love and man's love. Man's love
fails, gives up; but God's love does not. Man's love is finite, comes to an
end; but God's love is infinite and eternal. Man's love is dependent on
favorable behavior and circumstances; God's love is not. People place
conditions on their love, but God's love is unconditional.

According to God's Word, He loved us before the world was formed,
before we loved Him or believed in Him, or had ever done anything
either good or evil. God does not require us to earn His love, and we
must not require others to earn ours. As believers in Jesus Christ, the
love we are to manifest to the world is the unconditional *love of God*
flowing through us to them.

Loving people unconditionally is a very big challenge. I would be
tempted to say it's impossible, but since God tells us to do it, surely He
must have a way for us to do it. Sometimes we pray to be able to love
the unlovely and then do our best to avoid every unlovely person God
sends our way. Learning to walk in love with unlovely people and learning to be patient in trials are probably the two most important tools
God uses to develop our spiritual maturity. Believe it or not, difficult
people in our lives help us. They sharpen and refine us for God's use.

Love Others Today: "Lord, help me to love others today
without imposing 'ifs' or conditions. Let me remember
that as I do it, I'm being refined by You."

The Lord Will Provide

He has given food and provision to those who reverently and
worshipfully fear Him; He will remember His covenant forever and
imprint it [on His mind].   PSALM 111:5

Do you have financial worries or concerns about provision in your life
right now? If you find yourself worried that you will not have enough,
you're not alone. I have found that many people have the same fear.

Today's scripture teaches us that as long as we have reverence for
God and worship Him, we can count on Him to provide for us. I believe
this principle is an important key to having our needs met. If we maintain reverent attitudes toward God and are faithful to worship Him,
then we will be able to live in faith instead of fear when needs arise.

Maybe you are facing the possibility of losing your job or your home.
Maybe you are working as hard as you can, but your income simply
is not enough to support your family. Maybe you are living on Social
Security and wondering what the future holds for you. You see prices
rising continually and the enemy whispers, "You aren't going to have
enough to live on."

I encourage you to commit today's Scripture to memory. Meditate
on it often, and obey it. As you worship the Lord, remind yourself of all
the ways He has taken care of you throughout your life; thank Him for
all He has done for you; ask Him for wisdom; and tell Him that you love
Him and trust Him to meet every need in your life.

Love God Today: "Thank You, Lord, for being a faithful,
trustworthy Provider for me as I continue to worship You."

Praying God's Word

. . . Put the Lord in remembrance [of His promises], keep not silence.

ISAIAH 62:6

Today's Scripture instructs us to remind God of the promises He has made to us, and one of the best ways to do that is to pray His Word back to Him. God's Word is extremely valuable to Him and should be to us as well. In fact, Psalm 138:2 says, ". . . You have exalted above all else Your name and Your word and You have magnified Your word above all Your name!" This verse states that God magnifies His Word even above His name. If He honors it to that extent, we need to make a priority out of knowing the Word, studying the Word, loving the Word, and incorporating the Word in our prayers.

When we honor the Word and commit ourselves to it as I have just described, we are "abiding" in it. Jesus said in John 15:7, "If you live in Me [abide vitally united to Me] and My words remain in you and continue to live in your hearts, ask whatever you will, and it shall be done for you."

When we pray the Word of God, we are more likely to pray according to God's will and less likely to pray for things that are not His will for us. When we pray to God the same truths He has declared in Scripture, we know we are praying prayers He will honor.

Love God Today: Take some time to look at some of your favorite Bible verses and incorporate them in your prayers. God enjoys it when we speak His Word back to Him.

Worship in Spirit and in Truth

A time will come, however, indeed it is already here, when the true
(genuine) worshippers will worship the Father in spirit and in truth
(reality); for the Father is seeking just such people as these as His
worshippers.   JOHN 4:23

According to today's Scripture, God is seeking true, genuine worshippers who will really worship Him with all their hearts.

I have always been a bit saddened by the fact that God has to seek true worshippers. I think there should be an abundance of them and that we should dedicate ourselves to being the kind of worshippers God desires. But I find it interesting that He does not want just anybody to worship Him; He wants *true* and *genuine* worshippers. He is not looking for people who will worship Him out of fear or obligation, or even merely in their time of personal need, but out of a loving relationship.

True, sincere worship comes out of the heart and out of intimacy with God. It is much more than learned behavior or repeating certain rituals. Walking into a building called a church and kneeling at a certain time, standing at other times, and repeating certain phrases can be worship if these activities come from our hearts. But they are nothing if they are only memorized words and actions that are not sincere.

For worship to be genuine and sincere, truly we must have a heart connection and focus our attention on God when we are praying or worshipping Him. We would be better off to say less and mean it more, than to say more and mean it less!

Love God Today: "Lord, help me to be genuine and sincere each time I approach You."

Loving Others with Your Prayers

We give thanks to the God and Father of our Lord Jesus Christ,
praying always for you . . .   COLOSSIANS 1:93 NKJV

The term *intercession* simply means praying for someone besides your-self. It is going to God on someone else's behalf and taking their needs to Him in prayer—and it is a way of loving others. Intercession is one of the most important kinds of prayer because many people do not pray for themselves. Why? Because they have no relationship with God.

There are also times when people are hurting too bad to even know how to pray, or they have fought a long battle and are too weary to pray anymore. For example, I once visited a friend who had fought a valiant fight against cancer and prayed like a warrior, but she reached a point where she was not strong enough to pray the way she wanted to. She said, "Joyce, I just *cannot* pray anymore." She needed her friends to pray for her—not just to *pray* for her, but to really pray *for* her—to pray in her place because she could not.

I encourage you to draw nearer to God by joining Jesus in His min-istry of intercession. Your family and friends need your prayers; your neighbors and co-workers need your prayers; the people of your church, your community, and the world need your prayers. We live in difficult days, and we must pray for one another. Your intercession is the most powerful, most valuable gift you can ever give to those around you, and it will make an eternal difference in their lives and in yours. There may be times when you are the only person on earth praying for someone else—and your intercession can change that person's entire life.

Love Others Today: Ask God to put into your heart a person or a situation you can pray for right now.

Keep It Hot!

Above all things have intense and unfailing love for one another, for love covers a multitude of sins [forgives and disregards the offenses of others].   1 PETER 4:8

One of the most amazing truths I have ever learned, one that still thrills my soul, is that love is actually spiritual warfare.

If we fight our battles with love, then instead of appearing to be oppressed and discouraged all the time, we can actually look happy. We can be *on* the attack instead of *under* the attack.

Today's Scripture teaches us to have intense and unfailing love for one another. The New King James Version uses the word *fervent* to describe love; in Greek, *fervent* means "to be hot, to boil." Our love walk needs to be hot, on fire, boiling over, not cold and barely noticeable. Have you ever microwaved something for too long and not been able to remove it from the oven because it was too hot to handle? That's the way I want to be. If we are hot enough with love, Satan won't be able to handle us. We might say we will be "too hot to handle!"

I believe if we as the church of Jesus Christ, His body here on earth, will wage war against selfishness and walk in love, people will begin to take notice. We will not impress the world by being just like them. But how many unsaved friends and relatives might come to know Jesus if we genuinely loved them instead of ignoring, judging, or rejecting them? I believe it's time to find out, don't you?

———————————

Love Others Today: Start your own "love revolution" by declaring war on selfishness.

The Best Gift You Can Give the World

But those who wait on the Lord shall renew their strength; they shall mount up with wings like eagles, they shall run and not be weary, they shall walk and not faint.   ISAIAH 40:31 NKJV

We know from Scripture that we are not to live selfish, self-centered lives, but that does not mean we shouldn't take care of ourselves. Staying healthy requires making an investment of time, effort, and sometimes money.

Many Christians say they feel guilty unless they are at the bottom of their list of people they do things for. That's a wrong attitude! You cannot take proper care of your family and other loved ones, nor can you perform your own jobs properly, if you are physically, mentally, emotionally, or spiritually unhealthy.

The psalmist David prayed that he would eat his necessary food and get his necessary sleep. I think that is a good prayer for us to pray. I think David was actually praying to maintain balance in all areas of life. Do all you can do to be physically healthy. Eat enough healthy food, but don't overeat. Exercise enough daily to get your heart rate pumping and your muscles working. Get seven to eight hours of good sleep each night. Drink plenty of good, clean water. And don't forget to laugh a lot because laughter is like medicine for your soul and body. Laughter is internal jogging and lifts your spirit. Work hard, but remember to take time to do some things you enjoy because that will help you stay healthy emotionally. Get enough of everything, but not too much of anything. God's will is that you respect yourself enough to take care of yourself and give the world a healthy you.

Love Yourself Today: Move yourself to the top of your list of people you take care of. Then you'll be better able to care for others!

Loving God with Your Words

I will bless the Lord at all times; His praise shall continually be in my mouth.   PSALM 34:1 NKJV

It is good to have love for God in your heart, but even better to express it with the words of your mouth. Tell God several times each day that you love Him; say with the psalmist David: "I love You fervently and devotedly, O Lord my Strength" (Ps. 18:1). It isn't good enough to merely think, "God knows how I feel." Are you blessed when people tell you they love and appreciate you? Of course you are, and it blesses God when we verbalize our love and praise for Him. Verbal expression of love and gratitude improves all our relationships, including our relationship with God.

Don't offer your petitions to God without telling Him how grateful you are for what He has already done for you. As parents we are more likely to answer the request of a thankful child than we are a grouchy and ungrateful one. As an employer I want to do even more for employees who are appreciative. Offering our continual gratitude to God for His goodness and mercy in our lives moves Him to want to do even more for us. Our gratitude shows God that we are mature enough to handle even more blessing and responsibility.

Women often say, "I know my husband loves me, but I wish he would tell me more often." Let's try to be more diligent in telling God and the people in our lives that we love and appreciate them and what they mean to us.

Love God Today: It is impossible to love God with your whole heart, soul, mind, and strength, and not hear it come out of your mouth.

Loving God Through Obedience

If they obey and serve Him, they shall spend their days in prosperity and their years in pleasantness and joy.   JOB 36:11

One of the most important aspects of our Christian life is obedience, which reveals our love for God. We simply will not make progress with God unless we are willing to obey Him. Disobedience of any kind, on any level, is sin.

I encourage you to make up your mind that you are going to be extremely, even radically, obedient to God. First John 3:22 says: "We receive from Him whatever we ask, because we [watchfully] obey His orders." Does that mean we have to be perfect? No. It is true that God in His grace will bless those who make mistakes, but we should not be satisfied to stay the way we are. God blesses us even though we are not perfect, but at the same time, our hearts need to be longing for growth and improvement.

If we do the best we can and we are sincerely sorry when we make mistakes, then we know that God will continue blessing us because He is very merciful. But, on the other hand, if we remain in disobedience, knowing we are disobeying God, and not making an honest effort to grow spiritually, then we really do not need to be blessed because if God blesses us in the midst of that attitude or behavior, we will not want to change or grow.

We hurt ourselves every time we do not obey God. But when we do obey God, we position ourselves for great blessings and are people that God can work through for His glory.

Love God Today: "Lord, I repent for my disobedience and ask You to help me obey You in every way."

Don't Overreact

When Pharaoh let the people go, God led them not by way of the
land of the Philistines, although that was nearer; for God said, Lest
the people change their purpose when they see war and return to
Egypt.   EXODUS 13:17

No matter how carefully you plan your progress in any area of your life, you will have setbacks. That's part of the journey. Successful people are able to press through difficulty and delay and get right back on track without wasting time, feeling bad about themselves, or losing momentum.

Having a bad day does not mean you have to have a bad life. Don't be like the Israelites in today's Scripture who wanted to return to Egypt every time they had a bad day while traveling toward the Promised Land. You are being freed from the bondage of Egypt and heading toward the Promised Land, where God's purposes and promises will become realities in your life, but you will have days in the desert. When that happens, don't be too hard on yourself.

Be nurturing and supportive of yourself, as you would of anyone else you love. Remind yourself that ten steps forward and one step backward still gets you where you're going. Celebrate your successes, even small ones, and it will help you press past your setbacks.

Consider writing down your victories as you have them. Keep a journal of your journey and record all your little successes, and include the lessons you're learning along the way and the good experiences you're having. When you have a discouraging day or one when you feel you've done everything wrong, read your journal. You may be amazed at how far you've come!

––––––––––––

Love Yourself Today: Don't overreact to setbacks along your journey. Remind yourself often of the progress you've made.

Just You and God

And after He had dismissed the multitudes, He went up into the hills
by Himself to pray. When it was evening, He was still there alone.

MATTHEW 14:23

If you want to have victory in your daily life, spend time alone with God.

Jesus took regular times away for prayer and fellowship. He apparently had a sense that any time He felt He had given out all He had in Him to give, He would walk away from everybody and go somewhere, get by Himself, pray, talk to God—just do whatever He did in those times of solitude. Then He would come back ready to minister again.

Don't let yourself get burned out. When you feel you have given all you have to give, then go spend some time with God and get refilled. When your gas tank is getting low, you go and get it filled up again so you won't run out of gas. But when it comes to spiritual things, you may be running on fumes.

At times Jesus went off into the mountains to pray. He'd get up early in the morning to be alone with God. When He had a serious decision to make, sometimes He prayed all night. Why? He knew the value of being in the Presence of God.

When you are upset, go to Jesus and spend a little time with Him. In fact, run to Him.

I've said for years: "Don't run to the phone; run to the throne."

We need to honor God by putting Him first. We need to run to Him first, listen to Him first, give Him the first part of our money, the first part of our time, the first part of everything in our lives. According to Matthew 6:33, if we do so, He will supply our needs and bless us.

Love Yourself Today: Make God your number one priority,
and everything in your life will improve.

Love Can Change People

The righteous gives and does not spare.   PROVERBS 21:26 NKJV

I once read a story in *Guideposts* magazine, a remarkable account of how love changed a person's life. A Christian woman lived next door to an elderly lady who never came out of her house or even raised her window shades to let light into her home. This lady's husband had died, and she herself had endured a stroke, which had left her lonely and bitter.

The Christian woman and her two young children began trying to reach out to the elderly recluse, but every time they did, she rejected their advances. They baked cookies every week for a long time and delivered them to their neighbor's door. The first time, she opened the door just a crack, accepted the cookies, thanked them, and closed the door.

The neighbor's response was not what the Christian woman had hoped for, but she lovingly persisted. And eventually love did work! The elderly lady accepted a casserole from her and said more than just a short thank-you. As the visits continued, the elderly woman gradually began to chat longer. Finally one day, the Christian woman's children picked some flowers from their garden and delivered them to their neighbor. Eventually, they all became good friends. The elderly lady got her life back. She opened her blinds, her door, and her heart, and she began to live again—all because someone who loved God was determined to love her.

Many people in the world today are just like the elderly neighbor. They have had sadness or difficulties in their lives and have become bitter. They seem to reject love, yet love is what they need most. Be a person who gives of yourself and your resources to reach out and show love to someone who desperately needs it.

———————

Love Others Today: Do you know someone who is angry, sad, or bitter? How can you show love to that person?

Hold Them Loosely

Let no one then seek his own good and advantage and profit,
but [rather] each one of the other [let him seek the welfare of his
neighbor].   1 CORINTHIANS 10:24

Most of us struggle at times with wanting or trying to control people and situations because of fear. We are afraid we won't get what we want, so we try to orchestrate circumstances to get what we want and avoid what we don't want.

Neither you nor I should try to control the destiny of another human being. This is not our right, and God will not permit it. Try to influence others in a positive way, but don't cross the line and take away their liberty.

Fear is the emotion that influences us most in life, but that can be changed. What are we afraid of? Being needy or alone, suffering pain or loss? We try to manipulate people to be sure they are always in our lives and doing what we would like for them to do. Set people free, and if they really love you they will always come back.

Whatever God gives us, we must learn to hold loosely in our hands. If we don't own anything, we cannot lose anything. We are stewards over our children, not owners or masters. Everything really belongs to God, and He has endowed everyone with the right of free choice. We must learn to love people, not try to own them or make them over into our image; that's an act of selfishness, not love.

Give the gift of freedom. That will be a great expression of love from you, and people will love you for it in return.

Love Others Today: Remember, you are a steward over God's blessings, not the owner.

Real Giving

I will not offer burnt offerings to the Lord my God of that which costs me nothing.   2 SAMUEL 24:24

If God wants us to help people, why doesn't He make it easy and inexpensive? Let me answer that with another question. Did Jesus sacrifice anything to purchase our freedom from sin and bondage? I wonder why God didn't make the plan of salvation easier. After all, He could have devised any plan He wanted to and simply said, "This is going to work." It seems that in God's economy, nothing cheap is worth having.

I have learned the truth of today's Scripture, which teaches us that true giving is not giving until I can feel it. Giving away clothes and household items I am finished with may be a nice gesture, but it does not equate to real giving. Real giving occurs when I give somebody something that I want to keep. I am sure you have had those testing times when God asks you to give away something that you like. He gave us His only Son because He loves us, so what will love cause us to do? The simple truth is this: We must give in order to be happy, and giving is most effective when we feel the sacrifice of it.

The disciples of Jesus were all busy when He called them. They had lives, families, and businesses to take care of. But when Jesus said, "Follow Me," they left everything and followed Him.

They didn't ask how long they would be gone or what their salary package would be. They didn't even ask Him what their job description would be. They simply left all and followed Him. Perhaps the greater the opportunity, the greater the sacrifice must be.

———————————

Love Others Today: No matter what you own, don't let it own you. Be ready to sacrifice anything that God requires.

Power to Overcome

*But you shall receive power (ability, efficiency, and might) when the
Holy Spirit has come upon you...*   ACTS 1:8

No one's life is everything he or she wants it to be. We all have challenges and struggles, sometimes even heartbreaks and tragedies. I have
never met one person who could honestly say, "My life has always been
every bit as wonderful as I always dreamed it would be."

God's job is not to make us happy or to give us the lives we've
always hoped for. Often, we so desperately want unsaved people to
become Christians that we tell them their lives will be better if they will
just receive Jesus. In many ways, this is true, but sometimes we paint
such a rosy picture that we lead people to believe they will never have
another problem again if they will simply ask Jesus to be their Lord
and Savior. This is not true. Jesus did not come to give anyone a life of
leisure; Jesus came to give us *abundant* life, but not a trouble-free life.
Part of the abundance He offers is the power of His Spirit to overcome
what others cannot.

As believers, we have the power of the Holy Spirit to help us deal
with circumstances differently than nonbelievers do. When we are in
Christ, we are supernaturally anointed to live our natural, ordinary
lives in supernatural ways. We can be at peace in the midst of a crisis,
and we can be positive when everything around is gloomy and depress-
ing. Why? Because we can choose joy, peace, positive attitudes, and
stability. We can overcome the negative situations that are part of life,
but we must choose to do so.

Love God Today: "Lord, thank You for the power of the Holy
Spirit to help me deal with any circumstance that comes
my way."

What Can You Do for Him?

So we are Christ's ambassadors...   2 CORINTHIANS 5:20

I would like to suggest something for you to add to your daily prayers; it's a request I believe God would love to hear. Each day, ask Him what you can do for Him. I spent lots of years in my morning prayers telling the Lord what I needed Him to do for me, but a few years ago I added this new part: "God, what can I do for You today?"

Recently, I was asking God to help a friend who was going through a very difficult time. She needed something, so I asked God to provide it. To my surprise, His answer to me was, "Stop merely asking Me to meet the need; ask Me to show you what *you* can do." I have become aware that I often ask God to do things for me that He wants me to do myself. He doesn't expect me to do anything without His help, but neither will He do everything for me while I sit idly by. God wants us to be open to being involved.

I recently had two different people ask me to help a woman financially with some medical expenses. Both of them could have also helped, but neither one offered. They wanted me to do it all while they did nothing. God wants to work through all of us. If we all do what we can, some more and some less, people's needs will be met and we will be blessed by having been involved.

You and God are partners, and He wants to work *with* and *through* you. Ask Him to show you what you can do, and depend on Him to give you the ability to accomplish it.

———————————

Love God Today: "Lord, what can I do for You today?"

Let Yourself Grieve

Jesus wept.   JOHN 11:35

If you have had a painful loss in your life, whether it's been recent or quite some time ago, I want to offer hope to you today. Whatever your situation, God wants to heal you, and lead you to a place where you can enjoy life again. You need to grieve, and you can do it in healthy ways that will keep you from getting stuck in your pain and enable you to heal and move forward.

When you have suffered a loss, you need to go through the grieving process. In fact, the only healthy way to cope with loss is to grieve appropriately. Doing so is an important way of taking care of yourself.

The reason grieving is healthy is that your problems will deal with you if you don't deal with them. Sooner or later, they will catch up with you if you do not confront them honestly and work through them. Grieving is difficult and painful, but God will give you the grace to do it and He will be with you through it.

Part of healthy grieving is to squarely face your loss and embrace your pain. God gave you tear ducts for a reason. He knows you sometimes simply need to cry and cry and cry. Crying is not a sign of weakness. It's part of the process of healing from painful events and situations. Talk to God or someone you trust about how you feel. If you are a Christian and are having a hard time, just remember that weeping endures for a night, but joy comes in the morning according to God's Word. God is your Comforter, and He has good plans for your future. I also suggest that you keep reaching out to other people that are hurting. It may seem odd, but part of your healing will be found in helping someone else.

Love Yourself Today: If you have had a loss in your life, don't ignore it. Face it with God's help, grieve appropriately, and use your experience to help other people.

The Time Will Come

And the Israelites wept for Moses in the plains of Moab thirty days;
then the days of weeping and mourning for Moses were ended.

DEUTERONOMY 34:8

When Moses died, the Israelites mourned deeply over the loss of their leader. They wept for him for thirty days; then the days of mourning were ended.

I am not suggesting that the grieving process should only last thirty days. But I believe the principle behind this verse is important. I think it is letting us know that eventually we have to move on. Sometimes the best thing you can do when you are hurting is to do something. Find a place of new beginnings. Get up, get dressed, and keep moving. Go take a walk and talk to God. Do something for somebody else. As you work through your grief, you may have times when you simply need to get your mind off of what you're going through because you have done everything you can do about it; there is nothing else you can do except wait for the full healing to come.

It is proper to grieve, but don't let a spirit of grief control your life. If you have been through a recent tragic loss, you may not be ready to go on yet. Know, though, that the time will come when you do need to get busy again. It may not be easy, but it will be important to your healing. So, don't rush it, but when it comes, embrace it and trust the Holy Spirit to guide and comfort you as you move forward.

———————

Love Yourself Today: Always remember that no matter what you have lost, you still have a lot left, and God has a purpose yet to be fulfilled in your life.

The Power to Do Good

Do justice to the weak (poor) and fatherless; maintain the rights of the afflicted and needy. Deliver the poor and needy; rescue them out of the hand of the wicked.   PSALM 82:3, 4

I heard a story about former New York City mayor Fiorello LaGuardia. One winter night in 1935, LaGuardia paid a visit to night court in the poorest section of the city. He told the judge to take the night off, took his seat on the bench, and presided over the night's cases himself.

Soon a tired, despondent elderly woman appeared before him because she had been charged with stealing a loaf of bread. In her own defense, she said, "My daughter's husband left her. She is sick, and her children are hungry."

The storekeeper had no mercy.

With a sigh, LaGuardia said to the woman, "The law is clear. I have to punish you." He fined her ten dollars. As he was pronouncing the woman's sentence, LaGuardia was simultaneously reaching into his pocket to pull out a ten-dollar bill. He dropped it into his hat and said, "Here's the ten-dollar fine, which I now remit, and furthermore, I'm going to fine everyone in this courtroom fifty cents for living in a town where a person has to steal bread so her grandchildren can eat. Mr. Bailiff, collect the fines and give them to the defendant!" The total collected for the grandmother was $47.50.

I like the fact that the mayor of New York City used his position of authority to influence others to help the poor grandmother. Any time we can inspire or provoke others to do good, we need to do so.

Love Others Today: Whenever possible, use your influence to encourage others to do good.

Don't Fall for Pride

Pride goes before destruction, and a haughty spirit before a fall.

PROVERBS 16:18

Pride is something God hates. Pride precedes destruction and prevents promotion in our lives. It erases our compassion toward others and causes us to treat their problems and concerns as trivial. Pride will bring a person down and bring him down quickly.

It's amazing how someone can have a sweet heart and a right spirit and God will promote him—then suddenly he becomes a different person. He begins to believe he's better than everyone else—the president of his own fan club. He starts mistreating others and putting on airs. At that point, God must deal with him.

The apostle Paul said in Galatians 2:20: "It is no longer I who live, but Christ lives in me" (NKJV). Being able to honestly say, "It is no longer I" is a sign of real maturity because pride is all about "I." Pride says, "I'm better than you. I'm smarter than you. My opinion matters, yours doesn't."

Did you know that "me, myself, and I" are the greatest problems most people have? We are often full of ourselves, when in reality we're supposed to be full of God and empty of ourselves—totally empty. We're supposed to esteem others more highly than we esteem ourselves (see Phil. 2:3). That's one way to keep pride far from our lives.

Pride can sneak up on you. It's always lurking around the corner waiting to get you. But beware, because pride will destroy you.

———————————

Love Others Today: Value everyone and never think you are better than anyone else.

Quick to Judge

Judge not, that you be not judged.   MATTHEW 7:1 NKJV

Do you enjoy being around people who are judgmental? Surely not! Jesus clearly instructs us not to judge others and tells us that if we do judge, we can expect to be judged in return. Judgment toward others always begins in the mind. It starts in the privacy of our thoughts, with something like: *She shouldn't have spent so much money on that outfit,* or *That person says she is sick, but I think she is just lazy.*

All these judgmental thoughts come from an attitude of pride, and frankly, from minding someone else's business instead of our own. Most of us don't do a very good job of running our own lives, let alone trying to run the lives of others.

We need to remember that we are not responsible for what other people do. God is not going to ask us about them when we stand in front of Him. He'll ask us only about ourselves. We are responsible for our own obedience and our own relationship with God.

Religion, without a relationship with Jesus, leads to trouble, including a lot of judgmental attitudes. Religion is a system of rules and regulations, and when people value religion over relationship, their actions and attitudes say, "If you don't do it my way, you're wrong."

A person can be religious and follow many religious rules and regulations and still be very critical and judgmental, but if they are truly spiritual they will know that mercy triumphs over judgment.

Love God Today: "Lord, help me to walk in love, not judgment, toward others."

God's School of Wisdom

I have taught you in the way of skillful and godly Wisdom [which is comprehensive insight into the ways and purposes of God].

PROVERBS 4:11

True Christianity goes far beyond mere doctrine. We certainly need to know the principles of our faith in the form of doctrine, but real love for God is so much more than a set of basic beliefs; it is also a way of daily, practical living that comes from understanding the ways and purposes of God.

When we approach everyday situations from the perspective of God's ways and purposes, we ask questions such as: "How would Jesus talk to that person?" "How would Jesus deal with that person's obvious need?" When we begin to think along these lines, we are learning to be wise because we are seeking to understand the ways and purposes of God.

Moses was a very wise man, one who understood the importance of knowing God's ways. In Exodus 33:13, he cried out to God: "...If I have found favor in Your sight, show me now Your way, that I may know You..." God answered Moses' prayer, as we read in Psalm 103:7: "He made known His ways...to Moses, His acts to the children of Israel."

Notice the distinction between what God made known to Moses (His ways) and what He made known to the children of Israel (His acts). Some people are only interested in God's acts—what He will do for them. But wise people are like Moses; they hunger for a deep understanding of His ways. Let me encourage you to cry out to God as Moses did.

Love God Today: Ask God to show you His ways and help you understand His purposes.

Come as a Little Child

And He called a little child to Himself and put himself in the midst
of them, and said, Truly I say to you, unless you repent (change,
turn about) and become like little children [trusting, lowly, loving,
forgiving], you can never enter the kingdom of heaven.

MATTHEW 18:2, 3

One thing children are *not* is complicated. Children have no trouble letting you know what they want, running into your arms when they are afraid, or giving you a big generous kiss, sometimes for no apparent reason. They are not sophisticated enough to hide their hearts or feelings very well, and as a result, communicating with them can be easy and refreshing.

That's the way God wants us to be when we talk to Him. We need to approach God with childlike simplicity and faith. Just as children are naturally inclined to trust their parents completely, we also need to be guileless, pure, and free from doubt as we trust God. Then we can experience God's miracle-working power and see things change.

We do not want to be child*ish* in our relationships with God; we want to be child*like*. The Lord is not looking for complicated relationships. He is looking for sincere hearts and childlike faith. He wants us to approach Him as little children approach people they love. He wants us to let Him know what we want (see Phil. 4:6) and to run to Him when we feel threatened or afraid (Ps. 91:1–7). He wants us to show our affection for Him, sometimes for no apparent reason (see Ps. 34:1) and to share our hearts openly with Him (see Ps. 62:8).

Love God Today: "Lord, help me to have a pure, simple, childlike faith and love for You."

Don't Let the Devil Stop You

God, who got you started in this spiritual adventure ... He will never give up on you. Never forget that.   1 CORINTHIANS 1:9 THE MESSAGE

Several years ago, I was getting my nails done and a woman began to tell me about something that had happened to her son, who was four years old at the time. She said he was on a soccer team and so excited about it. He practiced and practiced and was thrilled to play his first game, but, in the mother's words, "It turned out horrible."

When I asked what happened, she said, "He was doing fine until about halfway through the game. Then a bigger boy came up and punched him in the stomach. The bigger boy then said something to him, and the four-year-old ran to the sidelines and began to sob uncontrollably."

He told his mother, "That boy punched me in the stomach and told me, 'You're no good. You'll never learn how to play soccer. You're not doing anything right, so get off this field and don't come back to try to play with us anymore!'"

The little boy said, "I'm never going back there again!"

This story provides a great illustration of what the enemy wants to do to God's people. He wants others to make fun of us or cut us down so we will feel rejected, lose our confidence, and stop trying to do anything in life. He often uses other people, just as he used the bigger boy to intimidate and crush the four-year-old. I urge you not to let anyone cause you to doubt yourself or to abandon the things God has called you to do. Move forward with confidence in His love for you and with a healthy love for yourself.

Love Yourself Today: What you think of yourself is much more important than what others think of you!

Fear Not

Have I not commanded you? Be strong, vigorous, and very courageous. Be not afraid, neither be dismayed, for the Lord your God is with you wherever you go. JOSHUA 1:9

The Bible says "Fear not..." in many different places. When we read these words, we sometimes think they mean that we are not to feel fear. There was a time in my life when I thought *feeling* fear meant that I was a coward. When I felt fear, I felt bad about myself. Many times, when I was ready to move forward in some area of my life, I suddenly felt afraid and got sidetracked. I prayed that I wouldn't be afraid anymore.

But then God showed me that when His Word says to fear not, it means not to give in to the kind of powerful fear that will keep you from moving forward. In our verse for today, God knew Joshua would be tempted to be afraid. Otherwise, why would God have told him to fear not? What God was really saying to Joshua was, "I'm sending you to do a job, but fear will be the enemy that tries to keep you from doing it." God wasn't telling Joshua not to feel fear; He was simply telling him not to run from his God-given assignment and destiny because of it. His message to Joshua—and to us today—was, "When you feel fear, stand your ground. Know that I am with you, and do what I've told you to do!"

Have you ever found that fear tries to hold you back when you begin to move forward in life? The only way to break free from that is to move forward anyway. When you believe God is leading in a certain direction, remember Joshua. Don't let fear catch you off guard or surprise you if it rears its ugly head; just look it straight in the face and keep on moving.

Love Yourself Today: Be courageous and do whatever you need to do, even if you have to "do it afraid."

Under Construction

My brethren, count it all joy when you fall into various trials,
knowing that the testing of your faith produces patience. But
let patience have its perfect work, that you may be perfect and
complete, lacking nothing.   JAMES 1:2-4 NKJV

As God is working out His perfect plan for us, we often want it to happen right now. But character development takes time and patience. James tells us that when patience has had its perfect work, we will be perfect (fully developed) and complete, lacking nothing. James also speaks about trials of all kinds, and it is during these trials that we are instructed to be patient. Patience is not the ability to wait; it is the ability to keep a good attitude while waiting. Patience is a fruit of the Spirit that manifests itself in a calm, positive attitude despite the circumstances.

"Due season" is God's season, not ours. We are in a hurry, but God isn't. He takes time to do things right—He lays a solid foundation before He attempts to build a building. We are God's building under construction. He is the Master Builder, and He knows what He is doing. God's timing seems to be His own little secret. The Bible promises that He will never be late, but I have also discovered that He is usually not early. It seems that He takes every available opportunity to develop the fruit of patience in us.

———————

Love Yourself Today: When you're feeling impatient, remember: You're still under construction.

Be Generous on Purpose

And let fall some handfuls for her on purpose and let them lie there for her to glean, and do not rebuke her.   RUTH 2:16

Today's Scripture is an instruction from Boaz, a wealthy man and leader in his community, to his workers. Telling them to leave grain in the fields for Ruth "on purpose" was his way of providing for her and her mother-in-law, Naomi, who were both poor widows. In their day the law demanded that some grain be left over after harvest so poor people could glean it and have something to eat. Boaz knew the law, but gave this instruction anyway to make sure that Ruth would have enough. We see repeatedly in Scripture that God always provides for the poor. But His provision does not fall out of the sky or just miraculously appear; He provides *through people.*

At Joyce Meyer Ministries, we have an account called "Love in Action." The ministry and employees can give money to this account specifically to be used for the needs of fellow employees who might be experiencing a difficult time financially for one reason or another. We decided we wanted to be prepared to help those among us who had genuine needs and could not help themselves.

If you have a Bible study group or a group of friends who want to love and bless others, you can select a treasurer or open a special bank account. Let everyone donate to that special fund when they can. If you cannot form a group, then find one or two people, and if you have to, do it by yourself; just do it!

Love Others Today: Needs *will* arise. Prepare ahead of time to be able to meet them—and ask others to join you.

Is This a Test?

And you shall remember that the Lord your God led you all the way these forty years in the wilderness, to humble you and to test you, to know what was in your heart, whether you would keep His commandments or not.   DEUTERONOMY 8:2 NKJV

Years ago a blind couple wanted to come to our Wednesday-night teaching sessions in St. Louis. They normally took the bus, but their usual route was canceled, and they could only continue coming if someone would pick them up and take them home. Nobody was willing to do it because the people lived in an area considered "out of the way."

In other words, providing transportation for this couple would have been inconvenient. Eventually we had to get one of our employees to do it, which meant we had to pay that person. We should not allow money to be our main motivator. We all need money, but we also need to do things for other people without being paid to do it; in fact, often, such opportunities are "testing times" from God. If you are willing to do something kind for someone else with no pay and perhaps no credit, that's a positive sign that your spiritual heart is in good condition.

When God wanted to see if the Israelites would obey His commands, He led them the long, hard way in the wilderness. He sometimes does the same with us. He may ask us to do something inconvenient. God may be using these things to test us. He may be looking to see what's in our hearts and to give us a chance to prove how much we love Him.

Love God Today: Next time you feel called to do something you don't really want to do, remember, it could be a test.

Celebrate Your Special Day

For you created my inmost being; you knit me together in my
mother's womb. I praise you because I am fearfully and wonderfully
made; your works are wonderful, I know that full well.

PSALM 139:13, 14 NIV

Are you the kind of person who considers your birthday a special day and makes the most of it? Or did you stop really celebrating your birthday and now simply let it pass without much fanfare?

I used to allow my birthday to pass without acknowledging it in significant ways, but I've recently changed that. I now celebrate not only the day of my birth, but sometimes the entire week of my birthday!

If you could see yourself from God's perspective, you would know that you have a huge reason to celebrate the anniversary of your birth. God made you for a special purpose, and without you the world would not be the same. Something would be missing if you were not here at this time, so rejoice and use your birthday as an excuse to celebrate you. God rejoices over us and enjoys us and wants us to do the same thing.

Celebrating another year of life is a way of honoring God and thanking Him for the gift of life. Why not celebrate that God kept your heart beating 38 million beats during the year? Why not celebrate that He protected you and provided for you and keeps loving you every minute you're alive?

Every day is worth celebrating, but especially the day of your birth. Go for it and don't hold back.

———————

Love Yourself Today: Make a note on your calendar to celebrate your next birthday in a big, wonderful way. And thank God for *you*—you are the work of His hand.

Change Is Part of Life

You, therefore, must be perfect [growing into complete maturity of godliness in mind and character, having reached the proper height of virtue and integrity], as your heavenly Father is perfect.

MATTHEW 5:48

Change and growth are processes that will continue as long as we live on earth in our human bodies. Progress is vitally important, but perfection is impossible. We can have perfect hearts toward God and His plan for us, but our behavior will always be lacking perfection in one way or another.

When God shows us a fault, He does not expect us to fix it without His help. He only wants us to acknowledge it, to be sorry for it, and be willing to turn away from it. He knows—and we need to know—that we cannot change ourselves, but He will change us as we study His Word and cooperate with His Holy Spirit.

I believe we should be thankful when God convicts us, and we truly should celebrate the fact that we have seen something that will help us change and honor God more. Each time you are convicted of sin, try lifting your hands in praise and saying, "Thank You, God, that You love me enough not to leave me alone in my sin. Thank You for changing me into the person You want me to be." This kind of attitude will open the way for you to make progress rather than being stuck in your sin.

Do your best and let God do the rest. As long as you are making progress, God is pleased.

———————————

Love God Today: Progress can't happen without change. When change comes to your life, embrace it.

Your Pain Is Someone's Gain

*Although He was a Son, He learned [active, special] obedience
through what He suffered. And [His completed experience] making
Him perfectly [equipped], He became the Author and Source of
eternal salvation to all those who give heed and obey Him.*

HEBREWS 5:8, 9

Have you ever needed a job, but every employment ad you read asked for someone with experience? You did not have any experience, and it frustrated you. I have been in that situation, and I remember thinking, *How can I get experience if nobody will give me a job?*

God also wants experienced help. When we go to work for God in His Kingdom, He will use everything in our past. No matter how painful it was, He considers it experience. Many of us have gone through difficult things, and those things qualify us to help take someone else through them, too. Our verses for today tell us that even Jesus gained experience through the things He suffered.

How could I write to you now if I had not gone through some difficult things and gained some valuable experience?

I encourage you to look at the wounds and difficulties you have survived from a new viewpoint. Take a look at how you can use your pain for someone else's gain. Can your mess become your ministry? I am a specialist in overcoming shame, guilt, poor self-image, lack of confidence, fear, anger, bitterness, self-pity, and other negative feelings. Let me encourage you to be positive about your past and your pain, and realize that it can all be used for good in God's Kingdom.

Love Yourself Today: Nothing you have been through will
be wasted. Everything that has been pain can become gain in
God's hands.

Protected in Every Way

*Behold, I have indelibly imprinted (tattooed a picture of) you on
the palm of each of My hands; [O Zion] your walls are continually
before Me.*   ISAIAH 49:16

Sometimes when we are really hurting, we can be tempted to think God
has forgotten about us and left us alone in our pain. This is not true! Just
take a look at the verse for today and see how God feels about us.

God is continually concerned about our protection, including our
emotional protection.

One way we need to be protected emotionally is in the area of rejection. An assault of rejection can happen quickly; and it can hurt so
deeply. Don't wait until someone hurts you to pray about your emotions. Every day, before you go out among people, take a minute to say,
"God, I'm believing You to protect me emotionally today. I trust that
You will protect my emotions."

If we trust God with our emotions instead of living in fear that
someone will reject us and wound us, we will not be devastated if rejection does come our way. In fact, it will hardly affect us at all.

When you encounter people every day, do so with an open heart, not
with your defenses up. Don't isolate yourself from people because you're
afraid they'll reject you. Interact anyway, trusting God with the results.

God doesn't want your self-esteem crushed by the fact that someone
rejects you. Jesus died to give you strength, security, and confidence in
Him, so I encourage you to resist all fear of rejection and trust God to
heal any emotional hurt that you may encounter.

Love Yourself Today: "God, help me enjoy all people without
fear of being rejected or hurt. I trust You to protect my
emotions."

Love Is a Privilege

I expect to pass through life but once. If therefore, there be any
kindness I can show, or any good thing I can do to any fellow being,
let me do it now, and not defer or neglect it, as I shall not pass this
way again.   WILLIAM PENN

In 1820, a wealthy English couple had a little girl named Florence. She was fully expected to marry well, and live the life of a sophisticated, privileged Englishwoman. But God had other plans for Florence. When she was seventeen years old, she received a "call" from Him and knew she was supposed to spend her life as a nurse. But her parents considered nursing a "low class" occupation and refused to allow Florence to seek the training she needed.

Finally, Florence's parents reluctantly agreed to let her take a three-month course in nurse's training.

Several years later, the Crimean War broke out, and wounded British soldiers couldn't receive proper medical care because of inadequate facilities at the front. At the request of an acquaintance of Florence's, she arrived near the battlefield in Turkey with thirty-eight nurses ready for duty.

As a result of her work, military hospital conditions improved dramatically and mortality rates dropped significantly.

Had Florence not been willing to answer God's clear call, even when people around her discouraged her, she would not have had the amazing opportunities she had to touch others with God's love and bring healing to them. God can do the same kind of remarkable work through anyone who follows Him, no matter what.

———————————

Love Others Today: "Lord, help me answer Your call, no matter what people think."

Make Mercy a Way of Life

It is because of the Lord's mercy and loving-kindness that we are not
consumed, because His [tender] compassions fail not. They are new
every morning; great and abundant is Your stability and faithfulness.

LAMENTATIONS 3:22, 23

Aren't you thankful for God's abundant mercy? It is new every morning. Surely we would all live miserable, defeated lives if it were not for
His compassion and willingness to forgive us.

When we meditate on God's mercy and truly realize how much He
willingly forgives us, we can much more easily show mercy to others.
Good relationships are impossible unless we are generous with mercy
and forgiveness. Being merciful simply means forgiving others even
though their actions would warrant our anger.

Jesus said that we are to forgive our enemies and be kind. In this
way we show ourselves to be like our Father in heaven, for He is merciful and kind.

God's mercy is new every morning, and I am glad—because I am
sure I use my allotted portion every day. I am grateful for a new, fresh
start each day. When we make mistakes, He does not want us to try to
sacrifice to make up for them. When others hurt or offend us, He wants
us to extend mercy to them.

Learn to give and receive mercy regularly; and let mercy become a
way of life for you.

———————————

Love Others Today: God's mercies are new for you right
now! Receive the mercy He has for you and extend mercy to
everyone around you.

Open Heart Surgery

*Nathanael answered him, [Nazareth!] Can anything good come out
of Nazareth? Philip replied, Come and see!*   JOHN 1:46

For years I did not understand Nathanael's question in today's verse,
and I couldn't figure out why, in the next verse, Jesus compliments
him, saying, "Here is an Israelite indeed, in whom there is no guile nor
deceit nor falsehood nor duplicity!"

Then one day I saw it. Nathanael had a negative opinion of Nazareth because the prevailing sentiment of his day was that nothing good
ever happened there. So when he heard that Jesus was from Nazareth,
Nathanael was initially closed to the idea that Jesus was the true Messiah simply because of where He came from.

So often we are like Nathanael. We decide that a person cannot be any
good because of where he lives or where he comes from. We can be very
opinionated, often without even realizing it. We have prejudices that have
been placed in us by others. This is why we have to carefully examine our
hearts to see if they are truly open and willing to embrace all people.

The thing Jesus seemed to like about Nathanael was that although
he seemed convinced that nothing good could come out of Nazareth,
he was willing to check it out. Even though he had a strong opinion, he
had an open heart. Let me encourage you to have an open heart toward
everyone you meet. Think of it. If Nathanael had been unwilling to
open his heart to Jesus, he would have missed the greatest blessing of
his life—a great relationship with the Lord. I believe God has blessings
in store for you through relationships, too, so keep your heart open.

Love Others Today: "Lord, give me an open heart toward
everyone I meet."

Look at Jesus

And the Lord said to Moses, Make a fiery serpent [of bronze] and set
it on a pole; and everyone who is bitten, when he looks at it, shall live.

NUMBERS 21:8

At one point in Israel's history, Israelites were dying in large numbers because a plague of snakes came upon them and were biting them as a result of their sin (see Num. 21:6). What did their leader, Moses, do? He prayed. To solve the problem, Moses turned his attention immediately to God, not to himself or anyone else.

I have found that victorious people in the Bible faced their problems with prayer. They did not worry; they prayed. I ask you today: Do you worry or do you take your needs to God in prayer? Moses did not make his own plan and ask God to bless it; he did not try to figure out an answer in his mind, nor did he worry. He prayed. God told Moses to make a bronze serpent, set it on a pole, and put it in front of the people. Every snake-bitten person who looked at it would live. The New Testament tells us that, "Just as Moses lifted up the serpent in the desert [on a pole], so must...the Son of Man be lifted up [on the cross], in order that everyone who believes in Him...may not perish, but have eternal life..." (John 3:14, 15).

You and I still sin today, but the message of the bronze serpent still applies: "Look and live." Look at Jesus and at what He has done, not at yourself and what you have done or can do. The answer to your problem, whatever it may be, is not worry, but praying and trusting that Jesus is leading you.

Love God Today: Look to Jesus for the answer to every problem that you have! He loves it when you lean on Him.

Where Is Your Trust?

[Most] blessed is the man who believes in, trusts in, and relies on the Lord, and whose hope and confidence the Lord is.   JEREMIAH 17:7

Sometimes in life we face problems or situations that seem absolutely overwhelming. When these things happen, it's human nature to look for help and support wherever we can find it! In our desperation, we sometimes turn to people instead of to God. People will often fail us, but God will *always* come through for us.

This is the confidence we need to have in the face of seemingly overwhelming problems. Rather than focusing on our own strength or good ideas, and rather than looking to other human beings for strength or advice, we need to first be looking to the Lord and trusting in His wisdom, strength, and power. No matter how many problems we're facing, the One who is with us is greater than all those who oppose us.

In Jeremiah 17:5–8 we read that those who put their trust in the arm of the flesh are cursed with "great evil" (Jer. 17:5). They are like a plant in the desert that is dry and destitute. They will not see any good happen. But those who put their trust in the arm of the Lord are blessed. No matter what comes they will flourish and not be anxious. Jeremiah says, "Blessed is the man who believes in, trusts in, and relies on the Lord, and whose hope and confidence the Lord is" (Jer. 17:7).

If we lean on the arm of flesh, meaning that we put our trust in other people or ourselves, we will end up being disappointed and perhaps devastated. God may use people to help us, but He wants us to come to Him first.

––––––––––

Love God Today: "Lord, help me to ask for Your help and advice first in every situation."

Everything God Has Is Yours

Let us revel and feast and be happy and make merry.
LUKE 15:23

A well-known Bible story tells of a young man who left his father's house to go out into the world and live life his own way. He wasted all his inheritance and finally ended up with a job feeding hogs and eating what they ate. He decided to return to his father's house, realizing that he would have a better life as a servant to his father than living the way he was.

His father saw him coming in the distance and immediately planned a party. He was extremely happy that his son had returned home. Everyone was enjoying the party, the music was loud, and the older son who was returning from working in the field heard it. He asked what was going on, and when he heard the news he became angry and refused to go to the party. His father pleaded with him, but he preferred to sulk. His bad attitude didn't cause his father to stop the party, but it did keep him from entering in.

The older brother reminded his father that he had served and worked for him many years and never caused any trouble, and not once had anyone given him a party. His father replied that he could have had a party any time he wanted one, because everything his father had was always his. To me, this is a most amazing lesson and one that we cannot afford to miss. God loves us, and all that He has is ours as long as we belong to Him. He appreciates our work and effort to please Him, but if we refuse to enjoy the benefits of being a child of God, that is our fault, not His.

Love Yourself Today: Don't refuse to celebrate and enjoy life . . . you're a child of the King!

Is It Okay to Have More Than Enough?

Then He said to them all, "If anyone desires to come after Me, let
him deny himself, and take up his cross daily, and follow Me."
                                                    LUKE 9:23 NKJV

Since Jesus told us to deny ourselves in order to follow Him, is it ever okay to have more than enough of a thing? Well, first let me say that God Himself is more than enough. He does exceedingly, abundantly, above and beyond all that we can ever dare to hope, ask, or think (see Eph. 3:20). God wants us to deny ourselves when we need to in order to help those in need, but He also wants us to enjoy abundance in our own lives as well. There is a time for everything, according to the book of Ecclesiastes.

Even though I have enough earrings or shoes, there are times when buying a pair is what I need to do for me. It lifts me emotionally and is a way of me enjoying the fruit of my labor. There are other times when I know by God's Spirit that I need to say no to myself and use what I would have spent on myself on someone else. I know people who are selfish and do too much for themselves, and I know others who don't do enough for themselves. If you don't do things for yourself occasionally, you may feel deprived and end up bitter. Don't be afraid to bless yourself, because there are times when you need it.

I have found that the safe way to live is to make all of my resources available to God for His use at any time, and in the meantime to enjoy all that I have. There is no law given by God on exactly how much of a thing we can have, but He does expect us to be led by wisdom and that means being led by His Holy Spirit.

Love Yourself Today: Make a decision to be more generous than you have ever been before and to also enjoy what you have fully.

Set Them Free

That fiftieth year shall be a jubilee for you ... You shall not oppress
and wrong one another, but you shall [reverently] fear your God.
                                                    LEVITICUS 25:11, 17

In Old Testament times, the Year of Jubilee happened every fifty years. During the Year of Jubilee, all debts were forgiven and all debtors were pardoned and set free.

As human beings, we often feel that other people are indebted to us— that they owe us something—when they have wronged us. Sometimes we even want to get revenge on them. But as believers in Jesus Christ, every day can be a type of "jubilee." We can say to those who are in debt to us through their mistreatment of us, "I forgive you and release you from your debt. You are free to go. I leave you in God's hands to let Him deal with you, because as long as I am trying to deal with you, He won't."

According to the Bible, we are not to hold a person in perpetual debt, just as we ourselves are not to be indebted to anyone else. We can have our sins forgiven continually through repentance and faith in Jesus Christ. We can live in and enjoy a continual Year of Jubilee.

Can you imagine a person who learns that he has been pardoned from a ten- or twenty-year prison sentence? That's the good news of the cross. Because Jesus paid our debt for us, God can say to us, "You don't owe Me anything anymore!" Our trouble is either that we are still trying to pay our debt to the Lord, or that we are still trying to collect debts from others. Just as God canceled our debt and forgave us of it, so are we to cancel the debts of others and forgive them what we feel they owe us.

Love Others Today: "Thank You, Jesus, for setting me free from all the penalties of my sin and paying the price for me so I can live in a continual state of jubilee, and I choose today to cancel the debts I feel others may owe to me."

Have an Intervention

*Oh, that there might be one who would plead for a man with God
and that he would maintain his right with Him, as a son of man
pleads with or for his neighbor!*   JOB 16:21

Your love for God and relationship with Him certainly benefits you,
but it can also benefit others. When people come to you with needs
or concerns, even if you don't have what they really need, God does.
When you have a relationship with God, you can say to people, "I don't
have what you need, but I know Someone who does. I'll ask Him! I will
intercede before God for you."

When you live in relationship with God, you know He has the power
to intervene in people's circumstances. The more intimately you know
God, the more confident you are in His willingness to help people. Out
of a heart of love and compassion, you can actually ask God to do you
a favor and help someone you love even when you know that they may
not deserve it.

Even though my father abused many people, including me, God gave
me the grace to forgive him and I wanted very much to see him love and
accept Jesus during his lifetime. One day, I boldly asked God to save
my father as a favor to me, praying basically, "Father, I have done everything You have asked me to do concerning my father. I boldly ask You
to save him; don't let him die and go to hell. Lord, I am asking you to do
this as a personal favor to me." Approximately two months later, he did
give his life to the Lord, and I had the privilege of baptizing him. Your
intervention in people's lives through prayer is very important and can
even be life saving!

Love Others Today: When you see a need, don't ever think
there is nothing you can do, because you can always pray.

First Response

Is anyone among you afflicted (ill-treated, suffering evil)? He should pray. Is anyone glad at heart? He should sing praise [to God]. Is anyone among you sick? He should call in the church elders (the spiritual guides). And they should pray over him . . .   JAMES 5:13, 14

Sometimes I marvel at how long Christians can struggle in a situation before we think to pray about it. We complain about our problems; we grumble; we tell our friends; and we talk about how God should do something about it. We struggle with situations in our minds and in our emotions, while we often fail to take advantage of the simplest solution there is: prayer. We are all guilty of having treated prayer as a last-ditch effort. We carry burdens we do not need to bear—and life is much harder than it has to be—because we do not realize how power-ful prayer is. If we did, we would pray about everything, not as a last resort, but as a first response.

In today's Scripture, the apostle James offers a simple, three-word solution to some of life's challenges: "He should pray." The message to us in this verse is that no matter what happens over the course of a day, we should pray. We should go to God immediately.

So, when you have a problem, pray; when you have a need, tell God what it is. When you are discouraged or you feel like giving up, pray. When you're offended, pray. When you don't know what to do, pray and ask God for wisdom. Whatever situation you find yourself in, pray before you do anything else.

Love God Today: Whatever happens, pray before you do anything else.

Our Greatest Privilege

Prayer is so simple that even the feeblest child can pray, yet it is at the same time the highest and holiest work to which man can rise. It is fellowship with the Unseen and Most Holy One.

ANDREW MURRAY

I believe prayer is the greatest privilege of our lives. It's not something we *have* to do; it's something we *get* to do. It's an important and intimate aspect of our love relationship with God because it's the way we communicate with Him. Prayer is also the way we partner with God to see His plans and purposes come to pass in our lives and in the lives of those we love. It's the means by which we human beings on earth can actually enter into God's awesome presence. It allows us to share our hearts with Him, listen for His voice, and know how to discover and enjoy all the great things He has for us. Communicating with God is indeed the greatest privilege I can imagine, but this high and holy work is also the simplest privilege I know.

I do not think prayer was ever meant to be complicated and that, from the very beginning, God intended it to be an easy, natural way of life by which we stay connected with Him all day, every day. Madame Jeanne Guyon wrote in *Experiencing the Depths of Jesus Christ* that "...God demands nothing extraordinary. On the contrary, He is very pleased by a simple, childlike conduct. I would even put it this way: The highest spiritual attainments are really the ones that are the most easily reached. The things that are most important are the things that are the least difficult!"

When you pray today, realize what a privilege it is and use the opportunity to tell God how much you love Him.

Love God Today: Make a priority of exercising the greatest privilege of your life: prayer.

Check Your Heart

*The Lord saw that the wickedness of man was great in the earth,
and that every imagination and intention of all human thinking was
only evil continually.*   GENESIS 6:5

In Genesis 6:5–8, part of the story of Noah, we see that wickedness and evil imaginations and intentions characterized the condition of people's hearts during Noah's day, and that's the reason God decided to send the flood and destroy everyone on earth except Noah and his family.

I believe Noah had a right heart toward God; otherwise, he would have been subject to destruction, just as everyone else was. One lesson we can learn from his life story is that people can protect themselves from destruction through simple, prompt obedience to God.

So many things in our lives would turn around and start to go well if we would simply maintain a right heart attitude toward God. Certainly, this starts with loving God, but we also need to deal with bad attitudes, impure motives, and wrong thinking.

The Bible says in Proverbs 4:23: "Guard your heart with all vigilance and above all that you guard, for out of it flow the springs of life." Keeping our heart right is a continual process. It involves a daily watching and a willingness to line up our thoughts, attitudes, and actions with God. For example, if someone offends us, we need to quickly forgive in order to keep our hearts pure and clean. If we hurt someone, we need to apologize.

I encourage you to spend some time examining your heart to be sure it is right before God. Study God's Word to find out what a "right heart" looks like. Check your attitudes and check your thoughts. Loving God means more than simply saying you love Him. It also means honoring Him and obeying His Word.

———————————

Love God Today: God, help me to diligently guard my heart and do my part to be pure and clean before You.

God Will Help You

Fear not, for I am with you; be not dismayed, for I am your God.
I will strengthen you, yes, I will help you, I will uphold you with
My righteous right hand.... Those who war against you shall be as
nothing, as a nonexistent thing. For I, the Lord your God, will hold
your right hand, saying to you, "Fear not, I will help you. Fear not,
you worm Jacob, you men of Israel! I will help you," says the Lord
and your Redeemer, the Holy One of Israel.   ISAIAH 41:10–14 NKJV

When we start reading today's Scripture, we might think, *Wow. God must be talking to people who really have their act together,* but the good news is that He is talking to ordinary people just like you and me. He helps us because He is good, not because we are. Fear comes against all of us, and God wants us to know that we don't have to let the feelings of fear defeat us. We can keep moving forward in the presence of fear because He is with us.

If someone has hurt you or treated you unjustly, remember that God promises to deal with them and make them as nothing at all... nonexistent!! When we read that God will strengthen us that means He will enable us to do whatever we need to do today and everyday. God is with you, and that makes you equal to anything that comes against you. Because God is with you, that makes you greater than any problem you have.

Fear is not God's will for you. He wants you to be bold, courageous, and confident, and you can be if you remind yourself often that you are not alone. God is with you!!

Love Yourself Today: Remember that God is with you at all times and you can do whatever you need to do.

The Value of Wisdom

Prize Wisdom highly and exalt her, and she will exalt and promote
you; she will bring you to honor when you embrace her.

PROVERBS 4:8

Today's Scripture teaches us that wisdom is one of the keys to promotion and increase in any area of life.

I believe many people fail to receive promotions they might otherwise be granted in their professions simply because they do not act wisely on their jobs. Brainpower alone is not enough; wisdom is also important.

I have had some extremely bright people with very good minds on my staff over the years. Some of them, however, did not use wisdom at work. Maybe they were unkind to co-workers, or unable to work with a team of people. Maybe they never seemed to be able to get back to their desks on time after lunch. Their skills were excellent, but they did not demonstrate wisdom in other ways, so I did not promote them. A wise person who also has good skills, on the other hand, can expect to advance anywhere he or she goes, because wisdom is what promotes us and exalts us.

When God gives us resources—which could include our time, talents and gifts, influence or authority, or our finances and possessions—we need to be wise stewards of those things, using them with discernment and understanding.

One way to love yourself is to learn to exercise wisdom in every area of your life. This will give you confidence in the decisions you make, and it will also cause others to look favorably on you and be inclined to bless you when they have the opportunity to do so.

Love Yourself Today: Are you behaving wisely at work and using wisdom God has given you?

Random Acts of Kindness

Wherever there is a human being, there is an opportunity for a kindness.   SENECA

Many media outlets have carried the story of a man named Chuck Wall, a human relations instructor at a college in Bakersfield, California. Reportedly, Wall heard a remark from a television news broadcaster, and it made an impact on him. At the conclusion of a sad story, the anchorman said: "Another random act of senseless violence."

That comment gave Wall an idea, which he turned into an unusual assignment for his students. He asked them to do something out of the ordinary to help someone else and then write an essay about it. After that, he decided to print bumper stickers that said: "Today, I will commit one random act of senseless kindness . . . Will you?" Wall's students sold the bumper stickers for one dollar each and gave the profits to a charity for the blind.

One student decided to pay his mother's utility bills as his random act of kindness. Another student bought thirty blankets from the Salvation Army and distributed them to homeless people who were living under a bridge.

The idea quickly became very popular. All the police cars in Wall's county soon had "kindness" bumper stickers on them. Pastors, teachers, businesspeople, and community leaders began talking about the "kindness campaign."

This all started in 1993, and today, many people are familiar with the phrase "random acts of kindness." I hope you not only know this phrase and appreciate the story behind it, but that you incorporate random acts of kindness into your everyday life as often as possible.

Love Others Today: Commit one random act of kindness today—you'll feel better, and so will someone else.

Playing Favorites

For God shows no partiality [undue favor or unfairness; with Him
one man is not different from another].   ROMANS 2:11

The Bible says in several places that God does not have favorites (see Acts 10:34; Eph. 6:9; 1 Pet. 4:9). In other words, He does not treat some people better than others and He is totally fair to everyone. He is very compassionate toward anyone who is hurting and works to bring justice into their lives. God gave Moses instructions for the Israelites concerning how to treat the strangers in their midst, and His primary directive was always basically, "Make them feel comfortable and at ease and be friendly with them. Do not oppress them in any way" (see Ex. 22:21; 23:9; Lev. 19:33). We can see that God cares about every person.

Let me ask you, have you ever been tempted to play favorites? Most of us have done this, but we need to grow out of it! We need to be friendly and kind to *everyone*.

The apostle James admonished the church not to pay special attention to people who wore splendid clothes to the synagogue or to give them preferable seats when they came in. He said that we were not even to attempt to practice the faith of our Lord Jesus Christ together with snobbery (see James 2:1–4). In other words, we are to treat all people as worthy of respect.

Jesus put an end to distinction between people and said that we are all one in Him (see Gal. 3:28). We simply need to see valuable people, not black, red, yellow, or white people, not the labels in their clothes, hairstyles, the cars they drive, their professions, or titles—just people for whom Jesus died.

————————

Love Others Today: Treat everyone you meet as if they had infinite value because in God's eyes, they do!

Don't Be a Hoarder

But do not forget to do good and to share, for with such sacrifices God is well pleased.   HEBREWS 13:16 NKJV

In his book *Lifesigns,* Henri Nouwen wrote a parable about a group of people called *the fearful hoarders.* They were people who looked at all the resources in the world and became fearful that they would not have enough when hard times hit. They began zealously gathering for themselves all the food and supplies they could find.

Other people soon noticed how much the hoarders were collecting for themselves. They asked the hoarders to share what they had stored because they were taking resources away from others. But the hoarders only guarded their supplies more vigilantly and grew more and more afraid they would need it all someday.

Other people began to suffer and die, so they demanded the hoarders share. The hoarders refused again. They also became afraid that the other people, in their desperation, would attack them in order to get what they had. They built walls so high they couldn't even see whether people were coming to attack them or not. They put bombs on top of the walls, so no one would risk even getting close to them and their provisions.

A funny thing happened. They soon became afraid of their bombs, realizing they could harm themselves more than their enemies. They realized that all their efforts to stay safe and secure only caused them to be trapped in a prison of their own making. Their efforts to protect themselves and their possessions made them miserable. Nouwen writes, "And they gradually realized their fear of death had brought them closer to it."

Love Others Today: There is a difference between saving wisely and hoarding fearfully. Refuse to let fear make you stingy!

Don't Get Separated

Who shall ever separate us from Christ's love? Shall suffering and affliction and tribulation? Or calamity and distress? Or persecution or hunger or destitution or peril or sword?   ROMANS 8:35

We have an enemy, Satan, who knows we cannot be confident and fearless unless we are established in God's love. Naturally, he desires to separate us from it. He wants to keep us weak and powerless so that we're no threat to the kingdom of darkness. Satan often uses our trials and tribulations to convince us that God does not love us. He might whisper to us thoughts such as, "If God really loved you, you would not have these problems," or, "God is all powerful; if He really loves you why doesn't He deliver you from your suffering?"

Paul was very clear in his writings in Romans 8:35–39. He said that we are to let nothing separate us from God's love, which is found in Christ Jesus.

Even when we are hurting or struggling, we need to choose to believe God loves us, has a good plan for our lives, and is helping us gain victory over our circumstances. Jesus said we would have tribulation in this world, but He also promised that He has overcome the world. Let us be persuaded beyond doubt that neither death nor life, nor powers, nor heights nor depth, nor anything else in all creation will be able to separate us from God's love, which is found in Christ Jesus.

Love God Today: "Thank You, Father, for loving me with a love so strong that *nothing* can ever separate me from it."

Be Conscious

And we know (understand, recognize, are conscious of, by
observation and by experience) and believe (adhere to and put faith
in and rely on) the love God cherishes for us. God is love, and he
who dwells and continues in love dwells and continues in God, and
God dwells and continues in him.   1 JOHN 4:16

You might be able to say, "I know that God loves me," and still not be experiencing or observing His amazing love. First John 4:16 challenged me to really begin to notice the many ways in which God shows His love for us. It might be something as simple as providing a parking spot in a very crowded lot or opening doors of opportunity that amaze me.

I believe we should form a habit of being conscious of God's love at all times and continue to be amazed at the fact that He shows His love for us even when we don't deserve it. One way I would encourage you to do this is to keep a book of remembrance, a book in which you write down special things the Lord does for you. It will help you be more aware of how often His love manifests in practical ways in your life. I believe, according to 1 John 4:16, that we should make an effort to *observe* God's love, to recognize and celebrate it with thanksgiving.

God's love contains the power to heal our emotional wounds. His love strengthens us to press on in difficult times, and it softens our hearts, enabling us to show more love to others. Can you imagine anything better to be "conscious and aware of" than this great love?

Love God Today: "Father, every time You do something special for me, no matter how small it is, let me be thankful for it."

Learn to Love Yourself

Do not merely desire peaceful relations with God, with your fellowmen and with yourself, but pursue, go after them!

1 PETER 3:11

The Bible teaches us not to be selfish and self-centered, but it never instructs us not to love ourselves in a balanced way. I always say, "Don't be in love with yourself, but love yourself." If you don't love yourself, you will be miserable because you are always with yourself. You are one person you will never get away from, not even for one second of your life.

Most people don't really like themselves. They are very self-critical; they reject themselves and may even hate themselves. I once heard a young woman ask a pastor to pray for her because she hated herself. He looked at her with a furrowed brow and took a step backward in shock. He said very firmly, "Who do you think you are to hate yourself after God sent His only Son to suffer so horribly and die in your place? If God loved you that much, surely you can learn to love yourself."

His statement opened her eyes to the mistake she was making, and she began her journey of learning to love and accept herself. I encourage you to do the same if you have not already done so. Take a step of faith and say, "I love myself with the love of God. I accept myself."

As you begin to think and talk differently about yourself, your entire attitude toward yourself will change. You will become a more positive, confident person, and you will begin to enjoy your life so much more. As you do, you will see the love of God flowing not only to yourself, but also through you to other people.

Love Yourself Today: Repeat several times, "I love myself with the love of God."

Make Yourself an Offering

I appeal to you therefore, brethren, and beg of you in view of [all]
the mercies of God, to make a decisive dedication of your bodies
[presenting all your members and faculties] as a living sacrifice,
holy (devoted, consecrated) and well pleasing to God which is your
reasonable (rational, intelligent) service and spiritual worship.

ROMANS 12:1

People need to see God, and the way they can do that is by watching Him work through us in practical ways that relieve human suffering. You and I can live selfishly, or we can lay our lives down willingly as "living sacrifices" and place ourselves at God's disposal every day.

In today's Scripture, Paul is pleading with Christians to offer all of themselves, every member of their beings to God, to dedicate and consecrate themselves to Him. What good does it do to go to church and sing songs that we call praise and worship and then live a lifestyle that doesn't worship God? He is looking for true worshippers who will worship Him in spirit and in truth (in reality). We may go to church and worship, but to be worshippers we must live our daily lives according to biblical principles.

Paul goes on in Romans 12:2 to say, "Do not be conformed to this world." In other words, don't be like the world, living only for yourself and what you can get. Live to give. God gave His best, and when we give we are more like Him than at any other time in our lives.

As human beings, we are naturally selfish, but God can and will change us. He can give us great joy as we become living sacrifices.

Love Others Today: "Father, I ask in Jesus' name that You give me the grace to become a living sacrifice, offering all of myself to You and holding nothing back."

Spice Things Up!

You are the salt of the earth, but if salt has lost its taste (its strength, its quality), how can its saltness be restored? It is not good for anything any longer but to be thrown out and trodden underfoot by men.   MATTHEW 5:13

I don't know about you, but I don't like bland food. My husband once had a stomach problem, and the doctor put him on a totally bland diet for a few days. At every meal, I heard him say over and over, "This stuff has no taste at all." His food needed a bit of salt, a little spice—and that is exactly what the world needs.

Each day as you leave your home to go into a dark, tasteless world, you can be the light and flavor it needs. You can bring joy to your workplace by being determined to consistently have a godly attitude. You can be "salt" through simple things like being thankful rather than complaining like most people do, being patient, merciful, quick to forgive offenses, kind, and encouraging. Even simply smiling and being friendly is a way to bring flavor into a tasteless society.

Without love and all of its magnificent qualities, life is tasteless and not worth living. I want you to try an experiment. Just think: *I am going to go out into the world today and spice things up.* Then get your mind set before you ever walk out your door that you are going out as God's ambassador and that your goal is to be a giver, to love people, and add good flavor to their lives. You can begin by smiling at the people you encounter throughout the day. Deposit yourself with God and trust Him to take care of you while you sow good seed everywhere you go.

Loving Others Today: How can you add some spice and flavor to the world around you today?

Stuff, Stuff, Stuff!

For the love of money is a root of all kinds of evil...
1 TIMOTHY 6:10 NKJV

Stuff, stuff, stuff, and more stuff...our society today is focused on *getting more things* and is filled with greed. I am amazed when I drive around and see all the strip malls that exist and the ones that are being built. Everywhere we look something is being offered for purchase—and it is all an illusion. Greed is the spirit that is never satisfied and always wants more. It promises an easier life and more happiness, but for many people all it creates is oppressive debt.

The pressure and temptation to purchase more and more keeps us rooted in selfishness, which keeps us from focusing on loving others. But, we can change if we really want to. Let's learn to buy what we need and some of what we want, and then let's learn to give a lot of our possessions, especially ones we are no longer using, to someone who has less than we do. Let us practice giving until it is the first and most natural thing we do every day of our lives. Being generous is the best way to avoid greed.

Today's Scripture says, "The love of money is a root of all kinds of evil." The only reason people love money and will do almost anything to get it is simply because they feel money can get them whatever they want and therefore buy happiness. Crimes are regularly committed for money—and this is all rooted in the disease of selfishness.

I pray that God will give you all the money and things you can handle and still keep Him first in your life. I encourage you to be very generous because greed and stinginess will make you miserable.

———————————

Love Others Today: Are you being greedy about something in your life? How can you turn that selfishness into loving generosity?

Do You Like Yourself?

Let him search for peace ... and seek it eagerly. [Do not merely desire peaceful relations with God, with your fellowmen, and with yourself, but pursue, go after them!]   1 PETER 3:11

Have you ever thought about your relationship with yourself? For years, it never occurred to me that I had a relationship with myself. In fact, I never thought about it until God began to teach me how to improve it. Maybe the idea that you have a relationship with yourself has never entered your mind, either. But the truth is, you spend more time with yourself than with anyone else! So getting along well with yourself is vital to your well-being.

Do you like yourself? Many people don't. Self-rejection and even self-hatred contribute to many of the struggles we have in life. Think about it: Rejecting or holding hatred toward others causes all kinds of problems in relationships with them, so why wouldn't rejecting or hating or disliking yourself cause the same kind of problems in your relationship with yourself?

Today's Scripture urges us to pursue and go after peaceful relations with God, others, and ourselves. I encourage you to embrace and accept yourself because God created you just the way He wants you to be and made every unique thing about you. He loves you tremendously, so let that truth empower you to not only *like* yourself, but also to *love* yourself. As you grow in this way, you'll notice that some of your problems will decrease and eventually go away.

Love Yourself Today: Make a list of your good qualities. Take a moment to think about how these positive attributes are a blessing to you and to others. Thank God for making so many good things about you!

Yes, Lord

For the Lord corrects and disciplines everyone whom He loves,
and He punishes, even scourges every son whom He accepts and
welcomes to His heart and cherishes.   HEBREWS 12:6

As we change and grow in God, we won't always do everything perfectly. As a result, we need to know how to receive God's loving correction. God corrects us and disciplines us because He loves us. In
Revelation 3:19, Jesus speaks this same truth when He says: "Those
whom I [dearly and tenderly] love, I tell their faults....So be enthusiastic and in earnest and burning with zeal and repent [changing your
mind and attitude]."

As I've dealt with my children and with hundreds of employees over
the years, I've discovered that in order for my correction to be effective, it's
essential that the people I correct know that I love and care about them.

The people who struggle most to receive correction are those who
do not know they are loved. Instead of feeling corrected for their own
good, they feel punished.

No one can receive God's correction properly without a revelation of
His great love. We may hear the correction and even agree with it, but
it will only make us feel condemned or angry unless we know it comes
from God's heart of love and will ultimately bring about the changes
needed in our lives.

Next time God corrects you, remember that He "dearly and ten-
derly" loves you and that He accepts you, cherishes you, and welcomes
you to His heart. Receive His correction as an act of love and respond
by saying, "Yes, Lord."

Love God Today: "When You correct me, Lord, I will welcome
it, receive it as an expression of Your love for me, and say yes
to You."

Things Unseen

Since we consider and look not to the things that are seen but to the things that are unseen; for the things that are visible are temporal (brief and fleeting), but the things that are invisible are deathless and everlasting.   2 CORINTHIANS 4:18

As believers, we know the spiritual realm exists and that what happens there affects what happens on earth. We know that there is more to life than meets the eye, and as we grow spiritually, we come to value the things that are invisible more than the things we can see. When we understand that there are invisible, everlasting spiritual realities that affect our earthly lives, we begin to perceive that God is inviting us to interact with Him, to perceive things spiritually, and to partner with Him to accomplish them on earth—and that only happens through prayer.

As we partner with God through prayer, we bring things out of the spiritual realm into our lives. These gifts of God that come from heaven are already stored up for us, but we will never have them unless we pray and ask God for them. He is doing such wonderful things for us, and we receive and enjoy those things through the power and the privilege of prayer.

The Lord's Prayer says, "Your will be done on earth even as it is in heaven." When we pray that way we are partnering with God through prayer so that the purposes and plans He has in the spiritual realm will come to pass on earth—in our lives and in the lives of those around us. Through prayer we have the privilege of bringing heaven to earth!

Loving God Today: Remember that the spiritual realm is real and that what happens there affects your life on earth.

Who Are *They* Anyway?

For where there are envy, strife, or divisions among you, are you not
carnal and behaving like mere men?   1 CORINTHIANS 3:3 NKJV

Have you ever thought about the fact that "they" seem to have a *lot* of influence in our lives? If we listen to our own conversation, we will hear ourselves saying, "Well, they say . . ." *They* decide what clothing is in style or which professions are "important" or respectable. So, who are *they*?

They are people who aren't much different from you or me, but they have set standards by doing certain things in certain ways—and now everyone seems to think what *they* say is right! If we listen to *them,* we will find ourselves trying to do the best at what *they* say we should do.

There came a time when I realized *they* were practically running my life, and I didn't like it. I decided I was tired of being enslaved by what *they* wanted and I was going to live my life free from what *they* said I should or shouldn't do. I realized that comparison and competition are worldly, not godly. The world system, which includes *them,* demands these behaviors, but God's system condemns them.

Jesus has set us free from needing to please people and from the division that competition creates. He has delivered us from jealousy and from being controlled and manipulated by *them;* and He has liberated us to discover and be what He has created us to be.

I hope you know that you are completely free to follow God's Spirit instead of people's opinions and to be the person God made you to be, free from the influence of *them*—whoever *they* are!

Love Yourself Today: In what ways do you need to break free from what *they* say you should do?

You Can Do All Things

I can do all things through Christ who strengthens me.
PHILIPPIANS 4:13 NKJV

Today's Scripture is a popular Bible verse; however, I believe it has been quoted out of context at times. It doesn't mean we can do anything we want to do or that we can do everything other people do. To think of it that way would leave many people frustrated because they would be trying to succeed and do things that are not part of their God-given callings and abilities.

This verse means we can do "all things" that are part of God's will for us. If you are called to be a missionary in the jungle, you will be able to "do" all things that are part of the rigors of jungle life. The same principle is true for any situation or calling.

In context the apostle Paul was saying he could be content with very little or with great abundance. He knew that whatever state he found himself in was God's will for him at that moment. Regardless of his circumstances, he knew God would strengthen him for what He was calling him to do.

This understanding of Philippians 4:13 has taught me to remain within the boundaries of what the Lord has called and equipped me to do and not try to undertake things that are not within the realm of my God-given talents and abilities to accomplish. This attitude allows me to enjoy peace at all times and in every circumstance.

I know God has called you to something great and that He will strengthen you to do all the things that are needed to help you fulfill His purposes for your life.

———————————

Love Yourself Today: "Lord, I thank You for giving me strength to do everything that is part of Your will for my life."

Mercy Wins

Mercy triumphs over judgment.   JAMES 2:13 NKJV

It is easy to judge a person or situation and dole out only what we think is deserved, but mercy is greater than that. It is a glorious thing for someone to overlook an offense. In order to help people in third world countries, I cannot look at the fact that many of them worship idols or animals or the sun or even demons. I could easily say, "No wonder they're starving—they have turned their backs on God." But perhaps I would be in the same situation they're in if I had been born in a different place. We must remind ourselves, "If it were not for the grace of God in my life, that could be me." That does not mean we need to embrace others' sin, but we should embrace *people* and help them in their time of need.

Mercy and compassion are two of the most beautiful qualities of love, and in fact there is no real love without them. Because I was forced to earn everything I got in my first thirty years of life, I was not big on giving people what I had worked for when it seemed to me that they had done nothing. Learning the difference between my human love and the love of God that had been deposited in me took some time. Mercy cannot be earned or deserved. Paul wrote to the Colossians and told them to "put on love" (Col. 3:14). I love the phrase "put on," which means to do something on purpose, without depending on feelings or reason. I have learned amazing life lessons from that tiny little phrase.

Unless we learn to live beyond our feelings, we may live our lives judging and condemning others. We will never be able to love people with the love of God or help the needy people of the world. We can decide to be people who allow mercy to triumph over judgment. Are you ready to put on mercy? Are you ready to put on love?

Love Others Today: What specific judgments in your mind need to be replaced with mercy? Ask God to help you; He will!

Keep the Secret

*But when you give to charity, do not let your left hand know what
your right hand is doing.*   MATTHEW 6:3

If you have ever walked through a large, bustling airport, you may have
noticed stores called "Duty Free Shoppes." One of the cofounders is
a man named Charles Feeney, and the *New York Times* once carried a
story that said Feeney gave away about $600 million during a fifteen-
year period. He kept about $5 million for himself.

You might think a man who has given more than $600 million to char-
itable causes would be well known. Feeney is not. In fact, his gifts were
all given anonymously. He sent them by cashier's checks so the recipient
could not trace the gift.

Apparently, Feeney decided at one point that he had enough money
for himself, and he began giving away the rest. He didn't own a house
or a car.

There's a similar story about Charles Spurgeon and his wife. When
their chickens laid eggs, they sold them; they never gave any away.
Only after Mrs. Spurgeon died did people learn the couple had used
all the egg money to support two elderly widows. They endured false
accusations of being stingy and mercenary because they didn't want
"the left hand to know what the right hand was doing."

Think about your neighbors or your friends at work or church. You
can probably soon come up with something you could do to help them.
Take the challenge and do it without letting anyone know where the
kindness came from.

———————

Love Others Today: What can you do, anonymously, to bless
someone today?

Let God Comfort You

Blessed be the God and Father of our Lord Jesus Christ, the Father of sympathy (pity and mercy) and the God [Who is the Source] of every comfort (consolation and encouragement).

2 CORINTHIANS 1:3

We all want to be accepted, not rejected. But most of us have felt the isolation and emotional pain that come from feeling rejected. It hurts! The good news is that we can do something about it.

Years ago, I reached out to someone who had hurt me greatly during my childhood. Instead of offering an apology, this person blamed me for something that wasn't my fault!

The emotional pain I suffered was intense. I wanted to hide and feel sorry for myself, but I now know how to respond differently. I know how to let God love me, comfort me, and heal me through the power of the Holy Spirit. I asked Him to heal my wounded emotions and enable me to handle the situation as Jesus would have handled it. As I kept turning to Him, I felt almost as though soothing oil was being poured over my wounds.

Maybe my situation sounds familiar to you. It's very hard to be your own comforter, and one of the best things you can do for yourself is to look to God for the comfort you need. Today's verse promises that He is the source of all comfort, consolation, and encouragement. He's the one who can provide them for you.

Love Yourself Today: Do you need comfort or consolation? Don't try to take care of it yourself, but go to God and let His healing grace give you everything you need.

Your Most Important Commitment

Then you will seek Me, inquire for, and require Me [as a vital necessity] and find Me when you search for Me with all your heart.

JEREMIAH 29:13

One Saturday years ago, Dave and I called my aunt and uncle and invited them out for a nice dinner. They couldn't go, my aunt said, because my uncle had to recharge the battery on the pacemaker unit on his heart. I wondered why he couldn't wait until later to charge his pacemaker; I didn't realize that waiting would be the difference between life and death. His pacemaker was a "vital necessity." It literally kept him alive.

According to today's Scripture, a believer's "vital necessity" is time with God. I wonder, what is the most serious time commitment on your calendar today? Your most important time commitment is the same as mine and as every other believer's: spending time seeking God, in His presence.

Perhaps because God is always available, we think we can spend time with Him "later," so we choose to respond to what seems urgent, instead of giving God a place of priority in our schedules. But if we spent more priority time with God, maybe we wouldn't have so many emergencies that rob us of valuable hours and minutes in our lives. When you sit in God's presence, even if you don't feel you are learning anything new, you are still sowing good seed into your life, seed that will produce a good harvest. With persistence, you will get to the point where you understand more of the Word, where you are having great intimate fellowship and conversation with God. You will sense His presence and begin to see changes in your life that will amaze you. If we seek God first, he will add everything else we need in life (Matt. 6:33).

––––––––––––

Love God Today: At what point in your day today will you take time to focus exclusively on God and be in His presence?

Deeper and Deeper

Again he measured one thousand, and it was a river that I could not cross; for the water was too deep, water in which one must swim, a river that could not be crossed.   EZEKIEL 47:5 NKJV

In the verses that precede today's Scripture, the prophet Ezekiel talks about a vision in which he saw waters issuing from the threshold of God's temple. I believe these waters represent an outpouring of God's Spirit. First, the water was only ankle deep to Ezekiel; then it reached his knees; then his loins. Soon the waters had risen deep enough to swim in.

In this story we see a picture that could represent four levels of commitment to God. Some people only want to get close enough to Him that they are ankle-deep in water. They like to feel their feet on solid ground so they can be sure they are still in control. They don't want to abandon themselves totally to the point that the river (representing God's Spirit) is in control. Others are willing to go knee-deep or waist-deep, while some want the river to be deep enough to swim in.

How far into the river of God's grace and power are you willing to let the Holy Spirit lead you?

We need God's presence in our lives; we need intimate fellowship with Him. Often we find ourselves in situations that we don't know how to handle; they may seem too "deep" for us or we may feel we're "in over our heads." But God is ready to lead and guide us by His Spirit if we make ourselves available to Him.

Seek God with your whole heart, and you will find Him.

———————————————

Love God Today: "Lord, I pray that You will continue to take me deeper and deeper in You."

Do What You Need to Do

But even in case you should suffer for the sake of righteousness, [you are] blessed (happy, to be envied). Do not dread or be afraid of their threats, not be disturbed [by their opposition].   1 PETER 3:14

Notice that today's Scripture mentions fear and dread. These two negative dynamics work together. They both try to hold us back from doing what we need to do, and they both waste our time. Almost everyone wrestles with them, but what is the point of dreading something we *have* to do?

Our lives would be so much better if we would simply reject fear and dread at their onset. We might say: "I dread getting up for work in the morning. I dread the traffic on my morning commute. I dread balancing the bank accounts." We can choose to stay in bed, get fired, and go bankrupt, but we probably won't. None of us would want the negative alternative, so why dread doing what we are going to do anyway?

A positive attitude can enable us to enjoy everything that we do. Don't dread things, because dread is a relative of fear, and fear always holds us back. Fear says, "Oh, I can't do this. I'm not up to this. It's too much for me." But God has not given us a spirit of fear. He has given us power, love, and sound minds (see 2 Timo. 1:7). We do not have to dread or live in fear of anything.

If you have to "do things afraid," then do them afraid. But do them! Work through your fears; stop running from them; do not allow fear or dread to steal one more minute of the time God has given you.

―――――――――――――

Love Yourself Today: Be a person of action and refuse to torment yourself with dread or fear.

Works That Work

For My people have committed two evils: they have forsaken Me,
the Fountain of living waters, and they have hewn for themselves
cisterns, broken cisterns which cannot hold water.

JEREMIAH 2:13

I believe one of the biggest ways people waste time is by doing what the Bible calls "dead works." I like to define a dead work as a "work" that doesn't work! That means that you are trying to make something happen, but no matter what you do, it simply does not work. When that happens, the reason is that the work is yours and not God's. When you stop planning and striving, and come to the end of yourself, then God will begin to move. That doesn't mean you have no responsibility; it simply means your work needs to be inspired and empowered by the Holy Spirit, not conceived in your natural mind and fueled by your natural strength.

There are many different kinds of dead works. For example, anything we do with a wrong motive is a dead work. Another type of dead work would be the efforts we make without asking God to get involved. Take another look at today's Scripture and imagine how frustrated you would be if you spent all day digging a well, thinking you would get water, and at the end of the day, tired and worn out, your only result was a big hole.

Things we do outside of God's timing or His will are also dead works. Learn to discern when you are working on something that is not working and refuse to do anything that is not in God's will and timing.

———————————

Love Yourself Today: What do you need to stop doing so you can use your time more wisely?

Strategically Placed

For behold, darkness shall cover the earth, and dense darkness [all]
peoples, but the Lord shall arise upon you [O Jerusalem], and His
glory shall be seen on you.   ISAIAH 60:2

I believe the lives of God's people are going to get better and better, but
the lives of those who are still in bondage to the world will get worse
and worse as they sink deeper and deeper into despair and depression.
The light of God will intensify in us as we allow Him to work in us and
make us the kind of vessels through which His glory can shine.

God is willing to purge us and cleanse us of the things in our lives
that are not like Christ, if we will welcome His fire into our lives. Ask
Him to work in you and cleanse you of anything that is hindering Him
from flowing through you. Like a gardener, God wants to prune off all
the dead things in our life so we can bear good fruit for Him.

I believe God has strategically placed His people all over the world,
in every company, every marketplace, every hospital, school, and so
on. As the darkness in the world becomes darker in these last days, His
glory will shine brighter on those who belong to Him. Then we will be
able to help the lost find their way.

This is the day for believers to shine and be used by God as never
before. The world will not be won through a handful of preachers. We
desperately need an army of people available for one-on-one ministry
in their neighborhoods, at their work, and in the marketplace. This is
why I implore you today to make a deeper commitment to God than
ever before. Not only do you need God; He also needs you!

Don't discount yourself by believing that God could not possibly
use you. He can; He wants to; and He will!

———————————

Love Others Today: God has strategically placed you where
you are right now. Be a light that shines in the darkness.

Love Through Serving

Whoever desires to be great among you must be your servant.

MARK 10:43

A servant is one who lives to benefit another, one who sacrifices for another's joy or fulfillment. Sacrifice is the only status symbol in the Kingdom of God. Jesus said servanthood makes a person great, and that no one can become great without it.

When it comes to serving others, we are often like children who don't want to eat our vegetables. We like the things that taste good, but often ignore the things we really need to be healthy. At one time in my life I would not touch vegetables. I liked pasta, fried foods, cakes, pies, potatoes, and meat. As a result I was overweight and I felt bad. Thankfully, I learned to like foods that were better for me. Now I actually crave vegetables!

In a similar way I have learned to enjoy doing things for others and serving them. At first I didn't like it at all; then little by little I began to see the importance of it, and now I actually crave it. Just as I make sure I eat my vegetables, I make sure I reach out to others in love.

When God began dealing with me about serving others it was hard, but it has freed me from myself. What a completely awesome delight it is to actually wake up in the morning and find God and others on my mind first.

Don't let selfishness rule in your life. Be aggressive and do things for other people on purpose. As you do, you will find that you are a more joyful individual.

Love Others Today: How can you deliberately incorporate walking in love into your everyday life this week?

Don't Keep God Waiting!

We must begin to believe that God, in the mystery of prayer, has entrusted us with a force that can move the Heavenly world, and can bring its power down to earth.   ANDREW MURRAY

Any healthy relationship includes a certain amount of asking for what we want and need from another person. The same principle applies in our relationships with God. I know this sounds simple, but our prayers are not answered when we do not pray. The apostle James said that "we have not because we ask not" (James 4:2).

God is waiting for us to make requests of Him in prayer.

I once had an employee who often complained about having so much work to do. I don't think he even realized he was complaining, but it irritated me. I actually began to complain about the employee who was complaining! Then one day I realized I had never actually prayed about his negative attitude. So, I simply asked God to cause him to stop complaining and to be thankful and positive.

The next day when I saw the man, he made the first positive comment I had heard in a long time about his job. God was ready to help us, but His hands were tied until someone prayed. My prayerlessness was just as wrong as my employee's complaining. I was hindering God by being too passive to open a door for Him to work. I thought about the problem, resented the problem, talked about the problem, and got aggravated about the problem, but literally months went by before I prayed. As soon as I did, God intervened.

Learn from my mistake and don't let prayerlessness hinder God from working in your life and the lives of your loved ones.

Love God Today: What do you need? Have you asked God for it?

Don't Compromise

*Oh, how great is Your goodness, which you have laid up for those
who fear, revere, and worship You, goodness which You have wrought
for those who trust and take refuge in You before the sons of men.*

PSALM 31:19

God is good to everyone, but I do believe He reserves special rewards
for those who are bold and never compromise their faith when they
are with unbelievers. Our verse for today says that He has goodness wrought for those who take refuge in Him *before the sons of men.*
We must be sure that we don't live one way in front of our Christian
family and friends and then another way in front of our unbelieving
associates.

Our calling as believers is to be lights in dark places. We must maintain our integrity at all times and never compromise our moral standards. However, if we desire the approval of men, we often do whatever
it takes to feel accepted by them, even at the cost of displeasing God
and going against our own conscience.

It is much better to please God than to please men. The apostle Paul
stated that if he had wanted to be popular with people he would never
have become an apostle (Gal. 1:10). He would have missed the privilege
of serving God as he did. It is tragic how often people say "no" to God in
order to say "yes" to men. We must obey God rather than man (Acts 5:29).

When we follow God we have peace, and we experience the rewards
of God in our life. I encourage you to take a stand for what is right in
your life. Don't let the fear of rejection pressure you to sin against your
own conscience.

Love God Today: Do you want God's goodness stored up for
you? Live your Christian faith openly in front of the people
around you.

Follow God with Boldness

... the righteous are bold as a lion.   PROVERBS 28:1 NKJV

God has uniquely created you and gifted you to fulfill His purpose for your life. It may be something others regard as "important," or "cool," or it may be something other people don't find impressive. For example, some believe leading a Bible study is somehow better than being a stay-at-home mom, but really, what matters is that you do what God is calling you to do. Regardless of your chosen profession, the only way to find joy and satisfaction is to live your life according to His will.

The Holy Spirit leads us into the will of God. I have discovered that boldness is necessary in order to be led by the Holy Spirit, because He may not always lead us to do what everyone else is doing. Some insecure people tend to feel "safer" doing what others do. They are fearful of standing alone or going against the crowd. But sometimes God calls us to do something new or different, and we need to be willing to "break the mold" and do whatever He asks.

Any time we step outside the boundaries of what other people say is permissible or "right," we risk being judged or criticized. We must be secure in God and not allow such things to keep us from following the Holy Spirit and fulfilling our God-given purpose.

Do you really believe you are doing what God created you to do, or have you allowed other people's opinions to cause you to hold back? Great joy and many good things are waiting for you as you move forward with courage into all God has called and created you to do!

———————————

Love God Today: What is it that you sense God is calling you to do, but have lacked confidence to do in the past? Break the mold, and be bold!

Confessing a Healthy Self-Image

I am alert and active, watching over my word to perform it.
                                        JEREMIAH 1:12

One of the most powerful things we can do as believers is to confess God's Word. His Word is truth, and when He hears us speaking His truth and living our lives according to it, great things happen. I encourage you to confess the Bible-based truths below repeatedly, so they can become part of the foundation of a strong self-image in your life.

1. I know God created me, and He loves me.
2. I have faults and weaknesses, and I want to change. I believe God is changing me little by little, day by day. While He is doing so, I can still enjoy myself and enjoy my life.
3. Everyone has faults, so I am not a complete failure just because I am not perfect.
4. I am going to work with God to overcome my weaknesses, but I realize that I will always have something to deal with; therefore I will not become discouraged when God convicts me of areas that need improvement.
5. I want to make people happy and have them like me, but my sense of worth does not depend on what others think of me. Jesus has already affirmed my value by His willingness to die for me.

Love Yourself Today: "Lord, help me today to be established and well grounded in the truth of Your Word concerning my self-image and to confess these truths in faith."

Say It Out Loud

I am alert and active, watching over my word to perform it.
JEREMIAH 1:12

Today, as I did yesterday, I want to share with you some powerful truths that are based in God's Word. I encourage you to confess these words over and over, so they will change your thinking and become part of your belief system about yourself. As you confess them with a heart full of faith, doing your best to believe them and act on them, you'll be well on your way to a healthy self-image.

1. No matter how often I fail, I will not give up, because God is with me to strengthen and sustain me. He has promised to never leave me or forsake me (see Heb. 13:5).
2. I like myself. I don't like everything I do, and I want to change—but I refuse to reject myself.
3. I am right with God through Jesus Christ.
4. God has a good plan for my life. I am going to fulfill my destiny and be all I can be for His glory. I have God-given gifts and talents, and I intend to use them to help others.
5. I am nothing, and yet I am everything! In myself I am nothing, and yet in Jesus I am everything I need to be!
6. I can do all things I need to do, everything God calls me to do, through His Son Jesus Christ (see Phil. 4:13).

———————————

Love Yourself Today: Review the list of six confessions that will help you gain a healthy, biblical self-image. Which one do you need to focus on most today?

Believe the Best

Love . . . is ever ready to believe the best of every person.
1 CORINTHIANS 13:7

We can quickly ruin a day with wrong thinking. In other words, if we don't have the right mind-set toward a person or a situation, we can cause trouble. Friendships are destroyed because of wrong thinking. Marriages fail. It's so easy to concentrate on everything that is wrong with your spouse or a friend instead of what is right, and soon you want to get away from the person, when what you really need to escape is your own negative mind.

A great way to develop the right mind-set is to believe the best. Replace doubt-filled thoughts with faith-filled ones; replace fear with love; replace suspicion and fear with trust. Trust breeds trust.

This is good old common sense. Consider the following scenario. You are admiring the flowers at a certain home, and a man comes out of his house and mutters, "What are you doing in my yard?" You act angry and suspicious right back. His unfriendliness boomerangs back to him, and probably makes him even grouchier. On the other hand, if you are somehow able to look past his suspiciousness toward you (maybe he was recently robbed) and act extremely friendly and relaxed toward him, chances are he will relax, too, and you'll have a friendly interaction.

Call this the "boomerang effect." Or call it "reaping what you sow." Sow kindness and pleasantness into other people, and you'll find yourself on the receiving end of kind actions and pleasant words. When you believe the best about others, they're likely to believe the best about you, too.

———————————

Love Others Today: I choose to believe the best about everyone with whom I come in contact.

One Step at a Time

He will teach us His ways, and we shall walk in His paths.

ISAIAH 2:3

Our verse for today speaks of learning God's ways and walking in His paths. As believers, we hear a lot about "walking" with God. We want to walk in truth, walk in the light, walk worthy, and walk by faith. Of course, we also want to walk in love.

A walk is made up of a lot of steps. In fact, there's absolutely no way to walk except to do it one step at a time. To walk from one place to another, we must decide to take steps and then put one foot in front of the other. With each step, we make progress toward our destination. We don't take steps accidentally; we take each one because we choose to take it.

If you want to walk in love and to give love a place of priority in your daily life, you will have to make lots and lots of decisions to do so. This means deliberate decisions to love, all day, every day. And most of these decisions will involve the way you choose to treat other people.

Love requires a decision, and it takes effort, just as any other kind of walk does. If you take a brisk walk through the park or around your block, you'll notice that you have to work at it, especially if it is something you are not accustomed to doing. Similarly, every time you love somebody, it will cost you something—some time, some effort, some money, some energy. You can't love and not have it cost you anything or expect it to always be easy. One of the greatest things that I learned about love is that you have to do it on purpose. You don't wait for a feeling to motivate you; love is allowing God to operate through you to bless and encourage other people.

———————

Love Others Today: Remember, every act of love requires a decision, and it's something you do on purpose, one step at a time.

God Chose You

"I have loved you, [just] as the Father has loved Me; abide in My love [continue in His love with Me]."   JOHN 15:9

Ephesians 1:4, 5 says that in God's love He chose *you*, actually picked *you* out for Himself as His own. He loves you because He wants to; loving you pleases Him. If you reject God's love because you don't feel worthy, that hurts Him. God knew all about you when He called you to Himself. You are no surprise to Him. God wants to meet you wherever you are and help you get to where we need to be. He will change you, but He will love you perfectly while He is doing so. This is part of what it means to abide in Him (see John 15:9).

God is love. Love is not something He turns on and off based on our behavior. Love is who God is. If we abide in His love, we abide in Him.

If you desire fellowship and intimacy with the Lord, you must abide (live, dwell, and remain) in His love. His love heals all of your emotional wounds and bruises. It is the medicine you need to recover from rejection, betrayal, abandonment, and other traumas.

Think of yourself standing under a massive waterfall with hands and face turned upward, allowing the water from the fall to pour all over you. Now imagine that the water is God's love. Receive it, bask in it, and let it make you confident and whole.

Don't look for love in all the wrong places; if you do, you'll just get hurt and disappointed over and over again. The free gift of God's love is extended toward you right now. Receive it and let it pour into you by faith.

———————————

Love Yourself Today: "Father God, I believe you love me perfectly, and I receive Your love right now. Thank you for loving me and making me whole!"

Need Some Help?

Behold, God is my helper and ally; the Lord is my upholder and is with them who uphold my life.   PSALM 54:4

There are many people who have received Jesus as their Savior and Lord who will live their Christian lives and go to heaven without ever drawing on the power of the Holy Spirit available to them, never experiencing the true success God intends for them. People can be on their way to heaven, yet not enjoying the trip.

We often look at people who have wealth, position, power, fame, and consider them to be totally successful. But many people who are viewed as successful still lack good relationships, peace, joy, contentment, and other true blessings that are available only in the context of a personal relationship with God through Jesus Christ.

Self-sufficient people often think it is a sign of weakness to depend on God. But by drawing on the ability of the Holy Spirit, they could accomplish more in their lives than they could by working in their own strength.

There are countless things we struggle with when we could be receiving help from the Holy Spirit. Many people never find the right answers to their problems because they seek out the wrong sources for advice and counsel instead of asking the Divine Counselor who lives within them for guidance.

I encourage you to lean on God for everything, and that means little things as well as big things.

———————————

Love God Today: The only way to experience the success God intends for you is to become totally dependent on the Holy Spirit.

Obedience and Authority

Therefore [because He stooped so low] God has highly exalted Him
and has freely bestowed on Him the name that is above every name,
that in (at) the name of Jesus every knee should (must) bow, in
heaven and on earth and under the earth.   PHILIPPIANS 2:9, 10.

The kingdom of darkness has no power over Jesus. Why? Because He was radically obedient.

As human beings we are not perfect, but we do need to do the very best we can to obey God in all things. The rewards of obedience are wonderful, but the rewards of sin are oppressive and bring every kind of misery. If there is any known disobedience in your life, I urge you to admit it, ask God to forgive you, and start today obeying God. Everything He asks us to do is for our good, so why delay.

In Ecclesiastes Solomon ended the book he wrote by saying that "The full duty of man is to obey God." He had tried every way possible to live his own way and still be happy and yet found nothing that worked except following God fully. We can learn from Solomon's mistakes if we are wise. Don't waste your life or for that matter, don't waste one more day being disobedient.

The door of disobedience is one of Satan's favorite entrances by which to gradually draw us into his web. The Bible teaches us the importance of obeying the Word. Obedience both proves our love for God and empowers us to enjoy authority over the enemy and his kingdom.

Love God Today: "Lord, reveal any areas of disobedience in my life that I might be ignoring, and continue to work with me until I am completely what you want me to be."

A Health Tip for Today!

Water is the single most important nutrient for our bodies.
DON COLBERT, M. D.

Many people feel bad physically simply because they are dehydrated. They don't drink enough water. Water is life-giving. Getting enough water every day is very important to your health. Here are five easy ways to do it.

1. *Make water taste good.* If you don't have access to good tap water try installing a filter on your tap; squeezing a wedge of lemon, lime, or orange into every glass; or making iced herbal tea.
2. *Carry water everywhere.* The only way you can drink water is to have it handy. Make drinking water easy for yourself by having a bottle with you all the time.
3. *Have water call you.* If you struggle to remember to drink water every hour or so, put technology to work for you. Set your phone alarm to ring at certain intervals as a reminder that it's time to drink up!
4. *Get water from fruit.* Fruit can be 80 percent water, or more. Eating several pieces of fruit each day basically counts as an extra glass of water.
5. *Install a water cooler.* Consider getting a cooler at home or asking if your workplace will provide one.

Jesus is the living water we need for our soul and spirit, and fresh, clean drinking water is what we need for our physical bodies. Stay hydrated spiritually and physically for good overall health.

––––––––––

Love Yourself Today: Taking care of yourself is a way of loving yourself. Do what you can to feel as good as you can.

Like the New You

Therefore if any person is [ingrafted] in Christ (the Messiah) he is a new creation (a new creature altogether); the old [previous moral and spiritual condition] has passed away. Behold, the fresh and new has come!   2 CORINTHIANS 5:17

You can be a blessing everywhere you go because Jesus lives in you and His life overflows from within you. Not only that, you can like yourself because of what Jesus has done in your life. According to today's Scripture He has completely recreated you. There's a new you!

The old you died with Christ. Now spiritually you're alive in Christ, a new creature, filled with possibilities. As you learn God's Word, He will use it to change you into His image. The new you that is inside will make its way to the outside where other people can see it.

God says that you are valuable, so don't determine your worth and value by the way other people have treated you and what they have said about you. God says you're accepted in Christ, and what He says is more important than what anyone else says (see Eph. 1:6 NKJV).

Why don't you decide right now to like yourself? Plunge into the ocean of God's love and say, "If You love me, God, I can love myself."

Stop letting people run your life, and be led by the Holy Spirit. Stop trying to please people all the time and be a God-pleaser instead. Enjoy the new you and maintain peace with yourself by refusing to live in guilt and condemnation, recognizing that God is greater than all your sins. Let go of your past mistakes and embrace all the new things God has for you.

Love Yourself Today: You are a new creation in Christ. I hope you like what He has made!

Christ's Credentials

*You yourselves are our letter of recommendation (our credentials),
written in your hearts, to be known (perceived, recognized) and read
by everybody.*   2 CORINTHIANS 3:2

Everybody wants to be loved, and God makes Himself known through
His love. For this reason I believe it is important to God's heart for us to
focus on expressing His love in order to draw people to Jesus.

People are hungry and they are looking for something real. When
people see the fruit of the Holy Spirit in us and see that it is good, they
will want to find the source of this fruit—this tree of life. They will
be ready to accept Jesus as the Way to form a personal, eternal relationship with God and to experience the abundant, exceptional life on
earth that He came to provide.

It is an amazing thought to me that we are personal representatives
of Jesus Christ and that He is making His appeal to people through us
(2 Cor. 5:20). Everyone in the world is looking for genuine love, and
when we let the love of God flow through us to them, we are representing Christ in the best possible way.

We are to go out into the world and let the Holy Spirit flow through
us to show people God's love—His patience, kindness, goodness, and
the other fruit. Let the way you live your everyday life be a tool that
God can use to draw other people to Him.

Follow the more excellent way of love. Receive God's love and let it
flow in its many forms and power to others.

———————————

Love Others Today: Everywhere you go, remember that you
represent Jesus to the people around you. Represent Him with
love.

What Do You Want People to Say About You?

A good name is rather to be chosen than great riches, and loving favor rather than silver and gold.   PROVERBS 22:1

I want to ask you an important question today: Once your life on earth is complete, how do you want people to remember you? What do you want them to say about you? Do you want them to say, "That person worked seventy hours per week and made millions of dollars that he spent on his own pleasure. I wonder what will happen to his fortune now that he is gone"? Or, do you want them to say, "That person was kind and helped bring the best out of me. She gave me a chance. She *really* loved me"?

Most of the things to which we devote our time and energy are currently passing away. They will not last; they are not eternal.

We strive to make more money, build businesses, be popular or own buildings, cars, clothes, and jewelry. Yet all of these things are temporal. In time, they will all fade away. Only love never comes to an end. An act of love goes on and endures forever.

I want to leave something as a result of my journey through life. I want to bless people in every way I possibly can. I want to be the type of person others can come to and have blessings dispensed into their lives. I want to make others happy, and I have discovered that as I do, I reap happiness in my own life. I want to put my time and energy into something lasting, don't you? Let's love.

Love Others Today: How you treat people today is the way they will remember you tomorrow.

God Gives Good Gifts

Having gifts (faculties, talents, qualities) that differ according to the grace given us, let us use them.   ROMANS 12:6

John the Baptist came to tell people to prepare the way of the Lord (John 1:23). That was his purpose on earth, and he knew it. But John's disciples were trying to incite him to jealousy over Jesus' ministry! They said, basically, "Here he is baptizing, too, and everybody is flocking to him!"

John responded to them by saying, "He must increase, but I must decrease. He must grow more prominent and I must grow less so" (John 3:30). (John did not have a jealousy problem!)

Heaven is the only source of gifts, and we need to be content with the gifts God has seen fit to give us (see John 3:27). So if your gift is teaching, then teach; if it is giving, then give, and do it with zeal. You might as well be content and enjoy the gift you have. After you decide to be content and give yourself over to your gift completely, you'll find that you enjoy using it. That enjoyment will grow as you continue to fulfill your purpose. It is very important to find out what your gift is and use it (see Rom. 12:6–8).

People who are spiritually mature know their gifts and abilities are needed to complete what God wants to do in a certain situation, but they also know their gifts aren't the only gifts. They can enjoy their gifts without being insecure or jealous of others, knowing that God has everyone on a journey toward fulfilling His purpose for their lives.

———————————

Love Yourself Today: "Lord, thank You for giving me the gifts I need to fulfill Your purpose for my life."

Love Jesus First

Teacher, [You are essentially and perfectly morally] good, what must I do to inherit eternal life [that is, to partake of eternal salvation]?

MARK 10:17

In today's Scripture a young man asked Jesus the question above and Jesus responded: "You know the commandments: Do not kill, do not commit adultery, do not steal, do not bear false witness, do not defraud, honor your father and mother" (Mark 10:19).

The man replied to Jesus that he had obeyed all the commandments for as long as he could remember. What happened next is extremely important: "And Jesus, looking upon him, *loved him*..." (Mark 10:21, emphasis mine). Jesus is about to give this man an instruction *because He loved him:* "You lack one thing; go and sell all you have and give [the money] to the poor, and you will have treasure in heaven; and come [and] accompany Me."

Many people do not like this verse because they do not understand the heart of love behind it. Does God want to make us sell everything we have and give the proceeds to the poor in order to serve Him? He would only ask us to do that if what we had was standing in the way of our being obedient to God. The point of this parable is that we should love Jesus first. We must love Him more than we love our "stuff," which was not the case with the man in the story.

If you have a job that keeps you from serving God, find another job. If you have a boyfriend or a girlfriend who doesn't want you to love God first, find someone else. If you really want a deeper walk with God, you may have to sacrifice some things that are keeping you from it.

———————————

Love God Today: Is anything standing between you and God? Make the situation right today.

Keep the Peace

Then He arose and rebuked the wind, and said to the sea, "Peace, be still!" And the wind ceased and there was a great calm.

MARK 4:39 NKJV

You cannot rebuke the storms in your life if there's a storm on the inside of you. The disciples could not rebuke the storm, because they lost their peace and were as "stormy" as the weather. But when Jesus spoke, "Peace, be still" out of the well of peace within Him, the wind and the waves immediately became calm.

We *must* have peace in our lives. To do that, we must learn to maintain peace in our relationships with God, with ourselves, and with others. Peace is a fruit of the Spirit, which is love. So when we stay at peace, we are also walking in love.

We maintain peace with God by believing and trusting Him. Don't be angry with God because you prayed and what you asked for didn't happen. Trusting God in every situation is the only way to stay at peace.

We also need to maintain peace within ourselves. We do that by refusing to live in guilt and condemnation, recognizing that God is greater than all our sins. We don't second-guess ourselves or worry about what we did or didn't do. We don't get anxious over what might happen. We keep our minds at rest.

We also maintain peace by keeping peace with our fellow man, by not allowing strife in our relationships with other people. Learn to recognize what strife is and eliminate it. Stop letting your emotions rule you. Learn to keep quiet when God says to keep quiet. Don't try to control other people; that will only steal your peace.

Love God Today: Stay at peace with God, yourself, and others.

God Is Pleased with Your "Who"

Before I formed you in the womb I knew [and] approved of you [as my chosen instrument], and before you were born I separated and set you apart, consecrating you; [and] I appointed you as a prophet to the nations.　　　　　　　　　　　　　　　JEREMIAH 1:5

God knows everything about us. He knows every mistake we will ever make, and He still loves and chooses us. I believe that we must live with a real sense of God's approval before we can enjoy life and bear fruit that will glorify God. Don't be afraid that God is angry with you; start believing that He approves of you. Do it in faith!

God does not approve of all of our behaviors and choices, but He does approve of us as His children. Our heavenly Father has a good plan for each of our lives before we ever show up on planet earth. Why then, do so many people live miserable, wasted lives? It is because they don't believe God's Word. They reject the truth and believe the lies of Satan, or they believe their own thoughts, opinions, and feelings more strongly than they believe what God says.

If God says He approves of us, then all we need to do is believe this truth. You might say, "Well, in today's Scripture God was talking to Jeremiah, not to me." No, He was talking to all who would believe. Every example in the Bible is given to teach us how to live. Jeremiah had faults; he was afraid of what people would think of him. God did not reject him, though; He helped him work through his fears and enabled him to be mightily used to help other people. Jeremiah's fear did not please God, but *he* did please God. There is a difference in a person's "who" and their "do." God may not always be happy with what you do, but He is always pleased with who you are.

Love Yourself Today: Remember, God always loves your "who," even when your "do" could use some improvement!

You Have to Have It to Give It

Freely you have received, freely give.   MATTHEW 10:8 NKJV

I have not always loved myself, but with God's help over the years, I did learn to receive His love, which helped me love myself in a balanced way, share His love with others, and love Him in return. This process didn't happen overnight and it wasn't easy, but it did happen for me and it can happen for you, too.

For a long, long time, I seemed to always have difficulties in relationships, and I really did not know why. I couldn't find people I liked and enjoyed, who felt the same about me. Through God's help, I finally realized what the problem was: I was trying to give away something I did not have.

I was desperately attempting to display loving behavior but had failed to receive God's love for myself. Therefore, I could not give love away to others. I didn't have any love to give. I had not received proper love during my life, so I didn't have the ability to love myself in the right way.

Maybe you can relate to my story; maybe you struggle in relationships because you have never been loved properly. This can begin to change only as you begin to believe His Word, which says over and over again that God loves you. Develop the mind-set that says, "I can love myself because God loves me. I can love what God can love. I don't love everything I do, but I love and accept myself because God loves and accepts me." As these thoughts take root in your mind, you'll find that you love yourself more and more—and then you'll have love to give away to others.

Love Yourself Today: "Lord, I declare that I love myself because You love me. The more I love myself, the more I can love others."

God's Construction Crew

We know that we have passed over out of death into Life by the fact that we love the brethren (our fellow Christians). He who does not love abides (remains, is held and kept continually) in Spiritual death...　　　　　　　　　　　　　　　1 JOHN 3:14

Life in this verse is the life of God, or "life as God has it." I don't want to be one of what I call "the walking dead"—someone who lives and breathes, but never truly lives as God desires. Loving others is the only way to keep the God kind of life flowing through you. It has been given to us as a gift; it's in us, but we need to release it to others through words and actions. Left dormant, it will stagnate like a pool of water with no outlet.

Are you a part of God's construction crew, or part of Satan's destruction crew? Do you build people up with your words and action, or tear them down? Do you strengthen or weaken them? If you ask these questions and get the wrong answers, it is easy to fix. Just simply begin today by making a plan to be a blessing to others. Use your words, facial expressions, and voice tones to lift up others. Smile at people; it will be a sign of approval to them. Live to put smiles on others' faces, and you will always have a smile on yours.

Love Others Today: Look for the needs around you and let God use you to meet those needs. Make sure you're part of God's construction crew!

Who's Number One?

*Give away your life; you'll find life given back, but not merely given
back—given back with bonus and blessing. Giving, not getting, is
the way. Generosity begets generosity.*   LUKE 6:38 THE MESSAGE

Sometimes we tend to live "backwards"—exactly opposite of the way
we should live. We live for ourselves and yet we never seem satisfied. We
should live for others—give away our lives—and learn the wonderful secret
that what we give away comes back to us multiplied many times over.

When somebody wants to be "number one," it automatically means
a lot of people will be disappointed. Only one person can be the number one runner in the world; only one can be the president of the company or the best-known actor or actress. Only one can be the top author
or the best painter in the world. While I believe we should all be goal
oriented and do our best, I don't believe we should want everything for
ourselves and care nothing about other people.

I have lived long enough to try a variety of ways to be happy and
have discovered by process of elimination what is effective and what is
not. Self-focus and striving to be number one at others' expense does
not make life work the way it was intended to work and is definitely not
God's will for our lives. Instead, He wants us to be aggressive about
loving others and helping them get ahead.

Love must be more than a theory or a word; it has to be action. It
must be seen and felt. Love is and has always been His idea. He came
to love us and to teach us how to love. When we do this, life is exciting,
beautiful, and rewarding.

Love Someone Today: "Lord, help me not to disregard or
compete with others in an effort to be number one. I pray for
opportunities to show love to others by helping others get
ahead and reach their goals in life."

Stick to Your Standards

*We have wronged no one, we have betrayed no one, we have cheated
or taken advantage of no one.*   2 CORINTHIANS 7:2

In 1893, a Missouri minister's son named James Cash Penney graduated from high school hoping to be able to further his education and
become a lawyer. Instead, he went to work as a salesman at a dry goods
store. Penney believed in honesty, integrity, respect, and hard work in
every area of his life, including his work.

The hardworking, ambitious young man soon had enough money
saved to start his own business, and he chose to open a butcher shop.
The business failed not because Penney wasn't a good businessman,
but because of his integrity. Penney believed in treating every customer
with kindness, fairness, and respect. When he refused to grant special treatment to a certain influential customer, that customer used his
influence to force Penney out of business.

Penney bounced back, though, and returned to the dry goods business, working for a chain of stores called Golden Rule. He eventually
became a partner in the company and soon opened his own Golden
Rule store. Penney earned a reputation for fair pricing and excellent
customer service.

Several years later, the owners of Golden Rule sold the company
to Penney, who renamed it JCPenney. He continued to operate with
integrity and kindness and built his company into a thriving business.

Love Others Today: Treating other people well and refusing
to compromise your standards of kindness and integrity has
its own rewards.

Keep Asking, Keep Seeking, Keep Knocking

For everyone who asks and keeps on asking receives; and he who seeks and keeps on seeking finds; and to him who knocks and keeps on knocking, the door shall be opened.   LUKE 11:10

Jesus encourages us to keep on asking, keep on seeking, and keep on knocking. We need to do these things, day in and day out, 365 days a year, so we can keep receiving what we need from God.

How many times do we stay awake all night wrestling with our problems and losing sleep over them instead of simply casting our cares upon the Lord and asking Him to meet our needs—then trusting Him to do so? How many hours and days have we wasted trying to reason or decide what is best in certain situations instead of simply asking God for wisdom?

Our mistake is failing to ask and seek and knock, failing to trust God, our living heavenly Father to give us the good things that we ask of Him. We should humble ourselves under God's mighty hand knowing that in due time He will bring to pass what is right for us (see 1 Pet. 5:5, 6). One sincere prayer will produce more good fruit than years of our trying to solve our own problems.

In Matthew 7:11, Jesus says, "If you then, evil as you are, know how to give good and advantageous gifts to your children, how much more will your Father Who is in heaven [perfect as He is] give good and advantageous things to those who keep on asking Him." I promise you, God has good and advantageous things for you. Just keep asking, keep seeking, and keep knocking.

Love God Today: "Lord, I commit to continually asking, seeking, and knocking."

Are You Set Up to Be Upset?

Rejoice in the Lord, O you [uncompromisingly] righteous [you upright in right standing with God]; for praise is becoming and appropriate for those who are upright [in heart].   PSALM 33:1

Do you ever wish your life would just *change*? Sometimes our lives do change quickly, but sometimes they don't, and we have to stay faithful, thankful, and positive in the midst of things we wish were different.

How do you approach every day and every situation? Do you decide ahead of time that you won't be happy or peaceful if you don't get what you want? People think in these ways quite often. I have heard people say things like, "If it rains tomorrow I am not going to be happy." When we think thoughts such as this, we are preparing ourselves to be unhappy and to lose our peace and joy before we even have a problem.

Instead of setting ourselves up to be upset, we need to think and speak things like, "I really hope the weather is nice tomorrow, but my joy is on the inside of me so I can be happy and have rest in my soul no matter what kind of weather we have."

The way we approach our lives makes all the difference in the quality of life we can have. When we can't fix life, let's remember that we can fix our approach toward it.

Make up your mind that you will be happy if you get your way today—and if you don't.

Love God Today: "Lord, today I will use my thoughts and words to set myself up for peace and joy."

Loved into Wholeness

The Lord appeared from of old to me (Israel) saying, Yes, I have loved you with an everlasting love; therefore with loving-kindness have I drawn you and continued My faithfulness to you.

JEREMIAH 31:3

Personal wholeness begins with receiving God's love. It is easy to believe and say, "God loves everyone," but each of us, as an individual, needs to know beyond any shadow of doubt and be able to say with all faith, "God loves *me*." It is impossible to love ourselves unless we receive God's love for us. Knowing He loves us individually is the one sure way we can finally accept and love ourselves properly.

How do we reach the point of being convinced of God's love for us? His Word is full of scriptures that speak of the ways He loves us. Confessing His Word aloud is extremely effective in renewing our minds and becoming established in truth in this area. Our minds, our emotions, the enemy, and even people around us may tell us we aren't lovable or that God doesn't really care about us, but we must learn to think the way God thinks and say what He says.

God has a great deal to say about you in His Word, including the fact He loves you with an everlasting, unconditional, perfect love. Don't wait until you feel loved or lovable to believe it. None of us deserves God's love; we can never be "good enough" to earn it. But God doesn't love us because we are good; He loves us because *He* is good! He is full of grace and mercy, and His love is everlasting and unconditional. Choose to believe what God says about you !

————————————

Love Yourself Today: I choose today to believe what God's Word says about me and to embrace the truth that He loves me and chose me to be His very own.

Dare to Be Different

*The sun is glorious in one way, the moon is glorious in another way,
and the stars are glorious in their own [distinctive] way; for one star
differs from and surpasses another in its beauty and brilliance.*

1 CORINTHIANS 15:41

I'm sure you've noticed how different human beings are! We're all
unique. Like the sun, the moon, and the stars mentioned in today's
Scripture, God created each of us to be different from one another, and
He did this on purpose. Each of us meets a need, and we are all part of
God's overall plan.

We're all born with different temperaments, different physical
features, different emotional makeups, different gifts and abilities—
different everything. Our goal should be to find out what makes us special and unique and to succeed at being the best individuals we can be.

When we struggle to be like others, we lose our distinctiveness and
even lose ourselves in the process. We also grieve God's Holy Spirit.
God wants us to fit into His plan, not to devise our own plans or try to
fit into someone else's design.

We need to find out what God wants us to have, who He wants us
to be, and what He wants us to do. That's where we'll discover our gifts
and find both success and enjoyment.

You are an individual, created on purpose for a unique role in God's
plan. I encourage you to recognize and celebrate the things that distin-
guish you from everyone else and enjoy the freedom that comes from
being exactly who God made you to be!

Love Yourself Today: "Thank You, Lord, for creating me to
be different from everyone else and for making me special on
purpose!"

Follow the Greatest Example

Then He poured water into the washbasin and began to wash the disciples' feet and to wipe them with the [servant's] towel with which He was girded.   JOHN 13:5

In John 13 we see the premier example of servanthood as Jesus washed the disciples' feet. In those days men wore sandals, and the roads were not paved; they were plain old dirt. By the time a day ended, the disciples' feet were really dirty, and Jesus offered to wash them. He chose this lowly task to teach His disciples a great lesson, saying, "Unless I wash you, you have no part with (in) Me [you have no share in companionship with Me]" (v. 8).

In verses 13–17, He explained clearly the meaning of His actions. I have learned from this passage that we must do things for each other; otherwise, we are really not part of one another. The things we do to serve one another are the things that bind us together.

Jesus was able to wash His disciples' feet because He was free. Only a person who is truly free, one who is not insecure, can do menial tasks and not feel insignificant as a result. Serving others is not typically viewed as a high position, and yet Jesus said it is the highest of all.

If someone knows full well he has done us wrong, and we return his evil with good, it begins to tear down the walls he has built around himself. Sooner or later he will begin to trust us and start learning from us what real love is.

That is the whole purpose behind being a servant, to show others the love of God that He has shown us so that they, too, can share in it—and then pass it on.

———————————

Love Others Today: What will you do to love people by serving them today?

Don't Get Cold!

*And the love of the great body of people will grow cold because of the
multiplied lawlessness and iniquity.*   MATTHEW 24:12, 13

We are familiar with most of the signs of the end times in Matthew
24:4–11—wars and rumors of wars, earthquakes, famines, and wide-
spread deception. But another sign of the end times is that love will
grow cold.

When I first read and pondered today's Scripture I realized that "the
great body" is the church, not the world. I saw that all the pressure of
rampant evil and the stress of our modern lifestyles was indeed producing an atmosphere so supercharged with problems that most people were totally ignoring their love walk and concentrating on looking
out for themselves.

This is something God never told us to do. Instead, we are to concentrate on representing Him properly, which is impossible unless we
are walking in love. As we do that, He will give us wisdom to deal with
our stresses and deliverance from our foes.

In my own life, I realized I was trying to solve all my problems,
thinking when my life got straightened out, then I could go forward in
ministry to others. The fact is, I had it backward. I needed to cast my
care on the Lord first. I needed to sow seeds in others' lives by helping
them, and then God would bring a harvest in my own life.

Refuse to let your love grow cold. Stir up the love in your marriage,
toward your family and friends. Grow to the point that early in the
morning your heart is filled with thoughts of how you can bless someone that day.

Love Others Today: Make a determined decision to refuse to
let your love grow cold.

Your Breakthrough Is on Its Way

*A man's mind plans his way, but the Lord directs his steps and
makes them sure.*   PROVERBS 16:9

Our mind plans based on what we know or think, but God often leads
us in an entirely different direction. We only know a little and we base
our plans on what we know, but God knows everything. He knows the
end from the beginning and will always direct our steps in what will
ultimately work out for our best, if we will cooperate with Him.

Proverbs 16:25 says, "There is a way that seems right to a man and
appears straight before him, but at the end of it is the way of death.
God's ways may not always be quick, or according to our desires, but
He does have an appointed time, and it will be the right time. In other
words, God has an appointment with your circumstance, with your
breakthrough, with your answered prayer.

In Acts 1:6, 7, some of the disciples said to Jesus, "Lord, is this the
time when You will reestablish the kingdom and restore it to Israel?"
In other words, they were saying, "Jesus, tell us when You're going to
come back. We want to know when these things are going to happen."

Jesus said to them, "It is not for you to know the appointed time.
Only God knows the appointed time."

So if only God knows the appointed time and if we believe He loves
us, then why can't we believe that at the appointed time we're going to
get our breakthrough? We can prove that we trust God by enjoying our
lives and being peaceful while we wait.

———————————

Love God Today: God has an appointment with your
breakthrough—so be patient while you wait.

Amazing Grace

I do not set aside the grace of God; for if righteousness comes through the law, then Christ died in vain.

GALATIANS 2:21 NKJV

In today's Scripture, the apostle Paul said that if he did not receive the grace of God, he would be treating His gift as insignificant. In the Amplified Bible, the first part of this verse says, "I do not treat God's gracious gift as something of minor importance and defeat its very purpose. I do not set aside and invalidate and frustrate the grace (unmerited favor) of God." In other words, the grace of God is so awesome and so wonderful that we need to highly esteem it, deeply appreciate it, and allow it to work in our lives.

I discovered years ago that every time I became frustrated, the reason was that I was trying to do something in my own strength instead of putting my faith in God and receiving His grace (help). I was frustrated and struggling with something most of the time in the early years of my walk with the Lord. Receiving a revelation of God's grace was a major breakthrough for me.

Maybe now is a time when you need to embrace God's grace in your life. He wants you to stop trying to do things in your own strength and simply rest in Him, trusting that He will handle everything in the best possible way.

God will not permit us to succeed in life without His help. If He did, we would take the credit that is due Him. Because He loves us, He wants to pour out His grace in our lives. When we receive it, we will be thankful, joyful, and amazed by what He accomplishes on our behalf.

———————

Love God Today: Have you been frustrating the grace of God that is available to you? Relax, receive it, and let God's grace do for you what you cannot do for yourself.

Love Money? Don't!

But Gehazi, the servant of Elisha the man of God, said, Behold, my
master spared this Naaman the Syrian, in not receiving from his
hands what he brought. But as the Lord lives, I will run after him
and get something from him.   2 KINGS 5:20

One day a military official named Naaman, who had leprosy, went to
the prophet Elisha for healing. After he was healed, he tried and tried
to give Elisha a gift, but Elisha refused to receive anything from him.

Gehazi was Elisha's servant, and he ran after Naaman, stopped him
on his journey home, and lied to him when he said Elisha wanted two
silver pieces and two changes of clothes. When Elisha asked him where
he'd been, Gehazi lied again, saying, "Nowhere."

But Elisha knew better and said as a result of Gehazi's behavior
that just like Naaman, leprosy would "cleave to you and to your off-
spring forever" (2 Kings 5:27). Gehazi's choice not only affected him, it
affected the generations who came after him. I wonder how many times
in his life Gehazi sat around with leprosy and thought about the man
he could have been.

Gehazi allowed the love of money to keep him from reaching his
destiny. How many people today lose their families because of the love
of money? This happens more than we like to admit. It's all because of
the love of money and things, and it leads to all kinds of trouble.

Working hard for a period of time is admirable. But working franti-
cally for the lust of more and more things is evil and always causes
trouble in the end.

Love God Today: Love God more than you love things, and
He will always give you what is best for you and will help you
fulfill your destiny.

Wisdom Is Calling

Wisdom cries aloud in the street, she raises her voice in the markets.
                                                        PROVERBS 1:20

God wants us to use wisdom, and according to today's Scripture, wisdom is not difficult to obtain; the Holy Spirit wants to reveal it to us; we simply need to pay attention.

For example, have you ever needed to make a decision and had your "head" (your intellectual abilities) try to lead you one way while your heart is leading you another? Have you ever had a situation in which your natural thoughts and feelings seemed to be guiding you in one direction, but something inside of you kept nagging you to go another direction?

Chances are, wisdom is crying out to you. One way to love yourself is to listen to it and obey. Many times, it cries out in your heart that you should or should not do a certain thing—you *should* eat healthily, you *should* be kind to other people, you *should* not spend money you do not have. These are all practical examples of using wisdom in everyday life. When you sense such leadings, the Holy Spirit, who speaks to your heart, is trying to help you make a wise decision, even though it may not be the choice you want to make or it may not seem to make sense in your present circumstances.

The Spirit wars against our flesh, and vice versa (see Gal. 5:17). When we know the wise choice and don't make it, the reason is often that we are allowing our flesh to lead us and to see if we can get away with unwise decisions—which are also known as "foolishness." The flesh leads us to foolishness, but God wants us to walk in wisdom and make choices now that we will be happy with later.

Love Yourself Today: What is wisdom saying to you today? Are you willing to follow it?

Just Do It!

Because of laziness the building decays, and through idleness of hands the house leaks.   ECCLESIASTES 10:18 NKJV

Do you truly believe that love can change the world? I do. But I also know the events and accomplishments that have brought lasting change to the world have not been accidental; they have been things people thought through and acted on deliberately. The Bible is filled with instructions for us to be active.

Wishing for something does not produce the results we desire, but we must aggressively do what needs to be done to achieve them. We will never find a successful man who spent his life wishing for success and attained it. The same principle applies to loving God, loving ourselves, and loving others. If we want to love people as Jesus instructed, we will have to do so on purpose. It will not happen by accident.

If we seek opportunities to love people we are sure to find them, and that will protect us from being idle and passive. We must ask ourselves if we are alert and active or passive and inactive? God is alert and active! I am glad He is; otherwise, things in our lives would deteriorate rapidly.

So much good can happen in your life and in the lives of those around you if you'll simply decide not to be passive, but to follow the Holy Spirit as He leads you. God-inspired, balanced activity will keep you from being idle and bless many people in the process.

Love Yourself Today: "Lord, I commit to being active and intentional, not passive or idle."

Entertaining Angels?

Do not forget or neglect or refuse to extend hospitality to strangers...
for through it some have entertained angels without knowing it.

HEBREWS 13:2

Today's Scripture teaches us to be careful how we treat strangers because we might be entertaining angels without knowing it. We should be kind, cordial, and gracious to them.

One time I was having coffee with several people, including a pastor from Birmingham, England. I remember looking at the hairstyle of the girl who was waiting on us. Her head was shaved except for what is called a Mohawk going down the middle, and it was black, blue, red, and white. She also had her nose, tongue, and her lip pierced. I remember feeling a bit uncomfortable because she was not anything like I am. I just wanted to order my coffee and try not to stare.

The pastor, on the other hand, started a conversation with her, and the first thing he said was, "I like your hair. How do you get it to stand up like that?" He continued the discussion with her, and the atmosphere that had felt tense suddenly relaxed. Soon we were all at ease. I learned a huge lesson that day—that I am not as "modern" as I might like to think I am. I still have some thinking that needs to be dealt with, and I need to do better making all people, including those who are a bit different from me, feel comfortable and included.

I believe God delights in variety. That's why He made so many people and made us all so different. Let's accept everyone and appreciate the uniqueness each person has to offer.

Love Others Today: "Lord, help me be especially kind and gracious to those who are different than I am."

Give It Away

Therefore I urge you, brothers, in view of God's mercy, to offer your
bodies as living sacrifices, holy and pleasing to God—this is
your spiritual act of worship.   ROMANS 12:1 NIV

For most of my life, I woke up every day and lay in bed making plans for myself. I thought of what I wanted and what would be best for me and how I could convince others to cooperate with my plans. When things did not go my way I became upset, frustrated, and even angry. I thought I was unhappy because I wasn't getting what I wanted, but I was *actually* unhappy because all I did was try to get what I wanted without any real concern for others.

Once I discovered that the secret of joy is in giving my life away rather than trying to keep it, my mornings became quite different. Now, in the mornings I pray and then take some time to think of all the people I know that I will come into contact with today, and ask the Lord to show me what I can do for them. I encourage you to pray through our Scripture for today. Set your mind to encourage and be a blessing to everyone that you come in contact with.

If you want to dedicate yourself to God so He can use you to love and help others, I suggest you pray like this: "Lord, I offer You my eyes, ears, mouth, hands, feet, heart, finances, gifts, talents, abilities, time, and energy. Use me to be a blessing everywhere I go today."

You will never know the joy of living like this unless you actually try it. I call it a "holy habit," and like all habits, it must be practiced to become one.

———————————

Loving Others Today: "Lord, flow through me and help me be aware of the needs around me that I can meet."

Learn to Receive

Now thanks be to God for His Gift, [precious] beyond telling [His indescribable, inexpressible, free Gift]!   2 CORINTHIANS 9:15

Have you ever tried to give a gift to someone who refuses to take it? That's frustrating and disappointing! I enjoy surprising people by giving them something they want or need. I've experienced planning a surprise, going shopping, spending money, and getting a gift ready, only to give it and have the recipient struggle to receive it graciously.

Most of the time, when people have trouble receiving from others, the cause is insecurity or feelings of unworthiness. They may even become suspicious, wondering what the giver wants from them or what the giver's motive is. I've even had the experience of trying to give something to someone and have to work so hard convincing them to take it that the whole situation becomes embarrassing!

If we as human beings feel this way, how much more do you think God feels the same when He tries to give us His love, mercy, favor, or grace and we refuse it because of a false sense of humility or a feeling of unworthiness? One way we show our love for God is to graciously receive His love and every good gift He brings into our lives.

You see, God has a plan: He wants us to receive His love; love ourselves in a balanced, godly way; generously love Him in return; and love everyone who comes into our lives. Learning to receive graciously helps us give graciously. When God reaches out to love us, He is attempting to start a cycle that will not only bless us, but others as well.

––––––––––––––––––

Love God Today: "Lord, please help me receive graciously all that You desire to give me."

No More Same Old Same Old

Do not [earnestly] remember the former things; neither consider the things of old. Behold, I am doing a new thing!

ISAIAH 43:18, 19

In today's Scripture, God says He is doing a new thing. As you move into the future He has for you, you will encounter all kinds of new opportunities, and challenges. The days ahead will be full of new experiences, things you have never done before. You may not know how to do them, but you will learn. Everything you are doing today was new to you at one time—and look, now you can do it.

Continuing to face new challenges and develop new abilities is extremely important to your growth and maturity. As you walk with God into your future, you will hear Him say, "You have not done this before, but don't be afraid. I'm taking you to a place you have never been before. I'm going to ask you to do something you don't know how to do!" God has already been where He is leading you, and He has prepared the way. Step out in faith and you will experience the faithfulness of God.

We think and say, "It's time for a change! I need something new," and then we hesitate to embrace that new thing when it comes. If you are ready for something new and fresh, don't be afraid to embrace it when it comes.

Don't stay trapped in the past. Let go of what lies behind and press into the great future God has planned for you. I can promise you: God is with you. He will lead you. He will strengthen you. He will help you.

Love God Today: With God's help, I will embrace every new thing He brings into my life.

God Has a Wonderful Plan for You!

Sanctify yourselves [that is, separate yourself for a special holy purpose], for tomorrow the Lord will do wonders among you.

JOSHUA 3:5

I believe God wants to do something special in your life and that just as He planned the Israelites to enter into the Promised Land, He has planned a good promise for you.

You do not have to be perfect, strive, beg, or bargain with God to do something good in your life. He is waiting on you to trust and believe Him to do what He has promised.

I am living proof of the goodness and mercy of God. Naturally speaking, there is no way for a person with my background to be where I am today. But with God, an abused little girl who became an angry housewife can be changed to the point that she can preach God's Word all over the world. I don't believe I could ever fully explain all the steps I had to go through, all the lies of the enemy I had to overcome, all the fears and insecurities I had to deal with to be transformed into the woman I am right now, but I can truly say that each step of faith I took released more of God's good plan for me.

God is excited about your future, and I hope you are also. Don't let the discouragement of the past steal the amazing future that is yours.

I believe you are called for a holy purpose—a purpose that has been in God's heart since long before you were born. I believe your future is bright with God's promise, and that His presence will be with you every day. I believe God will do wonders in your life, just as today's Scripture promises, as you continue to follow Him.

Love God Today: Agree with God and say ten times every day, "Something good is going to happen to me today."

Love Yourself, Laugh at Yourself

You grow up the day you have the first real laugh at yourself.
ETHEL BARRYMORE

Many of us take our personal faults and mistakes too seriously. We spend too much time opposing ourselves, being our own worst enemies. We often judge ourselves more strictly than we judge others and we focus on our faults far too intensely. We should always be serious about our sin and want to improve. But many of the little, everyday things we treat as monumental are really not so terribly important. So give yourself a break!

God knew every flaw and weakness you would have and every mistake you would make when He called you into relationship with Himself. Nothing about you surprises Him.

God knows—and has always known—everything about you. He knows what you will think, do, and say every day for the rest of your life on earth. He also knows how He will help you, teach you, correct you, encourage you, and give you grace for all your faults and failures. He is always for you, never against you, no matter what you do. This truth should set you free to lighten up, enjoy being who God made you to be, and have a laugh at your own self.

You are who you are. You do what you do, and it's not always perfect. In fact, sometimes you really mess up! That's part of being human. But if you also love God, have a heart to change, and ask Him to help you, then you can relax. God is working on you, changing you every day, helping you grow. God is not mad at you! Enjoy Him, and enjoy yourself even though you are not perfected yet.

Love Yourself Today: Don't be so serious all the time. As often as possible, have a good laugh!

It's Okay to Walk with a Limp

And as he passed Penuel [Peniel], the sun rose upon him and he was
limping because of his thigh.   GENESIS 32:31

Jacob was a man with many weaknesses, yet he pressed on with God and was determined to receive God's blessing. God likes that kind of determination. He actually told Jacob in Genesis 32:28 that he (Jacob) had contended with God and man, and that God would be glorified in him. God can always be glorified through people who will not allow their personal weaknesses to stop Him from flowing through them.

In order for God to flow through us, we must first come face-to-face with the fact that we have weaknesses—and then we must determine not to let them bother us. Our imperfections will not stop God from working through us unless we let them. We need to accept ourselves completely—weaknesses and all—because God does.

I am going to ask you to do something very important. Right now, stop and wrap your arms around yourself. Give yourself a great big hug and say aloud: "I accept myself. I love myself. I know I have weaknesses and imperfections, but I will not let them stop me, and I will not allow them to stop God from working through me." Try doing that several times each day, and you will soon develop a new attitude toward yourself, a new outlook on life, and a greater level of confidence in God.

God will bless all of us even though we limp (are not perfect in all of our behavior). Remember, God looks at our hearts. If we have faith in Him and hearts that long to obey Him and bring Him glory, then He will work wonders through us in spite of our weaknesses.

Love Yourself Today: Don't let your weaknesses stop you. Be determined to let God work through you in spite of them.

Fight for Others

But let justice run down like waters and righteousness like a mighty and ever-flowing stream.   AMOS 5:24

Today I want to share the story of a well-known champion of freedom and justice, an Englishman named William Wilberforce. In 1780, this well-educated son of a wealthy merchant became the youngest Member of Parliament, at age twenty-one.

In 1785, Wilberforce had what many believe was an unmistakable encounter with God. After that, he wanted to do everything he could do to serve God. By 1787, Wilberforce had emerged as Parliament's dominant voice against the slave trade. Very few people supported him because slavery was a powerful part of the British economy in those days. Wilberforce believed this was wrong and endured hardship, controversy, ridicule, and betrayal as he worked passionately to stop human trafficking. He wrote a bill to abolish the slavery and presented it before the British Parliament eighteen times.

In 1807, the slave trade was officially abolished. However, the new law did not liberate people who were already enslaved, so Wilberforce fought to free slaves who were being held at the time. The law passed about a month after his death.

All kinds of injustice run rampant in our world today. Treat people with dignity, stand up for what is right in your life, and help those who cannot stand up for themselves.

———————————

Love Others Today: Be a person whose convictions are based on God's Word, and do what God calls you to do to act on them.

Check Your Motives

The righteousness of the upright...shall deliver them, but the treacherous shall be taken in by their own iniquity and greedy desire.   PROVERBS 11:6

Here's an important question for you: When you do things to bless other people, why do you do it? Do you bless others because you love them, or do you do it to get them to love you?

There was a time in my life when I tried to "buy" protection for myself. I thought if I was extremely nice to people and gave them gifts, I could protect myself from their rejection. It took me a while to learn that my motives were impure and therefore my act of kindness was not acceptable to God.

I was deceived. I really thought I was walking in love until God revealed to me that I was not giving my love freely to others without strings attached. I was giving my love to others in order to get them to love me.

When we give gifts, we should always do so for the joy of giving, not with the ulterior motive of trying to manipulate the recipients in some way so they feel they owe us something.

When our behavior is excessive and out of balance people can sense that something isn't right about our attitude toward them. When you do things to bless others, be sure to do so out of a heart of love, care, or appreciation for them, not out of a personal need for security.

———————————

Love Others Today: Take an honest inventory of your relationships. Are you trying to buy anyone's friendship for your own benefit instead of blessing that person out of sincere love?

God Restores and Leads

He refreshes and restores my life (my self); He leads me in the paths of righteousness [uprightness and right standing with Him—not for my earning it, but] for His name's sake.   PSALM 23:3

The twenty-third Psalm, where today's Scripture is found, is so comforting. He causes us to lie down and rest, and He "refreshes and restores" our lives. The King James Version of this verse says: "He restoreth my soul."

When God restores our souls, He restores our minds, wills, and emotions. With our souls, we process our circumstances; we entertain thoughts; we feel and express our emotions; and we make decisions. What a wonderful promise—that God will restore our souls! The word *restore* means, "to bring back into existence or use" or "to bring back to an original state or condition." *Restore* can also mean, "to make restitution, to cause to return or to refresh." If you have been hurt and your soul has been wounded, you can claim the promise of restoration.

When David says God will restore our souls and our lives, I believe he means that God will return us to the state or condition we were in before we were hurt or erred from following the good plan He predestined for us before we were born and before the enemy attacked us to draw us out of His plan for our lives.

God has a plan for your restoration. If you will allow Him to do so, He will guide you by His Holy Spirit along the unique way that leads to healing and wholeness, and to being able to fulfill the great purposes He has for your life.

Love God Today: "Thank You, Lord, for restoring my soul and my life, and for leading me in the way that is right for me."

The Power of Private Praise

But when you pray, go into your [most] private room, and, closing
the door, pray to your Father, Who is in secret; and your Father,
Who sees in secret, will reward you in the open.

MATTHEW 6:6

I sincerely believe that if you bow down and worship God the way King David did, you will see some marvelous things take place in your life; if there is bondage in your life, I believe that you will experience release.

As Jesus told us, there are some things we are to do in private. There are times when I go into my bedroom, lock the door and praise and worship the Lord, sometimes crying and sometimes laughing all by myself. If anybody saw me, they might think I needed to be locked up! But in private, I can express myself freely to God with no inhibitions.

If you do these things openly, the world will tell you that you're crazy! But you can do them in private, between you and God alone, and you will see good fruit develop in your life. The fruit comes from what God sees, not what people see.

I believe that all of us ought to get in a private place and rejoice before the Lord, bow down before Him, lift up our hands to Him in praise, and, if we need to, even weep in His presence.

―――――――――――

Love God Today: Worship God in private today—with no inhibitions!

Do You Love Him?

"Simon, son of Jonah, do you love Me?" He said to Him, "Yes, Lord;
You know that I love You." He said to Him, "Tend My sheep."

JOHN 21:16 NKJV

In the story that contains today's Scripture, Jesus asked Simon Peter
three times if he loved Him and all three times, when Simon Peter said,
"Yes," Jesus answered with, "Then feed My sheep," "Tend My sheep,"
or "Feed My lambs" (see John 21:15–17). On several occasions He
referred to Himself as a Shepherd and to His people as sheep, so Peter
knew He was telling Him to love and help His people.

I believe Jesus was saying in these verses that if we love Him we
should be helping other people, not simply gathering in buildings on
Sunday morning to follow rules and rituals. If a church is not involved
in reaching the lost and helping oppressed people, then they are not
functioning as God fully intends.

The apostle John said that we know we have passed over out of
death into life by the fact that we love the brethren and He who does
not love is held and kept continually in spiritual death (see 1 John
3:14). If a church is not overflowing with the genuine love of God, how
can it be filled with life?

The early church grew rapidly and had a wonderful reputation
because it was filled with people who genuinely loved one another.
What the world needs is love. It needs God; and God is love. If we
get involved in helping and genuinely loving people, we can shape the
world once again for the glory of God!

Love God Today: Do you love God? Then feed His sheep by
helping others.

Know the Hope of Your Calling

The eyes of your understanding being enlightened; that you may know what is the hope of His calling, what are the riches of the glory of His inheritance in the saints.   EPHESIANS 1:18 NKJV

God wants us to know what His eternal plan and purpose are. As you can see in today's Scripture, He wants us to know the hope of our calling. He has chosen us in Himself to be holy, to live before Him without blemish and in love. This is God's call and it is great indeed.

How can we fulfill such a high calling since we are filled with weakness, inability, and the susceptibility to temptation? It is beautifully simple when we have revelation. We are made holy in Jesus Christ and we can lift our voices and confess, "I am holy in Jesus Christ; I am blameless and perfect in Him." When believers come to the place of knowing by revelation what belongs to us in Christ *right now*, we no longer need to search relentlessly for that "something more," because we know we already have it. It is finished! The work is complete! It belongs to us. God loves you now! He sees you as perfect in Christ now! He is leading and guiding you now!

In order to help others, we must know the hope of our calling and what our inheritance is in Christ. Perhaps the reason we have difficulty accepting that holiness, peace, joy, righteousness, redemption, deliverance, wisdom, victory, and literally hundreds of other blessings that are ours right now is that we don't see ourselves as God sees us. We need to look at ourselves through the eyes of faith as children of God. As we do, we'll realize the hope of our calling.

Love Yourself Today: "Help me, Lord, to realize what I have in You right now."

Truth Precedes Change

And you will know the Truth, and the Truth will set you free.
JOHN 8:32

Is there something you'd like to change about yourself or the way you live? Change begins with truth. It's almost impossible to see the need for change or to know how we should change if we don't face the truth about where we are. In the process of change, admitting the truth about ourselves is often the hardest part. We don't need to feel guilty about the way we are, we just need to ask for God's forgiveness and be excited about change.

Let me share a practical example of how facing truth and changing has worked in my life. If I'm eating too much and don't want to face the truth about that, I will make excuses. "My metabolism must be slowing down." "The dry cleaners shrank my pants." Excuses can be endless! Excuses, though, are actually reasons stuffed with lies.

Once I decide to stop making excuses, I can admit the truth. "I've been eating too much and that's why I've gained weight." When I say that I am taking responsibility for the problem. That's the truth, and it will set me free.

I have had to face many truths in my past and still do. If we want to change, we have to start with the truth. Ask God to reveal truth to you about you! When He does if it begins to hurt just realize that the pain you feel is actually a healing pain that is working toward your freedom and increased peace and joy.

————————————

Love Yourself Today: "Lord, help me to see and admit the truth about every area in my life, and, with your help, make the changes I need to make."

God's Love Will Change You

In this is love: not that we loved God, but that He loved us and sent His son to be propitiation (the atoning sacrifice) for our sins.

I JOHN 4:10

Meditate on God's love for you. That's what is going to change you. If you don't like something about yourself, "knowing that you know" that God loves you is going to change it.

God wants you to spend time with Him in fellowship and worship on a daily basis. That's what will change you. It is the private time you spend with Him, just loving Him and letting Him love you, that is going to cause you to grow up and be strong in your spirit.

The devil will give you one excuse after another for not spending time with God. Get serious with God and cry out to him. The Word of God and fellowship with Him will change you. Paul says in Philippians 4:13, "I can do all things through Christ which strengthens me." In other words, there is nothing in all creation you can't do through the power of Jesus Christ.

Use the problems that come against you as opportunities to grow. Find out what God will do because He loves you! If you will lean on God and let God love you and you love Him, you can forget all the trying to operate in faith and enter into rest.

Love Yourself Today: After all, God loved you first!

Get the Devil Back

If your enemy is hungry, give him bread to eat; and if he is thirsty,
give him water to drink; for in doing so, you will heap coals of
fire upon his head, and the Lord will reward you.

PROVERBS 25:21, 22

One day, I tried to buy a cup of coffee for a woman who was in line behind me in a coffee shop and she flatly refused. Actually, she made such a scene that it embarrassed me, and at first I thought, *Well, I won't do that again.* Dave was with me, and he reminded me that my response was exactly what the devil wanted, so I changed my mind. That was a difficult moment, but it made me sadly aware of how many people don't know how to receive a blessing—probably because it never happens to them.

Each act of kindness is my way of obeying God and overcoming the evil in the world. I don't know what bad things have happened to people, and perhaps my acts of kindness will help heal the wounds in their souls. I also believe kindness toward others is a way for me to get the devil back for the pain he caused in my life. He is evil to the maximum degree; he is the perpetrator of all the evil we experience in the world, so every act of love, goodness, and kindness is like stabbing him in his wicked heart.

If you've been mistreated and wished you could get back at the devil for the pain he has caused you, then be good to as many people as you can. It is God's way, and it will work because love never fails!

Love Others Today: Have you ever been discouraged when trying to do something nice for someone? Keep being nice anyway!

Get Rid of the Failure Syndrome

[God] disarmed the principalities and powers that were ranged against us and made a bold display and public example of them, in triumphing over them in Him and in it [the cross].

COLOSSIANS 2:15

Many people lack confidence. They are often shame-based and guilt-ridden, and they have a very poor self-image. The enemy knows that and begins his assault on personal confidence whenever and wherever he can find an opening. His ultimate goal is total destruction of that person and his or her self-esteem.

The devil knows that someone without confidence will never step out to do anything edifying for the Kingdom of God. He does not want you to fulfill God's plan for your life. He can make you believe that you are incapable, and then you won't even try to accomplish anything worthwhile. Even if you do make an effort, your fear of failure will seal your defeat, which you probably expected from the beginning because of your lack of confidence. This is what is often referred to as the "Failure Syndrome."

God wants you to know that the devil is already a defeated foe. Jesus triumphed over him on the cross and made a public display of his disgrace in the spirit realm. Jesus' victory means that you can get rid of the failure syndrome. His ability to bring His will to pass in your life is determined by your faith in Him and in His word. *That* is reason for confidence!

Love Yourself Today: Remember: the destroyer of your confidence, the enemy, has already been defeated by God.

Absolute Trust

For we have heard of your faith in Christ Jesus [the leaning of
your entire human personality on Him in absolute trust and
confidence in His power, wisdom, and goodness] *and of the love
which you [have and show] for all the saints (God's consecrated ones).*

COLOSSIANS 1:4, (EMPHASIS MINE)

According to today's Scripture, when you and I exercise our faith,
we place our trust and confidence in three specific attributes of God's
character: His power, His wisdom, and His goodness.

When we approach God in faith, we must first realize that He has
the power, the supernatural ability, to meet our needs and solve our
problems. He is able to work any kind of miracle we need. God has the
power to do *anything.*

Faith also involves placing absolute trust and confidence in God's
wisdom. When we do not know what to do or how to do it, God does.
In His power, He can do anything, but in His wisdom, He may choose
not to do everything He is able to do. He always works in our lives with
our best interests in mind. When He answers our prayers in ways we
do not understand, we need to trust His wisdom.

God is a good God, and we need to have faith in His goodness. He
always wants the best for us! He has good plans for our lives and will
always do us good, not evil (see Eph. 2:10 and Jer. 29:11).

When you put your faith in God, you have complete confidence in
the God who has the *power* to accomplish anything on your behalf, the
wisdom to know exactly what you need, and the *goodness* to work in
your life in ways that bring the greatest possible blessing.

Love God Today: "Lord, I place my absolute trust in your
power, your wisdom, and your goodness."

Yes, You Can

Say not, I am only a youth; for you shall go to all to whom I send you, and whatever I command you, that you shall speak. Be not afraid of them [their faces], for I am with you to deliver you, says the Lord.   JEREMIAH 1:7, 8

In the first chapter of Jeremiah, God spoke plainly to the young prophet and gave him a specific call. But Jeremiah did not embrace it with enthusiasm. Instead, he said: "Ah, Lord God! Behold, I cannot speak, for I am only a youth" (Jer. 1:6). God told Jeremiah he was to be a prophet to the nations, and Jeremiah responded, basically, "No, I can't. I'm too young."

God corrected Jeremiah when he resisted the assignment God had for him. Jeremiah's biggest problem when confronted with God's call on his life was that he focused on himself. Everything was about him! "*I* can't, God! *I'm* too young!" When we focus on ourselves, we will never develop confidence to fulfill God's will, but when we focus on His strength, wisdom, and power—then we realize we can do whatever He asks of us.

I wonder how many times God has told somebody what an awesome purpose He has for him or her, and heard in response: "No, God! I can't do that!" In the strictest sense, that answer is true. But when God gives us an assignment, He also plans to give us the grace and strength we will need to accomplish it. He does not expect us to do it alone. So when we respond to Him, we need to say, "Okay, God. This is a big assignment, but you are a big God and I know I can do anything with your help!"

———————————

Love God Today: "Lord, I believe I can do *anything* with your help!"

A Very Valuable Possession

But man is freer than all the animals, on account of his free-will, with which he is endowed above all other animals.

ST. THOMAS AQUINAS

One of the gifts God gives us because He loves us is free will. If we did not have free will, then we would have no responsibility, either. We could wander through the days like robots waiting for the next thing to happen to us. But God did give us free will, and this puts tremendous responsibility on us. It also opens up to us possibilities of total joy and fulfillment.

God will give you all the tools you need on earth to fulfill the great plans He has for your life. But it's up to you to take up those tools and use them effectively. We are partners with God. We never have to do anything without His help, but He also expects us to make a willful choice to do our part.

Many are called to do great things, but not everyone is willing to take the responsibility for what they are called to do. God helps us, but He does not do everything for us. My brother died at age fifty-eight in an abandoned building in Los Angeles because he wasn't willing to take responsibility for his past mistakes and do the work involved in seeing his life restored. As long as someone else did everything for him he was fine, but as soon as he had to make right choices on his own, he always drifted back to living for the moment instead of making hard choices that would produce good results in the future.

I wanted to help my brother, but he would not help himself. God wants to help us, but we must do the part He gives us to do. We have free will, and we can make right and good choices just as easily as we can make bad ones. The choice is ours either way.

Love Yourself Today: "Thank You, Lord, for the gift of free will. Help me to exercise wisdom as I make my choices."

Rejoice in This Day

This is the day which the Lord has brought about; we will rejoice and be glad in it.   PSALM 118:24

One of the most important lessons we can ever learn is to enjoy every day of our lives as we look forward to the future. One of my greatest desires in ministry is to see people thoroughly enjoy the quality of life Jesus died to give us—not just to read about it or talk about it, but to walk in it and experience it as a daily reality.

Many people, myself included, are extremely goal oriented. We are so focused on tomorrow that we often fail to appreciate and enjoy today because we are always thinking ahead, looking to the next event, working to complete the next assignment, and seeing what we can check off of our to-do lists. Our fast-paced, high-pressure society urges us to accomplish as much as we can as quickly as we can—so we can then accomplish even more. Over the years, I have learned that the intense pursuit of one goal after another can cause us to miss out on some of the enjoyment life offers us. God does have purposes and plans He wants us to fulfill during the course of our earthly lives, but He also wants us to enjoy and make the most of every day we live.

Maybe you desperately want to enjoy everyday life, but fear that actually enjoying something might not be "holy" or pleasing to God. For some reason, many people have come to believe that enjoying life is not okay. Often, we aren't even aware we think or feel that way. God wants us to enjoy today and every day. As today's Scripture teaches us, today is the day He has given us; let's choose to rejoice and be glad in it.

Love Yourself Today: Be sure that you enjoy every day God gives you.

Trust and Do Good

Trust (lean on, rely on, and be confident) in the Lord and do good...

PSALM 37:3

I spent several years studying the subject of love, and I believe that's a worthwhile pursuit for every believer. During the time I was focused learning about love, I realized that faith only works through love. According to Galatians 5:6, faith is actually "activated, energized and expressed" through love.

At one point, the Holy Spirit led me to study Psalm 37:3, our verse for today, which teaches a similar lesson. I was startled to realize that I had only half of what I needed to know to connect properly with God. I had the faith (trust) part, but not the "do good" part. I wanted good things to happen to me, but I was not overly concerned about being good to others, particularly when I was hurting or going through a time of personal trial.

I don't want to sound as though I was totally self-absorbed, because that wasn't the case. There were times I did acts of kindness to help people, but helping others was not my number one motivator.

What about you? Are you walking in faith and pure-hearted good works? Are you trusting God, but also concentrating on doing good, with love as your primary motivation? We must walk in both faith *and* love, both trust in God *and* doing good to others.

One of the greatest things you can ever do is learn about love and practice what you learn every day, in every way you possibly can. Your life will change completely if you will simply apply what you read about it in God's Word.

Love Others Today: What motivates you more than anything else? Is it love? If it isn't, are you willing to change your focus?

Love Is a Verb

And let us not grow weary while doing good, for in due season we
shall reap if we do not lose heart.   GALATIANS 6:9 NKJV

We often think of love as a "thing," but the word *love* is a verb. Love must *do something* in order to remain what it is. Part of the nature of love is that it requires expression. The Bible says that if we see a need and close our heart, how can the love of God live and remain in us (see 1 John 3:17)? Love becomes weaker and weaker if it cannot be demonstrated; in fact, it may become snuffed out.

The ultimate act of love was Jesus' laying down His life for us. And we should lay down our lives for one another. That sounds extreme, doesn't it? Fortunately, the great majority of us will never be called upon to give up our physical lives for someone else. But we have opportunities every day to "lay down" our lives for others. Every time we put aside our own desires or needs and replace them with an act of love for someone else, we lay down our lives for a moment, or an hour or a day.

If we are full of God's love, then we must let love flow out of us. If it becomes stagnant through inactivity, it is good for nothing. It is useless to say we love people if we do nothing for them. Put a sign in your house that asks, "What have I done to help someone today?"

Love is all about action. It is not a theory or merely a word. Let's use all means possible to keep on showing love to people.

———————————

Love Others Today: What can you do to show love to someone today? Take the time to think about it and make a plan.

Time Is a Gift

To everything there is a season and a time for every purpose under heaven.   ECCLESIASTES 3:1 NKJV

Time is a resource God gives us, and we must use our time to be fruitful. One of the phrases we should avoid, both verbally and in our attitudes, is: "I just have a little time to kill." Time is not a commodity to kill or to "pass"; it is a gift to steward.

If you are like I am, you like to be productive with every minute.

When you have five, ten, or fifteen minutes, don't just "kill" your time. Use it to bear fruit. Keep a book or a Bible with you and use those few minutes to read something. Listen to worship music or part of a sermon. Pray. Make a few phone calls. Write someone a note of encouragement. When you have a few minutes, make them count.

To me, one of the worst things that can happen to people is to grow old and look back upon their lives and realize they never took time to do what they thought they were supposed to do or what they wanted to do. I do not want you to look back in your later years and think you wasted your life or feel you never really did anything worthwhile. No matter what your age is today, it is not too late to start right now using your time to bear fruit.

***

Love Yourself Today: "Lord, help me today to use wisely the gift of time You have given me."

How Wisdom Works

The reverent fear and worship of the Lord is the beginning of
wisdom...   PSALM 111:10

Proverbs 2:1–5 gives us great insight into the way wisdom works and
into the value of making the effort to seek wisdom in life.

My Son...if you cry out for insight and raise your voice for under-
standing, if you seek [Wisdom] as for silver and search for skillful and
godly Wisdom as for hidden treasures, then you will understand the
reverent and worshipful fear of the Lord and find the knowledge of
[our omniscient] God.

This passage encourages us to seek wisdom as diligently as we pursue other things in life and to understand that the reverential fear of the
Lord is essential to living a wise life.

This kind of awe toward God is the first step toward wisdom; without it, we will never be wise. When I use the words *reverential fear,* I do
not mean we should be afraid of God, but I do mean we should have
great respect for Him and treat Him with honor. The reverential fear
and awe of God means that we know God is mighty and that He means
what He says, that He can do anything He wants to, anytime He wants
to, to anybody He wants to, and no one on earth can stop Him.

If we are going to relate to God in reverential fear, as the Bible
instructs, we will understand that we need to love, honor, and obey
Him. We will be blessed with wisdom if we do.

***

Love God Today: "Lord, give me the kind of reverential fear of
You that is the beginning of wisdom."

Teach the World to Smile Again

For God did not send His Son into the world to condemn the world,
but that the world through Him might be saved.   JOHN 3:17 NKJV

Pastor Paul Scanlon has a great understanding of love, and he is the writer of today's devotion.

"God so loved the world that He sent us an alternative, not an ultimatum. Our leader, Jesus Christ, overcomes by replacing, not condemning. If the church is to love the world, we must find new ways of loving.

"While traveling through an airport recently, I noticed an older lady with a cane, struggling to place her belongings on the security-screening belt. The security agent was stern with her and, although she was struggling, did nothing to help her. I instinctively started loading her things onto the conveyer belt. On the other side, I waited with her to help retrieve everything. I will never forget how she looked at me and said, 'Thank you so much; your kindness compensated for that man's unkindness.'

"That lady put into words my deepest conviction about the church: the church is God's compensation factor for a hurting world.

"To compensate is 'to reduce or balance out the bad effect of loss, suffering, or injury by exerting an opposite force or effect.' We are God's opposite effect; we balance out the pain and suffering. Compensation doesn't change what happened, but it can reduce the effect. Christians who know how to love are part of God's great compensation plan for a world that has forgotten how to smile."

Love Others Today: How can you "compensate" for some kind of pain or loss in the life of someone you know?

Something Good

And God saw everything that He had made, and behold, it was very good (suitable, pleasant) and He approved it completely.

GENESIS 1:31

Everything God made is good; in fact, according to today's Scripture, it's "very good." Since He created you, He calls you "very good," and I wonder if you can say the same about yourself. Many people do not think there is anything good about them, but that contradicts God's Word.

The Bible asks an important question in Amos 3:3: "Can two walk together unless they are agreed?" (NKJV). If we want to walk with God we must agree with Him. He says He loves us and accepts us. We need to agree with Him by loving and accepting ourselves.

To accept ourselves does not mean that we're going to approve of everything we do. We may still do things that frustrate us or displease God, but we don't have to reject ourselves because of them. God doesn't. When we accept ourselves, we can begin working on those things with God's help, confident in the fact that He loves us.

When we don't accept ourselves, we fall into self-rejection. Rejection actually multiplies our problems. People who reject themselves feel something is wrong with them. They see only their flaws and weaknesses, not their beauty and strength. This is an unbalanced attitude that doesn't agree with God's truth.

You can choose to accept yourself or you can choose to reject yourself. You can also choose whether or not to agree with God and see yourself as "very good." I know from experience that agreeing with God is always the best choice!

Love Yourself Today: Lord, I choose to agree that everything You have made is good—including me!

God Sees Your Possibilities

Not that I have already attained, or am already perfected, but I press on, that I may lay hold of that for which Christ Jesus has also laid hold of me.   PHILIPPIANS 3:12 NKJV

None of us is perfect. We are sometimes painfully aware of our short-comings and imperfections, but God always looks at us through the eyes of possibility. He sees who we can become and He is always hopeful concerning our future. It takes time to grasp for ourselves the hope that God has for us, but I hope you'll begin that journey today.

To realize how much hope God can have for a person, all I have to do is think about what I was like when He called me into full-time ministry.

When God began using me to minister to others, I still had a lot of bad habits. I sincerely loved God, and I wanted to do what was right, but I had very little revelation of His precepts. I tried to "be good" and to do good works, but I also had a shame-based, guilt-ridden person-ality as a result of my childhood. I didn't like myself, had a poor self-image, and was terribly insecure and extremely fearful. Inside, I was a mess, but God filled me with His Holy Spirit and let me know He wanted to use me to minister to others.

The Lord did not wait until I was "fixed" before He got involved with me, because He looked beyond my current reality and saw possi-bilities. He started working with me right where I was and is responsi-ble for getting me to the point where I am. He will do the same for you!

Love Yourself Today: "Lord, help me to remember that when you see me, you see possibilities."

Overcome Evil with Good

Do not let yourself be overcome by evil, but overcome (master) evil with good.   ROMANS 12:21

An old movie entitled *El Cid* tells the story of the man who united Spain and became a hero because he chose to overcome evil with good. For centuries, a battle raged between the Christians and the Moors in Spain. These two groups hated each other, and much killing took place on both sides during their conflict. In battle, El Cid captured five Moors but refused to kill them because he realized that killing had never done any good. He believed that showing mercy to his enemies would change their hearts. Although his actions initially earned him the label of "traitor," they eventually worked and he was honored as a hero.

One of the Moors who had been captured said of El Cid, "Anyone can kill, but only a true king can show mercy to his enemies." Because of El Cid's one act of kindness, his enemies offered themselves to him as friends and allies from that point on.

You may be fighting a different kind of battle, but at some point everyone runs into conflicts, hurt feelings, or disagreements. Sometimes people encounter the pain of betrayal or deliberate disrespect from others. When these things happen, we have a choice to make: Will we obey God's Word or will we simply handle the situation as our emotions lead us? Jesus says: "But love your enemies and be kind and do good [doing favors so that someone derives benefit from them] ..." I encourage you to obey God and overcome evil with good.

Love Someone Today: Can you think of anyone to whom you could show love by extending mercy? Is there someone who has treated you wrongly to whom you can be kind? Go ahead and do it. It may be one of the most powerful things you have ever done.

Top Priority

A new commandment I give to you, that you love one another; as I have loved you. JOHN 13:34 NKJV

Most people live their lives according to priorities. Simply put, this means that we do the things that are most important to us. If you want to see what your priorities are, look at your calendar and your bank statement. How you spend your time and invest your money says a lot about what you value and prioritize in life.

I believe Jesus gave us a clear instruction about priorities when He commanded us to love each other as He has loved us. He was saying that loving people needs to be our top priority, the main focus of our lives; we need to concentrate on demonstrating love to others above everything else.

It took me about forty-five years to realize that my priorities were mixed up and I was not making love the most important activity of my life. It was not my first priority. The commitment to learn how to walk in love has been the single best decision I have ever made as a Christian.

How can love take first place on your priority list? Study the many scriptures about love; take the lessons of this book to heart and read other books about love; pray and ask God to help you love Him, love others, and love yourself. As you fill your mind with good, biblical insights about love and as you put those lessons into practice in concrete ways, you'll learn to live a life in which love takes priority over everything else.

Love Someone Today: Assess your priorities and find out where "love" is on your list. Make a commitment today to make loving others the most important thing in your life. Then do something practical for someone else as a way of showing love to that person.

You're Okay and You're on Your Way

Who will deliver me from [the shackles of] this body of death? O thank God! [He will!] through Jesus Christ (the Anointed One) our Lord!   ROMANS 7:24, 25

There was a time when I felt like the apostle Paul when he wrote the words of today's verse. I wondered if I could ever break free from a constant sense of failure and a feeling that I simply didn't "measure up" to what God wanted from me. I even wondered at times if God was frustrated with me for not making more progress. After struggling with these thoughts for a while, I finally developed a new attitude. Realizing God was happy just to see me making any progress at all, I started saying, "I am not where I need to be, but thank God, I'm not where I used to be. I'm okay and I'm on my way!"

I know now with all my heart that God is not angry with me because I have not arrived. He is pleased that I am pressing on, that I am staying on the path. If you and I will just "keep on keeping on," God will be pleased with our progress.

God knows our spiritual growth and maturity will take time. He doesn't expect us to arrive at our destination quickly. We don't think something is wrong when a one-year-old child cannot walk perfectly. We expect him to fall down frequently; when he does we lovingly pick him up, dust him off, and set him on his feet to try again. Without a doubt, God treats us with just as much affection and grace—always willing to set us on our feet again and encourage us as we keep putting one foot in front of the other.

———————————

Love Yourself Today: "Lord, I confess today that I'm okay and I'm on my way!"

Do It for God—and Yourself

That you may walk (live and conduct yourselves) in a manner
worthy of the Lord, fully pleasing to Him and desiring to please Him
in all things...   COLOSSIANS 1:10

When you get dressed and prepared for each day, do you ever consider that you should dress to please the Lord? I believe we should consider Him in all things, and often when I am choosing my clothes for the day I say, "Lord, I want to look nice for You today." I firmly believe that we should dress appropriately and be neat and tidy. We might have the kindest heart in the world, but if we look like a sloppy mess, people will usually form an opinion based on what they see first.

If I dress sloppy and don't comb my hair I feel sloppy and lazy, but doing my best to look nice makes me feel more professional and energetic. I am not suggesting that we can't be comfortable, but we should do it and still look nice. I see people in clothes that have sat in the clothes dryer too long and are wrinkled all over, and it immediately says to me, "lazy and sloppy." I see women in clothing that is way too revealing and totally improper, and I don't think God is pleased. You may have never considered that God cares about the way we dress, but I firmly believe that He cares about everything we do and that we should do our best in every area of life.

The next time you get dressed to go somewhere, go look in the mirror and ask yourself, "Am I dressed in a way that will be pleasing to the Lord?" Take good care of yourself in every area. Do it for God and for yourself. We don't have to be wealthy to look nice, all we have to do is do the best we can with what we have. Be an excellent person in all areas of life and do it unto the Lord.

Love God and Yourself Today and Everyday: What areas can you improve in to be more fully pleasing to the Lord?

There's More

For He satisfies the longing soul and fills the hungry soul with good.

PSALM 107:9

Have you ever done everything you knew to do as a Christian, yet found yourself thinking, *Is this it? Is this all there is?* Have you tried to be "a good Christian," but wondered if there's a new level of fullness, if there's more to loving God and receiving His love for you than you are currently experiencing?

I spent many years as a believer just going through the motions of serving God. In my heart I felt that something was missing from my relationship with Him, though I didn't know what it was. God had done many wonderful things for me, but my life was frustrating and not really much different from the lives of those I knew were not Christians. At the same time, I could not believe life as a Christian was meant to feel so meaningless and empty at times.

I finally asked God to give me whatever I was missing and God gave me the answer! I learned that growing in the knowledge of who God is and seeking intimate fellowship with Him is a vital necessity of being deeply satisfied and joyful in life. Intimate fellowship with God releases His power to help us accomplish what He has called us to do.

When Christ made the final atonement for our sins, God immediately invited us into the holy place of His presence. God wants us to come close to Him and see that His attitude is filled with love toward us. We can now enjoy intimate fellowship with God!

Love God Today: "Lord, teach me how to enjoy intimate fellowship with You."

Be Active, Not Idle

But put on the Lord Jesus Christ, and make no provision for the flesh, to fulfill its lusts.   ROMANS 13:14 NKJV

In today's Scripture, the apostle Paul teaches clearly that the flesh is lustful. He also describes the flesh as lazy and desirous of many sinful things. Thank God we are more than flesh! We also have a spirit, and the spiritual part of a Christian is where the nature of God dwells. With our spirits, we can discipline and rule over the flesh—but doing so requires effort and cooperation with the Holy Spirit who strengthens and enables us to do good things.

Paul says we are not to make provision for the flesh. I believe one way we provide for the flesh is by being lazy and doing nothing. Doing nothing is addictive. The more we do nothing, the more we want to do nothing.

In situations where our flesh tempts us to be lazy, we can begin to overcome by asking God to help us and by making determined decisions to be active instead of idle. Then, as we go forward and act on our decisions, we'll find that our feelings catch up with them.

One way to love yourself is to be active and enjoy the benefits of getting up and doing the things you need and want to do! There is nothing wrong with a day of rest, but just remember that God said we should work six days and rest one, not rest seven and work none.

Love Yourself Today: Always remember that you don't have to *"feel"* like doing the right thing in order to do it. You can do it on purpose!

Loving Yourself with Your Words

. . . let us hold fast our confession [of faith in Him].
HEBREWS 4:14

According to today's Scripture, Jesus is the High Priest of our confession. It is important that we work with His plan for our lives by saying about ourselves, and our lives, what He says in His Word. God says good things about us in His Word, and we need to agree with Him. He says He loves us, wants to spend time with us, forgives us for our sins, gives us favor and literally thousands of other good things. Have you been saying what He says? If not, there is no better time than right now. Ask God to help you never say negative, critical, faultfinding things about yourself. If you do something wrong, admit it and ask God for His amazing forgiveness, then confess aloud that you trust Him to change you as you study His Word (see 2 Cor. 3:18).

If you have a weakness, don't keep talking about it and acting as if you are afraid you will never enjoy freedom. Start saying that God is working in your life right now and that you have the fruit of self-control. The devil wants you to focus on what you do wrong and to be "sin conscious," but God wants you to be "righteousness conscious"— aware that you are forgiven, knowing He has given you right standing with Himself through your faith in Jesus.

Knowing who you are in Christ is one of the most valuable lessons you can ever learn. We are new creatures in Him, with a glorious future in front of us. God sees the good things about you!

Love Yourself Today: God has declared in His Word that you have value, so why not begin this day by saying, "I am valuable!"

Want More Light in Your Life?

*Then shall your light break forth like the morning, and your healing
(your restoration and the power of a new life) shall spring forth
speedily...*   ISAIAH 58:8

We all want more light in our lives—more clarity, better understanding, and less confusion. Isaiah declared that if we would stop hiding ourselves from the needs around us, our light would break forth (see Isa. 58:7, 8). He also said that our healing and the power of a new life would spring quickly. That sounds good, doesn't it?

Isaiah said justice would go before us, leading us to peace and prosperity, and that the glory of the Lord would be our rear guard. If we actively help the oppressed, God goes before us and He also has our back!

The Lord will guide us continually, and even in dry times He will satisfy us, and our lives will be like a watered garden (see Isa. 58:11). All of this happens as a result of living to bring justice to the oppressed.

Isaiah further said that if we will pour out our own lives to satisfy the need of the afflicted, our light will rise in darkness and any gloom we experienced will be comparable to the sun at noon (see Isa. 58:10). It sounds to me like helping people is the way to live in the light.

———————————

Love Others Today: What can you do to help someone in
need this week?

A Gift for Others—and for Yourself

Forgive, and you will be forgiven.   LUKE 6:37 NKJV

Do you hold unforgiveness toward anyone for any reason? If so, it needs to be eliminated from your heart and mind right away because it's keeping you in bondage.

You may be thinking, *Well, Joyce, that's easy for you to say. You haven't been hurt like I have.*

That is true, but I have been hurt in life to a very deep degree. I was abused, abandoned, rejected, blamed, lied about, misunderstood, and betrayed by family and friends, and I allowed the enemy to fill my heart with hatred for those who hurt me. But when I began to learn about love, I moved from hatred to bitterness to mild resentment and finally to freedom, which only comes through forgiveness. The Lord graciously brought restitution into my life.

God promises to bring justice into our lives and to give us a double reward for our former shame, pain, and unfair treatment (see Isa. 61:7). When we try to bring justice ourselves through vengeful acts, we only prevent God from working on our behalf.

The absolute key to unlocking the recompense of God for past hurts, however, is to do things His way and not our own. We are to love our enemies, pray for them, and bless them. If you have been hurt, God knows all about it, and He has a plan for your vindication. He, and He alone, is the Vindicator (Heb. 10:30).

Love Others Today: Do you need to extend forgiveness to someone? Make the choice to do so right now. It will be a gift to that person and a gift to you.

Everyone Can Use a Blessing

As it is written, He [the benevolent person] scatters abroad; He
gives to the poor; His deeds of justice and goodness and
kindness and benevolence will go and endure forever!

2 CORINTHIANS 9:9

When we think about giving, we often think primarily about giving to the poor. I certainly encourage you to bless those who are financially needy. But everyone needs a blessing—even the rich, the successful, and those who appear to have everything.

We often hear people say, "What do you buy the man or woman who has everything?" What to buy or do for them is not the real issue; it's the act of love that is important.

Dave and I once felt led to make a financial donation from our ministry outreach fund to a well-known gifted Christian music artist. He wrote to us, saying that the gift was very timely and that in twenty-three years no national ministry had partnered with him.

Everyone loves this man. He is a tremendous blessing to the body of Christ. Why had no other national ministry ever reached out to him financially? I believe it is because we have been trained to give to the poor and needy, but have had little or no instruction regarding the needs of the successful or "wealthy" of the world.

Those with wealth or riches have emotional needs, just as other people do. Everyone needs a blessing. We all need to be encouraged, complimented, and appreciated. We all get weary at times and need other people to say to us, "I just wanted to let you know I appreciate you and all you do."

Love Others Today: "Lord, show me who You want me to bless, even if they don't appear to need a single thing!"

The Difference Is Doing What God Says

You shall walk after the Lord your God and fear Him, and keep His commandments and obey His voice.   DEUTERONOMY 13:4

I remember a woman who attended one of my conferences. It was a banquet, and she was sitting with a group of ladies. She came to me and said, "You know, I really learned a lesson this weekend. As I listened to all those ladies talk about their problems, their breakthroughs, and about what God has done for them, I realized that many of them have gone through the same thing I went through."

Then she said, "Every single thing God has spoken to these ladies, He has spoken to me over the years. Everything He has told them to do, He has also told me to do. The only difference is, they did it, and I didn't."

The woman received a great revelation that day. She realized that she was no different from anyone else, that her problems were no worse than many other people's. What she needed to do was begin doing what God told her to do.

The devil tries to convince us that we are different from everybody else so we will keep asking, "Why is everybody else getting their breakthrough and I'm not?" God delivers people at different times—yours may come soon, or it may take some time. But it is also possible that God has told us the same thing He has told others. The difference may simply be that they have done what He said, and we haven't.

You are going to spend your time doing something. All God is asking is that what you do is what He says.

Love God Today: Be willing to do everything God asks of you.

Follow Jesus, No Matter What

Though he slay me, yet will I trust in him. JOB 13:15 KJV

Jesus said, I am Living Bread that came down from heaven. If anyone eats of this Bread, he will live forever." Later in the same chapter He said, "whoever continues to feed on Me [whoever takes Me for His food and is nourished by Me] shall [in his turn] live through and because of Me."

Jesus said that He was living bread and living drink and that anyone who ate and drank of Him would never hunger or thirst. He was, of course, speaking of spiritual hunger and spiritual thirst (the void people feel when they don't spend enough time in God's presence and with His Word). Material things cannot satisfy a hungry soul; only God can truly satisfy.

When Jesus presented to His disciples and followers this message about eating His flesh and drinking His blood, many found it offensive and hard to bear: "After this many of His disciples drew back (returned to their old associations) and no longer accompanied Him."

I believe many people are willing to follow Jesus if He is taking them where they want to go and doing for them what they want done. But when it comes time for this very needful transition in their relationship with Him, many cannot make the turn. Their carnal desires get the upper hand and they backslide.

We must decide that we will serve God even if we never get what we want. Like Job said in today's Scripture, we must say, "Though he slay me, yet will I trust in him." This is what it means to truly love Him.

Love God Today: Are you discouraged or disappointed about something? Keep following Jesus anyway.

Who Are You? No, *Really*...

And you are in Him, made full and having come to the fullness of life...   COLOSSIANS 2:10

How would you respond if I asked: "Who are you?" Would your first response be a list of things you do and roles you play in life? Would you say: "I am a flight attendant," "I am a banker," "I am a wife and a mother," or "I am a high school student"? Any of these answers would describe *what you do,* but none of them would tell me *who you are.*

As a believer, one of the most important realities for you to experience is who you are in Christ, your identity in Him. This will enable you to see yourself in a whole new way and love yourself because you realize who God made you to be. Understanding "who you are in Christ" is vitally important because being in Christ provides you with certain rights and privileges that belong to the children of God. Being in Christ is not about what you do, but about who you are. It's not about your activity; it's about your identity. It's not about your "do"; it's about your "who."

There is a big difference between who we are in Christ and who we are in ourselves. In and of ourselves, we are nothing, we have nothing, and we can do nothing. In Christ, though, we can be, do, and have everything God promises us in His Word.

———————

Love Yourself Today: "Thank You, Lord, for giving me such a strong identity in You, one that is totally separate from anything I do."

Try Some Shrug Therapy

Do not be quick in spirit to be angry or vexed, for anger and vexation lodge in the bosom of fools.   ECCLESIASTES 7:9

There are some things you can control in life—who your friends are, what you eat, and when you go to bed, for example. There are other things you can't control, such as what other people say or the flat tire you got last night. The way you respond to things you can't control helps determine your stress level and your quality of life and health. I have two suggestions about dealing with things you can't control. First, if you can't control them, don't take responsibility for them. And second, I like to say, "Do your best, pray, and let God do the rest!"

People who regularly get upset over small things suffer in many ways. People who shrug them off do much better. Shrugging off certain things doesn't mean you are indifferent; it simply means you've accepted the fact that you can't do anything to change them at that time. The flat tire has already happened. Calling someone to come fix it makes sense; throwing a tantrum and kicking the tire does not. We need to deal appropriately with each stressor as it arises so that we don't end up exploding in frustration over the unavoidable bumps on the road of life.

God works in mysterious ways. You never know when He may use some inconvenience or frustration for your good. He is in control, and if you trust Him to work things out, you'll be able to ride the ups and downs of life with peace, joy, and strength.

Love Yourself Today: Refuse to live in frustration. Take life one day at a time, and when things happen that you don't like, say, "It is what it is and God is still in control."

You Can't Take It with You

For we brought nothing into the world, and obviously, we cannot take anything out of the world.   1 TIMOTHY 6:7

Our society is filled to the brim with commerce. Everyone seems too busy making money so they can buy more things. I can hardly believe there are enough shoppers to buy everything that's available.

Things in themselves are not evil, but they can become so if they lure us away from godly priorities. First Timothy 6:10 says: "For the love of money is a root of all evils; it is through this craving that some have been led astray and have wandered from the faith and pierced themselves through with many acute [mental] pangs."

God wants His children to be blessed. He wants us to have nice things. He delights "in the prosperity of His servant" (Ps. 35:27). But, as our verse for today teaches us, we came into the world empty-handed and when we leave it, we can't take anything with us.

The more we use our resources to bless others, the more God will bless us. His Word promises: "Give, and [gifts] will be given to you; good measure, pressed down, shaken together, and running over, will they pour into [the pouch formed by] your bosom [of your robe and used as a bag]. For with the measure you deal out [with the measure you use when you confer benefits on others], it will be measured back to you" (Luke 6:38).

––––––––––––––––

Love Others Today: "Lord, help me to enjoy Your blessings, but not to hoard them or think too highly of them. Help me to use them to bless others."

Think on Purpose

And be constantly renewed in the spirit of your mind [having a fresh mental and spiritual attitude].   EPHESIANS 4:23

A real breakthrough came for me in my love walk when I realized that love was something I needed to do on purpose. I could not wait to *feel* loving; I had to choose to *be* loving. The same rule applies to our thoughts. We must learn to think good thoughts about people on purpose.

We must learn to look for the good, not the bad, in everyone. We all have faults and weaknesses, but we all also have good qualities. I admit that we must look harder to find the good in some people than in others, but to be like Jesus, that is what we must do.

Jesus finds the good in everyone and magnifies that instead of the bad. He found the good in me and started developing it until it finally surpassed a lot of the things that were wrong with me. He has done the same thing for many of us, and He expects us to do the same for people we encounter every day.

Take a moment and try this experiment. Just sit and think some good thoughts on purpose about someone you know, and see how much better you feel about yourself. If you keep it up, you will begin to notice changes in that person's attitude toward you. One reason that individual will change is that you will have changed.

Thinking good thoughts opens the door for God to work. If we want the Lord's good plan to manifest in our lives, we must get into agreement with Him (Amos 3:3). He is not negative in any way, and according to the Bible, we have been given the mind of Christ (1 Cor. 2:16)—but we must choose to use it.

Love Others Today: Choose to think good thoughts today—even if you don't feel like it.

They're Just Things

Do not love the world or the things that are in the world, if anyone loves the world, love for the Father is not in him.   1 JOHN 2:15

Remember, love people and use things to bless them. That is hard for us to do if we love things excessively. You and I must strive to keep things in their proper place. We must not allow ourselves to put them ahead of people.

One day my previous housekeeper was cooking a roast for us in the pressure cooker. She did something wrong, and the valve blew off the top, shooting steam, roast, grease, potatoes, and carrots straight up into the air. The ceiling fan caught the food and grease and sent them flying all over the kitchen walls, ceiling, floor, furniture—and the housekeeper.

When I arrived home from work, she was sitting in a corner of the kitchen, crying. I finally got her to tell me what had happened, and when she did, I started laughing. By the time Dave came in, she and I were both laughing hysterically.

She said, "I've destroyed your kitchen!"

I remember telling her, "The kitchen can be replaced, but you can't. You're more important than the kitchen. Thank God you're not hurt."

There was a time in my life when that would not have been my response. Before I learned that people are more important than things.

If we love people, God can replace things, but if we love things excessively, we may lose people who cannot be replaced.

Love God Today: "Lord, I declare that I love You and I love other people more than I love the things of this world."

Right Thinking Brings Blessings

Blessed (happy, fortunate, to be envied) is the man whose strength is in You, in whose heart are the highways to Zion. Passing through the Valley of Weeping (Baca), they make it a place of springs; the early rain also fills [the pools] with blessings.   PSALM 84:5, 6

When our strength is in God, even difficult places in life can be turned into blessings. That's why we need to constantly keep our hearts and minds focused on Him and not on our circumstances.

I have discovered that when I am unhappy, I am tempted to blame something or someone around me. I think many people are the same way.

Looking outward at circumstances or people, instead of inward at our own attitudes, can cause us to go around the same mountain again and again, caught in a repetitive cycle.

I now know that when I am unhappy, it is because of some wrong thinking on my part. Even if I am in the midst of negative circumstances, I can stay happy by having right thoughts toward them. If I know the Word of God and have it in my heart and mind, I know what kind of right thoughts I should be thinking.

God has satisfaction, fullness, completeness, and joy in mind for us. He wants us to experience abundant life. Fullness comes from being in the center of His will and agreeing with Him through thinking in accordance with His Word.

Love God Today: Next time you're tempted to blame something or someone for your unhappiness, take time to examine your thoughts. How could you think differently? Give it a try, and watch your mood improve!

Just "Be" with Him

And Moses said to the Lord, If Your Presence does not go with me,
do not carry us up from here.   EXODUS 33:12, 14, 15

When God called Moses to go to Pharaoh and tell him, "Let My people go," he asked the Lord, "Who am I going to say sent me? Pharaoh is
not going to listen to me and set the children of Israel free." Moses was
afraid; he was upset. But God said to him, "My presence will go with
you." I love Moses' reply: "Okay, but if Your presence is not going to go
with us, then don't send me!"

We need to really understand the awesomeness of God's presence.
Why in the world would we not want to spend time with God? We
spend time staring in store windows at the mall; we spend time on the
Internet. But most people admit it is hard for them to spend regular
time with God. The devil fights us when it comes to spending time
with God.

Why not begin dedicating a portion of time for that purpose? Try to
be as regular about it as you can. Read the Bible and any other Christian books that minister to you. Talk freely to God about anything you
would talk to a good friend about. Listen to Christian music and worship; or just sit there and enjoy the silence. If you will do that, you will
begin to feel and sense the Presence of the Lord and you will begin to
see wonderful changes in yourself and your life.

I guarantee you, there is nothing in life you need more and nothing
He would enjoy more than spending time with you.

Love God Today: Take time today to do nothing but sit in
God's presence.

Peaks and Valleys

But he himself went a day's journey into the wilderness and came and sat down under a lone broom or juniper tree and asked that he might die. He said, It is enough; now, O lord, take away my life; for I am no better than my fathers.   1 KINGS 19:4

Have you noticed that after experiencing a real emotional high, people may bottom out with an emotional low? Today's Scripture reveals that this happened to Elijah the prophet. He went from doing miracles one day to hiding from Jezebel the next. One day he was at the height of his victory. The next day he was sitting under a tree in the wilderness, asking God to let him die because he felt so depressed.

The emotion of excitement can make you tired after an exciting event, just as hard work does.

When we are excited, often we get the idea, *Oh, if I could just stay on this emotional high forever!* But God wants us to learn to be level in our emotions. That doesn't mean that we can't get excited, but we cannot live that way.

Elijah was tired from his exciting victory on Mount Carmel and what he needed was rest. When I have finished an extensive ministry trip and I feel completely drained, I have learned to rest. I need to sleep, spend extra time with God, do something fun for my emotions, and not make big decisions.

When you feel "low" after an emotional high, do not allow the devil to take advantage of you during those times. Use wisdom and get the rest you need—it will make a huge difference.

———————

Love Yourself Today: "Lord, give me the wisdom I need to take care of myself emotionally."

Embrace Freedom!

Fear not, for you shall not be ashamed; neither be confounded and depressed, for you shall not be put to shame....   ISAIAH 54:4

Do you often feel ashamed or somewhat embarrassed about who you are, as though you are "less than" other people? If so, it's possible you have a shame-based nature. The good news is that the power of shame can be broken off of you through the power of God.

We know from today's verse that the Lord has promised to remove shame and dishonor from us so that we remember it no more. In fact, God has promised that in their place He will pour out upon us a two-fold blessing. We will possess double what we have lost, and we will have everlasting joy (see Isa. 61:7).

Ask the Lord to work a healing miracle in your mind, will, and emotions. Let Him come in and fulfill what only He came to do: heal your broken heart, bind up your wounds, give you beauty for ashes, joy for mourning, a garment of praise instead of a spirit of heaviness, and double honor for double shame (see Isa. 61:1–3).

By faith, boldly declare that you are healed from the pains and wounds of your past; you have been set free to live a new life of health and wholeness. Continue to praise the Lord and confess His Word over yourself, claiming His forgiveness, cleansing, and healing.

Stop blaming yourself and feeling guilty, unworthy, and unloved. Instead begin to say, "If God is for me, who can be against me? I am no longer filled with shame and guilt. God loves me, and I love myself. Praise the Lord, I am free in Jesus' name, amen!"

Love Yourself Today: "Thank You, Lord, for promising to heal my broken heart and set me free from the shame of my past."

Givers and Takers

Let all men know and perceive and recognize your unselfishness
(your considerateness, your forbearing spirit).   PHILIPPIANS 4:5

I encourage you to model a life of generosity before all of those with whom you have contact. If you are a giver rather than "a taker," it won't take them long to realize you are quite different from other people. As they witness your joy, they may realize that giving makes a person happier than being selfish does. People are watching, and it's amazing what they notice and remember.

Today's Scripture urges us to let all men know and see our unselfishness (Phil. 4:5). This reminds me of Jesus' encouragement to let all men see our good and kind deeds so they will recognize and glorify God (see Matt. 5:16). Jesus did not mean we should be show-offs or do things for the purpose of being seen; He was encouraging us to realize how much we affect the people around us.

As you begin to live a life of generosity, I want to encourage you to be patient with yourself. The "self life" is deeply ingrained in every fiber of our being and does not die easily.

I've been trying to live unselfishly for several years, and it has been quite a battle. I have read books about love, gone over and over what the Bible says about it, and prayed about it, preached about it, and done all I can to keep it foremost in my thinking. At times when I realize I've been selfish again, I don't get upset with myself, because that only keeps me involved with me. When I fail, I ask God to forgive me and start fresh; and I believe that's the way to keep making progress.

Love Others Today: Without drawing undue attention to it, live in a way that makes your unselfishness evident.

It's Not About You

The Spirit of the Lord God is upon Me...He has sent Me to...
proclaim liberty to the captives, and the opening of the prison to
those who are bound.   ISAIAH 61:1

Dave and I have been married almost forty-five years, and I am appalled at how selfish I was during the early years of our marriage. I can honestly say I did not know any better. In the house where I grew up, all I ever saw was selfishness and "taking" instead of giving.

So when I became an adult, I was a selfish person who knew very little about giving to others. I was always on my mind, and nothing changed until I got weary of my entire life being about me, me, and more of me. According to today's Scripture, Jesus came to open prison doors and set captives free. He has set me free from many things, the greatest of which is myself. I have been set free from me! I continue to grow daily in this freedom, but I am thankful to realize that real joy is not found in getting my way all the time.

Perhaps, like me, you also had poor examples in life and need to "un-learn" some things you learned growing up. Be honest: How do you respond when you don't get what you want? Do you become angry? Do you grumble and complain? Are you able to trust God to take care of you or do you live in fear that if you don't take care of yourself, no one will take care of you? Believing you have to take care of yourself leads to selfishness, which leads to an unhappy life.

The Holy Spirit is a great teacher. He will help you learn the lessons you need to know in order to truly value, care for, and love others.

Love Others Today: "Lord, help me un-learn every bad lesson
I have learned in the past and set me free to learn to love
others they way You want me to love them."

Only God Knows the Future

There shall not be found among you anyone who . . . uses divination,
or is a soothsayer, or an augur, or a sorcerer, or a charmer, or a
medium, or a wizard, or a necromancer. For all who do these things
are an abomination to the Lord.   DEUTERONOMY 18:10–12

Today many people go to fortunetellers or psychics, or consult horoscopes, or watch movies and read books that make occult activities seem attractive. These activities were once geared mostly to adults, but have now become popular with children.

The Bible has much to say about witchcraft, consulting mediums, and other activities that offend God and that He considers off-limits.

The Bible tells us God is the only one who knows the future and that His Holy Spirit is the one who leads us into truth (see John 16:13). If you want to know what's ahead for you, read the Book by the one who can tell you and cultivate an intimate relationship with Him through the Holy Spirit. I can't say what all God will tell you about your future, but I guarantee that seeking to know it any other way will cause problems. God will tell you what you need to know, but in His mercy, He will conceal what He knows is best to reveal at a later time.

People who have sought to know the future using means that God deems "an abomination" often find themselves tormented. But when you trust God with your future and believe He will tell you what you need to know at the proper time, you can live in peace.

Love God Today: Seek God for your future and trust Him to bring it about in His timing.

Break Your Box

And being in Bethany at the house of Simon the leper, as He [Jesus]
sat at the table, a woman came having an alabaster flask [box] of
very costly oil of spikenard [perfume]. Then she broke the flask and
poured it on His head.   MARK 14:3 NKJV

I believe that breaking (saying no to) the flesh is what today's Scripture
is about. The woman broke that box so the expensive perfume could be
poured out. In the same way, we have to "break" our flesh.

We all have sweet perfume in us. But our alabaster box (our flesh)
has to be broken so the perfume (the good things of God) can flow
out of us. We are "pregnant" with the good things of God. We each
have the fruit of the Spirit—love, joy, peace, patience, gentleness, faith,
meekness, and temperance. But many times our alabaster box (our
flesh) keeps them from being poured out.

Oh, but we love our alabaster box. We don't want to break it
because, after all, it is such a pretty box. We spend so much time taking
care of it; we don't want it to be broken. But we must love God more
than we love anything else. We need to circumcise our flesh and be
willing to let go of the things of the flesh, so God's blessings can flow to
us and through us.

Love God Today: "Lord, I choose to break my alabaster box
in order to express my love for You and receive everything You
have for me."

The Worst Kind of Pride

Everyone proud in heart is an abomination to the Lord; though they join forces, none will go unpunished.   PROVERBS 16:5 NKJV

As a young Christian, I was so excited when I began to understand the power of faith. Admittedly, I got a bit out of balance about it at times. In fact, I was proud of it! Being proud of our faith is the worst kind of pride. We start to think that if others just had as much faith as we do, they wouldn't have some of the problems they have.

During that time, I had a problem with my back and was determined to walk in faith that God would heal me. I was determined to have a miraculous healing, and I am quite sure that I would have given "my faith" the credit.

One day, after I'd been hurting for years, God put on my heart the idea of going to a chiropractor. I told Him, "I am not going. I've been believing You for healing all these years, and I am going to be healed. I am not going to a doctor."

But my back continued to get worse. I woke up one morning and couldn't walk. I *had* to do something. So I finally decided to go to the chiropractor. In my pride I had decided how God had to heal me, not realizing then that He uses many methods and the choice is His. I was proud of my ability to trust God, but true faith is humble and completely dependent on God. It doesn't dictate to God what, how, and when He is to do things.

When asking God to do something for you, don't ever try to dictate the terms to Him. Ask for what you want and need, and tell God you will be happy to have the answer in His way and timing.

Love God Today: Have faith in God, but realize that faith is not the price that buys God's blessings, it is the hand that receives them.

Break Free from Criticism and Judgment

But [as for me personally] it matters very little to me that I should be put on trial by you . . . I do not even put myself on trial and judge myself . . . I feel blameless; but I am not vindicated and acquitted before God on that account. It is the Lord [Himself] who examines and judges me.   1 CORINTHIANS 4:3, 4

Criticism and judgment are rampant in today's society. It is unfortunate that people choose to degrade others instead of offering encouragement and affirmation. For most people, being criticized and judged by others is difficult to bear. It's hard on us mentally, and it can be very painful emotionally. But the more we learn to love ourselves in a godly way, the less susceptible we are to the wounds criticism and judgment can inflict.

Certainly, being critical and judgmental toward others is a sin; God's Word instructs us repeatedly not to treat people this way. But, it is equally sinful to allow the adverse opinions of others to affect us negatively or influence the decisions we make.

Most of the time, people who criticize and judge others are extremely insecure. Because they are not comfortable with themselves, they struggle to be at ease with others or to accept what others choose to do. We need to be secure enough in God to be who we are and do what He has called us to do, whether people around us approve or not.

Understand that criticism and judgment are the devil's tools. He will try to use them to keep you from fulfilling your destiny, to limit your liberty, and to steal your creativity. The way to resist them is to be secure in the fact that God loves you and to love yourself appropriately.

Love Yourself Today: "Lord, I pray that I will continue to grow to love and accept myself in godly ways so the criticism and judgment of others will not hurt me or affect me negatively."

Believe in Yourself

David was greatly distressed, for the men spoke of stoning him because the souls of them all were bitterly grieved, each man for his sons and daughters. But David encouraged and strengthened himself in the Lord his God.   1 SAMUEL 30:6

Do you ever encourage yourself in the Lord? Sometimes, if we don't encourage ourselves, we won't get any encouragement at all; and we need to be encouraged! It's important that we learn to be our own encouragers through Christ.

When David and his men found themselves in seemingly hopeless circumstances, which the men blamed on him, David didn't wait for someone else to pat him on the back; he encouraged and strengthened *himself* in the Lord. Later, that situation turned around completely (see 1 Sam. 30:1–20).

On a previous occasion, when David was just a boy, everyone around him discouraged him when he decided to fight Goliath. They told him he was too young and too inexperienced, and that he didn't have the right armor or the right weapons. Many of the discouraging things people said were true, but they didn't deter David. He provided his own encouragement because he was confident in God.

The key to being able to encourage yourself in the Lord is having confidence in His love, His ways, and His Word—and you can decide to believe or not. If you do believe, you will have confidence in God and you can encourage yourself in Him.

———————————

Love Yourself Today: In what specific ways can you encourage yourself in the Lord today?

Don't Put It Off

*Do not say to your neighbor, Go and come again; and tomorrow
I will give it.*   PROVERBS 3:28

Many people struggle with procrastination. As we see in the verse for today, we can easily say, "I'll do it tomorrow." We can have the best intentions, but if we don't act on them we will still be disobedient. Procrastination is very deceptive. We don't see it as disobedience because we intend to obey God; it's just that we are going to do it *when*—*when* we have more money, *when* we are not so busy, *when* Christmas is over, or *when* the children go back to school.

There is no point in saying, "I will be a giver when I have more money or more possessions to give away." If you aren't giving out of what you already have, you're not likely to do it when you have more.

Dave and I tithed from the beginning of our life together, but it never occurred to us to "live to give," to excel in giving. But, the closer we got to God, the more we wanted to give. We learned that true giving often means sacrificing something that we really would like to keep.

We were not in a financial position to give more money than our 10 percent tithe, but strong desire caused us to search for ways to give more. So we gave away personal possessions, extra clothes, household items, and an old car we decided to pass on to a needy friend.

In the process of giving, we discovered that we did not have to have money to be a blessing to others. We could start with what we did have, and as we did God increased us and enabled us to give even more.

———————————

Love Others Today: What acts of love or kindness have you been putting off? Do them today.

Love Never Fails

Love bears up under anything and everything that comes, is ever ready to believe the best of every person, its hopes are fadeless under all circumstances, and it endures everything [without weakening].   I CORINTHIANS 13:7

The God-kind of love bears up under anything and everything that comes. It endures everything without weakening. It is determined not to give up on even the hardest case. The hard-core individual who persists in being rebellious can eventually be melted by love. The Bible says, "while we were yet in weakness [powerless to help ourselves], at the fitting time Christ died for (on behalf of) the ungodly" (Romans 5:6).

It is hard to keep showing love to someone who never seems to appreciate it or even respond to it. It is difficult to keep showing love to those individuals who take from us all we are willing to give, but who never give anything back.

We are not responsible for how others act, only for how we act. We have experienced the love of God by His mercy, and now He commands us to show that same kind of love to the world. Our reward does not come from man, but from God. Even when our good deeds seem to go unnoticed, God notices and promises to reward us openly for them. Your Father who sees in secret will reward you openly.

Love Others Today: It isn't always easy to love, but God commands it. Love the unlovable in your life today.

Take Care of Your Temple

Do you not know that your body is the temple (the very sanctuary)
of the Holy Spirit Who lives within you, Whom you have received [as
a Gift] from God?   1 CORINTHIANS 6:19

I want to ask you today the same question Paul asked the believers in
Corinth centuries ago: Do you know that your body is the temple of the
Holy Spirit? Are you loving yourself by caring for your physical body,
treating it well, and using it for God's purposes?

Paul also writes: "You are not your own" (1 Cor. 6:19). In other
words you do not belong to yourself, and that means you don't have
the right to mistreat or ignore your body. You belong to God. You are so
special to Him that He purchased you with the highest possible price:
the life of His Son. His Spirit lives within you, so your body should be
used to glorify Him.

Some Christians focus so much on trying to be "spiritual" that
they fail to properly care for their bodies. Other people have such low
self-esteem or shame-based nature that they don't feel their bodies are
worth caring for. But God's plan for us involves maintaining spiritual,
emotional, *and* physical health. He wants us strong in every way!

No matter what shape you are in physically, it's never too late to do
some repair or maintenance on your temple. You can start by learning the basic principles of good nutrition, stress management, exercise,
and rest. It's amazing how much better you can feel if you will begin to
make positive changes in these areas. Give it a try; I promise, you'll be
glad you did.

————————————

Love Yourself Today: What can you do to improve your
physical health or well-being? Do you need to learn how to
make good food choices or get out and exercise? Whatever you
do, just get started on a new path of health and wellness!

One Life to Give

I die daily [I face death every day and die to self].
1 CORINTHIANS 15:31

You and I were not born knowing how to love others. In fact, we were born with a selfish, "all about me" attitude. The Bible refers to this as "sin nature." Adam and Eve sinned against God by doing what He told them not to do, and the sin principle they established was forever passed to every person who would ever be born.

God sent His Son Jesus to die for our sins and to deliver us from them. He came to undo what Adam did. When we accept Jesus as our Savior, He comes to live in our spirit, and if we allow that renewed part of us to rule our decisions, we can overcome the selfish, sin nature of our flesh. It won't go away, but the greater One who lives in us helps us overcome it daily (see Gal. 5:16). That does not mean we never sin, but we can improve and make progress throughout our lives.

Paul wrote our verse for today: "I die daily." In other words, even this well-known apostle struggled with putting others first; he found that doing so was a daily battle and required daily decisions. Each of us must decide how we will live and what we will live for; there is no better time to do so than right now. You and I have one life to live and one life to give, so the question is: How are you going to spend your life?

———————————

Love God Today: Remember that whatever you do for others, you are doing for God.

Who Do You Trust?

The Pharisee took his stand ostentatiously and began to pray thus
before and with himself...   LUKE 18:11

In Luke 18:9–14 Jesus tells a story of two men who went to the temple to pray. One was a Pharisee and the other was a tax collector. The Pharisees were revered, and the tax collectors were hated.

The Pharisee said, "God, I thank You that I am not like the rest of men—extortioners (robbers), swindlers, [unrighteous in heart and life], adulterers, or even like this tax collector here" (Luke 18:11).

Most of us would never pray that prayer, but that doesn't mean we've never thought we were holier than someone else. Maybe you feel that you give more than others, or study your Bible more. Beware of thinking more highly of yourself than you should.

In the parable that contains today's Scripture, the tax collector "would not even lift up his eyes to heaven, but kept striking his breast, saying, O God, be favorable (be gracious, be merciful) to me, the especially wicked sinner that I am!" (Luke 18:13).

The Pharisee was trusting in himself and his eloquence, trying to impress people. The tax collector was truly crying out to God. God doesn't want us trusting in ourselves. He wants us to trust in His mercy and His love, and to let His love and kindness flow through us to others.

Love God Today: "Lord, cause me to trust in your mercy and love, not in anything I think I can do for myself."

Enjoy!

The thief comes only in order to steal and kill and destroy. I came that they might have and enjoy life, and have it in abundance (to the full, till it overflows).   JOHN 10:10

I have a few questions for you. Are you enjoying your life? Are you generally happy and satisfied with who you are and what you do each day? Do you take time to appreciate the everyday experiences that make life rich and rewarding? Or do you race through each day to get to the next one? Do you take breaks and find things to laugh about on a regular basis, or do you allow the pressures of your responsibilities to carve a frown on your face as you keep your nose to the grindstone?

God wants you to be happy today and every day. He doesn't want you to merely exist, but to *enjoy* being alive. In fact, we know from today's Scripture that Jesus did not come to us simply to give us physical life, or to give us just enough to get through life's challenges and difficulties. He came to impart to us true life and authentic happiness—the rich, deep, joy-filled life God intends for us, the kind of life that is "in abundance, to the full, until it overflows."

I challenge you to go to a whole new level of enjoyment in your daily life. Don't wait for a special occasion to enjoy life. Enjoy it moment by moment, day by day. Learn to be happy in ordinary experiences such as waiting in traffic or doing the dishes. You'll find your level of joy steadily increasing in your life. Whatever your current level of happiness is, I invite you to step into greater joy. Live with more passion; laugh more; relax more; smile more; and simply *enjoy* more.

———————————

Love Yourself Today: What can you do in order to enjoy your life more?

Don't Wait for "When"

The greatest part of our happiness depends on our dispositions, not our circumstances.   MARTHA WASHINGTON

Many people allow circumstances to determine their attitudes. If their circumstances are favorable, they look at life through a positive lens. If their circumstances are negative, they see every situation from a negative point of view. We must be more mature than that; we must develop an optimistic outlook on life no matter what happens. We need to be as positive when the car breaks down or when we need a root canal as when we receive a raise or promotion. We cannot wait until our circumstances change to decide to adjust our attitudes. We need to be stable and consistent in every situation and not allow circumstances to dictate what our attitude in life will be.

To develop the stability we need, we have to eliminate the mind-set that says, "I will enjoy life when I don't have this problem anymore."

The fact is "when" rarely comes. When one issue finally goes away, something else will arise. This is not a negative statement; it simply reflects the way life usually works.

Life is full of surprises; some are wonderful and some are challenging. Whatever comes your way, decide now that you will meet it with a predetermined, positive mind-set.

The ability to choose how we respond to circumstances is a gift from God, and we should use it to our benefit. Don't waste a day being negative or letting circumstances affect your attitude.

Love Yourself Today: "Lord, help me to be consistent and stable, and to have a positive attitude, no matter what my circumstances."

What Was the Problem?

Behold, this was the iniquity of your sister Sodom: pride,
overabundance of food, prosperous ease, and idleness were hers
and her daughter's, neither did she strengthen the hand of the
poor and the needy . . . therefore I removed them when I saw it.

EZEKIEL 16:49, 50 (EMPHASIS MINE)

You've probably heard of Sodom and Gomorrah and the terrible wickedness in those cities. But what did they actually do that was so displeasing to God? We often think their sexual perversion finally caused God to destroy them, but it was actually something quite different.

I was shocked when I first read today's Scripture and saw the truth behind the destruction of these cities. The problem with Sodom and Gomorrah was that they had too much and were not sharing it with those in need. They were lazy and lived excessively convenient lifestyles, which led them to commit abominable acts. Failing to share what we do have with those who have less than we do is actually dangerous because this selfish type of lifestyle opens the door for evil to progress. Not only are these things not good for us, they are offensive to God. He expects us to be channels for Him to flow through, not reservoirs that hold everything we have for ourselves.

I believe we need to make an effort not to complain when we don't have things the way we want them. Inconvenience is often part of helping others, and in fact it is part of everyday life. No life is perfect, and when it isn't we should still be very grateful for what we have and be willing to share it with others.

———————————

Love Others Today: Think about ways in which you have both abundance and convenience in your life? How can you use these things to bless others?

Love Does Something

Let them do good, that they be rich in good works, ready to give,
willing to share . . .   1 TIMOTHY 6:18 NKJV

Our ministry has taken various people on mission trips to minister to desperately needy people, but they don't all respond the same way. Everyone feels compassion, but some individuals become quite determined to find ways to make a difference. Indifference makes an excuse, but love finds a way. Everyone can do something!

I remember a woman who decided she *had* to help in some way. For a while she couldn't figure out what to do because she had no extra money to contribute and she couldn't go live on the mission field. But as she continued to pray about the situation, God encouraged her to look at what she had, not at what she did not have. She realized she was very good at baking cakes, pies, and cookies. So she asked her pastor if she could bake during the week and offer her baked goods for sale on Sundays after church as long as the money went to missions. This became a way for her and other church members to be involved in missions, and it kept her active doing something to help someone else.

Another woman is a massage therapist, and she organized a special spa day and donated all the proceeds to help poor people. She raised one thousand dollars for missions and also testified that the day of giving was life changing for her, those who worked with her, and those who attended.

We all need to be loved, but I believe our personal joy is strongly connected to loving others. Something beautiful happens in our hearts when we give.

Love Others Today: "Lord, help me to not only feel compassion, but to find creative ways to express my love for others."

It's All About Others

And the people looked for Him until they came up to Him and tried
to prevent Him from leaving them.   LUKE 4:42

Today's devotion is written by my friend Pastor Paul Scanlon from England, a man who has practiced loving God and others in remarkable ways.

"In the early days of Jesus' ministry, He went to a town called Capernaum. The people loved Him so much that on the day he was about to leave town, they tried to keep Him from leaving (see Luke 4:42).

"His response was both stunning and profound. Stunning in its simplicity, and profound because of the insight it gives into His priorities and driving force. Jesus looked into the eyes of all those blessed people and simply said, 'I can't stay here with you any longer because I was sent to reach other people in other places and I must go and preach the good news to them also.' Did you get that? I was sent to reach others, others, others! It's all about others.

"If you could cut God, He would bleed others. But if we could cut the church, sadly, we would bleed ourselves. This fundamental misunderstanding about what matters most to God is at the heart of the church's failure to impact a hurting world.

"We are blessed to be a blessing; we are saved to seek and save others. We are healed to heal, forgiven to forgive. It is not about me, mine, us, or ours. It has always been about others."

Love Others Today: Is your life about others, or is it still about you? What can you do to become more others-minded?

Praise Has Power

But You are holy, enthroned in the praises of Israel.
PSALM 22:3 NKJV

Many people are familiar with the statement: "There's power in praise." It's true, and when we praise God from our hearts, we exert power in the spiritual realm. God Himself inhabits the praises of His people, according to our Scripture for today.

Before I speak to an audience, I make sure I have entered into praise and worship—not because God needs it, but because *I* need it. I need to engage my heart to focus on Him and my mouth to speak about Him; I need to tap into the power that is released through praise. I do all this because I love God, but also because praise creates an opening in the spiritual atmosphere which enables people to hear the Word clearly, receive it, and hold on to it through faith.

Think about how this applies to your life. How many times have you walked into a church service or a conference and felt "blah" when you first arrived, but then felt better after a few minutes of praising God? You see, praise brings a release of our burdens; it takes our focus off ourselves and our problems and puts it on God—and that always makes us feel better.

I encourage you to praise at home, in the car—and everywhere you possibly can. Live every day with praise on your lips, and you'll find that your power for living everyday life just keeps increasing.

———————————

Love God Today: "Thank You, Lord, that there is power in my praise."

We Can't Do Anything Without Him

I am the Vine; you are the branches. Whoever lives in Me and I in him bears much (abundant) fruit. However, apart from Me [cut off from vital union with Me] you can do nothing.   JOHN 15:5

According to today's Scripture, we cannot do anything—*anything*—apart from Jesus. I've certainly found this to be true in my life, and I'm sure you have, too. One time I was trying to fix my hair and had one piece that simply would not curl. The rest of my hair curled fine; my curling iron was red hot. I'd put the iron on that curl and turn it, then take it off, and that one piece of hair would fall flat. I didn't know about trusting in God and leaning on Him for *everything*. I was a self-sufficient, independent, strong woman. I had spent most of my life thinking I didn't need anybody because I'd been abused and was afraid to trust people. My attitude was: "Who needs you? I'm just fine by myself!"

I knew I needed God, but I didn't realize that I *desperately* needed God. I began to sense in my heart that God wanted me to pray and ask Him to help me with my hair. My first thought was, *I am not going to ask God to help me fix my hair. I am a grown woman, and I have been doing my hair for a long time. I'll try it again and put some hairspray on it, because sometimes that works.* It didn't work that time!

Finally, I conceded, saying, "Okay, Holy Spirit, would You please help me fix my hair?" I curled the same piece of hair again, and when I removed the iron that time, it had a nice little curl in it. I learned a valuable lesson from that experience: If we don't do things God's way, we're not going to do them at all. We honor Him when we show our dependence on Him by asking for help for big things and little ones.

———————————

Love God Today: I encourage you to lean on God and ask Him to help you with all kinds of things, little things as well as big things.

Understanding the Chastening of God

Now no chastening seems to be joyful for the present, but painful;
nevertheless, afterward it yields the peaceable fruit of righteousness
to those who have been trained by it.   HEBREWS 12:11 NKJV

When God is chastening or dealing with you, endure it. Don't try to get away from it because God chastens us just as a loving father chastens his children. Notice in today's verse that God's chastening brings "the *peaceable* fruit of righteousness" into your life (italics mine).

I have peace in my life now for only one reason. I have endured the chastening of the Lord (see Deut. 8:5). I've let God do what He wanted to do in my life. I let Him show me that I was prideful, haughty, obnoxious, selfish, self-centered, and hard to get along with. I've let Him show me these things because the truth about our behavior will set us free (see John 8:32).

It's not easy to endure that kind of godly chastisement. God won't let us off the potter's wheel until He's ready. It doesn't matter how tired we get of going around and around. God is the Potter and we're the clay, and He is going to make what He knows we can be.

Staying in bondage is much harder than enduring the chastisement of God. Had I not been willing to endure the chastisement of God, I'd still be back in the same old mess I was in thirty-something years ago. Allowing God to deal with you may not be comfortable or fun or easy. But He only chastises you when absolutely necessary and only for your good because He loves you. Love yourself by submitting to the work He wants to do in your life.

Love Yourself Today: Is God dealing with you in a certain area? Don't resist; let Him do it and see what good results from it.

Do You Want Everything God Has for You?

When Jesus noticed him lying there [helpless], knowing that he had already been a long time in that condition, He said to him, Do you want to become well? [Are you really in earnest about getting well?]
JOHN 5:6

The story where we find our verse for today tells of a man who had lain by a pool for thirty-eight years, waiting for the angel to stir the waters so he could get in and be healed of what John 5:5 calls his "deep-seated and lingering disorder." Perhaps you too have dealt with a "deep-seated and lingering disorder"?

Jesus hasn't changed, and He is asking us the same question he asked the man at the pool of Bethesda. He is saying, "Do you want to get well?" In other words, He is saying, "Do you really want everything I have for you? Are you willing to do whatever it takes to see these things happen?"

If we really want something enough, we will do whatever it takes to get it. I once reached a point in my life where I could not stand to be upset anymore. I resisted the devil; I prayed for peace, but nothing worked.

Finally, I just humbled myself before God and said, "Lord, I have got to have peace. I don't care what I have to do. I don't care how You have to change me or how I have to adjust to everyone around me. I just have to have peace!" Now I do have peace in my life, but I had to go through certain things to get it. I had to learn to do whatever God told me in His Word and in my heart to do, and it has been worth it.

Love Yourself Today: Do you want everything God has for you? Then be willing to do everything He asks of you.

Good Fruit on a Daily Basis

The fruit of the righteous is a tree of life, and he who wins souls is wise. PROVERBS 11:30 NKJV

When people hear we are Christians, they often take a close look at our lives. They want to see what kinds of standards we have; they want to know how we live. They aren't usually open to learn about our faith or receive from us until they have assessed the fruit of our lives, to see whether it is good. When we show people that what we have is real, then they will listen to what we say and be receptive to what the Holy Spirit wants to give them through us.

You can show people that what you have is real by responding with good fruit to the little incidents that happen in your daily life. If someone bumps into you at the grocery store or steps on your toe, you can be nice about it. To turn the situation into a pleasant experience, you could even laugh with the person, who certainly didn't intend to bump, or step on you. People can see Jesus in your patient, joyful, response to something as small as that.

Anyone could make an ugly face and utter a heavy, frustrated sigh over a little mishap. Christians are called to be better than that, to live above the petty responses we so often encounter in the world.

We learn how to develop love by reading and applying the specifics the Bible gives us and by seeking God and praying. But we also develop it on a daily basis by simply making little choices that display love through our actions. This will open the way for others to be interested in the Source of love they see in you.

Love Others Today: As you go about your day today, you will probably have some frustrations. Choose to respond with love.

No Pressure

They tie up heavy loads, hard to bear, and place them on men's shoulders, but they themselves will not lift a finger to help bear them.   MATTHEW 23:4

One of the many ways we can love people is to allow them to be who they are. What I mean by this is that we shouldn't pressure others to be or do anything; we should accept who God has created them to be and what He has called them to do.

We often expect more out of people than they are able to give, and when we continue to put pressure on them over a period of time, our relationships with them often fail. We should expect the best of people, but at the same time we need to remember that they are only human.

All of us need the freedom to be who we are. We want to be accepted unconditionally. This doesn't mean we don't know we need to change in certain ways. It means we don't want other people telling us how we need to change in order to be accepted by them.

When we disapprove of others they can sense it. It is in our tone of voice and in our body language, even if it isn't in our words.

When we want people to change, we cannot accomplish that by pressuring or nagging them. For change to be lasting, it must come from the inside. Only God can affect that type of heart change in someone. But one thing is for sure, God won't change people when we are trying to change them. He has a "hands off" policy when working in human lives. We keep our hands off and He works!!

––––––––––

Love Others Today: Do you need to take the pressure off some people in your life? Think it over. If so, I urge you to do it.

The Antidote for Doubt

No unbelief or distrust made him waver (doubtingly question)
concerning the promise of God, but he grew strong and was
empowered by faith as he gave praise and glory to God.

ROMANS 4:20

You may know the story of Abraham (see Gen. 12:1–7, 21:7). Basically, God promised Abraham a son, but at the time, he was one hundred years old and his wife was ninety, so their childbearing years were long gone! But Abraham knew God had spoken and was determined not to focus on the natural impossibility that he and Sarah could have a child. Instead, he planted his faith in God's promise and held on to that promise by praising God. His story is so remarkable that Paul made reference to it in Romans 4:18–21.

Abraham had absolutely no reason to hope. In fact, if any situation has ever been beyond hope, it would be the possibility of two people past ninety being able to have a biological child. Nevertheless, Abraham kept hoping; he kept believing God's promise. He did not waver in his faith or question God's promise. Instead, "he grew strong and was empowered by faith" as he praised God.

The same thing will happen when you praise God. You gain more and more strength, your faith increases, and the things that are coming against you to defeat you are dissipated as you praise Him. That's why it's important to be diligent to listen to praise and worship music. I encourage you to play it in your home and in your car; learn songs and sing them; thank God and praise Him!

———————

Love God Today: God never responds to complaining, but He does respond to praise and an attitude of gratitude.

Live a Consecrated Life

Unto You, O Lord, do I bring my life.   PSALM 25:1

I love to lift up my hands in the morning and pray the prayer of consecration found in today's Scripture. When we pray a prayer of consecration, we are saying to the Lord: "Here I am, God. I give myself to You. Not just my money, but myself. Not just one hour on Sunday morning, but myself. Not just a portion of my day, but myself. Unto You, O Lord, do I bring my *entire* life. I lay it on Your altar. Do what You want to do with me. Go places through my feet today. Make a difference in my world through me today. Here's everything about me; here are all the resources You have loaned me." That is what we mean when we say, "Unto You, O Lord, do I bring my life." Complete, voluntary surrender to the Lord—that's what *consecration* means.

When we consecrate something, we set it apart for God's use. Therefore, when we consecrate our lives, we turn our backs on our fleshly desires, worldly values, carnal thinking, undisciplined living, and everything else that does not agree with God's Word. Consecration may not be easy, but it is easier than sin and disobedience. It is worth the discipline.

When we consecrate ourselves to the Lord, we give Him everything we are, but we should also know that we give Him everything we are not.

God knows everything about you and loves you unconditionally, so hold nothing back from Him. Let go of everything as an offering to your Lord, and you will be amazed at how free you will feel.

———————————

Love God Today: If you are ready to consecrate yourself to God, lift your hands to Him and simply say, "Lord, I give you my life . . . everything I am and everything I am not!"

Give God Everything

For those whom He foreknew ... He also destined from the beginning ... to be molded into the image of His Son [and share inwardly His likeness].   ROMANS 8:29

If we really are serious about loving God, we must ask ourselves if there are any areas of our lives in which we are holding out on Him. What are the things about which we say, "Well, God, You can have everything but *that*," or "Lord, just don't ask me to quit doing *that*"?

God doesn't want to take everything we enjoy away from us, but everything must be available to Him. He makes the choices about what is really good for us and what is not; our job is to trust Him completely.

According to today's Scripture, one of God's primary goals in our lives is to make us like Jesus. This means that He wants us to continue to become more like Jesus in our thoughts, in our words, and in our actions.

God has given us a free will, and the only way we will ever belong to Him is to make deliberate decisions to give ourselves freely to Him. He will never force us to love Him or serve Him. He will lead us and prompt us, but He will always leave the decision to surrender up to us. If God has been dealing with you about anything, I encourage you not to put off surrendering it any longer. In your thoughts you may intend to surrender at some later time, but remember that good intentions do not equal obedience—and obedience is not only what God requires, it's also what proves our love for Him.

Love God Today: Go ahead and do it: Give God *everything*.

The Importance of Accepting Yourself

And this [salvation] is not of yourselves [of your own doing, it came not through your own striving], but it is the gift of God.

EPHESIANS 2:8

In 1718, a young child named David Brainerd was born in Connecticut. David lost his father to death when the boy was only eight years old, and his mother died six years later, when he was fourteen.

Brainerd became a well-known American missionary and a powerful preacher, but he felt an unusual burden of guilt, as though he could have been in some way responsible for his parents' deaths. As a result, he worked very hard to try to earn God's love and approval.

People who have written about Brainerd agree that he exhausted himself trying to please God because he always thought he had to earn God's love. He tried to please God so much that he wore out his body and became too ill to carry out his ministry or even to pray. The young man with so much ability and potential to do great things for God died of tuberculosis at the age of twenty-nine.

Brainerd's story holds a sobering lesson for all of us. We can love God and serve Him with all our might, but we must also receive His love for us. We must believe that He loves us and accepts us completely—and that we cannot do anything to earn His love or merit His grace. As our verse for today reminds us, our position in God is all because of what He does for us, not what we can do for Him.

———————————

Love Yourself Today: Nothing you can do will ever cause God to love or accept you more than He already does, so follow His example: Love and accept yourself.

Love Yourself, Discipline Yourself

*For the time being no discipline brings joy, but seems grievous and
painful; but afterwards it yields a peaceable fruit of righteousness to
those who have been trained by it.*   HEBREWS 12:11

I believe discipline is one of the most important character traits a person can have. We know that God disciplines those He loves (see Prov.
3:12), and if we love ourselves, we will require ourselves to be disciplined. Without discipline, we miss much of the enjoyment life has to
offer, but when we do discipline ourselves, we have the time, energy,
and resources to enjoy our lives.

Generally speaking, I believe disciplined people feel better about
themselves and enjoy more self-respect than undisciplined people do.
Undisciplined people tend to want "the perks without the works." In
other words, they want the benefits and advantages life has to offer
without making any effort.

Today's Scripture teaches us that discipline is something we do for
ourselves; it does not bring immediate joy or results, but later on it
produces good things for those who submit to it. Discipline is a tool
we can use for our good—not a taskmaster for us to resent or despise.

Don't think of discipline as difficult, but see it as a vehicle that
brings blessings, peace, fun, and great enjoyment to your life. Don't
see discipline as your enemy, but as a good friend that will help you
become everything God wants you to be and empower you to do everything He wants you to do.

———————————

Love Yourself Today: In what specific area of your life do you
need discipline? Make a commitment to God and to yourself
to work on it with His help.

It's Unconditional

But God shows and clearly proves His [own] love for us by the fact that while we were still sinners, Christ (the Messiah, the Anointed One) died for us.   ROMANS 5:8

According to God's Word, He loved us before the world was formed, before we loved Him or believed in Him. God does not require us to earn His love, and we must not require others to earn ours. We should realize that love is something we are to become; it is not something we do and then don't do. We cannot turn it on and off, depending on whom we want to give it to and how they are treating us.

As believers in Jesus Christ, the love we are to manifest to the world is the unconditional love of God flowing through us to them. Our love has conditions and limits; His does not.

Loving people unconditionally is a very big challenge. I would be tempted to say it is impossible, but God tells us to do it, and He never commands us to do something and then leaves us to perform it on our own. His grace (His power, ability, and favor) is sufficient for us, which means He enables us to do what He has called us to do.

God actually sends some people into our lives to function as "sandpaper" to help smooth our rough edges. Learning to walk in love with unlovely people is one of the most important tools God uses to develop our spiritual maturity.

———————

Love Others Today: "Lord, give me grace to love everyone in my life, even the difficult ones."

Make the Effort

*Eagerly pursue and seek to acquire [this] love [make it your aim,
your great quest].*   1 CORINTHIANS 14:1

True Christlike love is not found on the surface of life. It's not always an easy thing to do.

Today's Scripture tells us that we must "eagerly *pursue* and *seek*" love and that we are to make it "our great quest." If you have read about great quests and adventures throughout history, you know that they take a lot of effort. This tells me we will have to work at love if we are going to walk in it.

The words *pursue* and *seek* are both strong action words, terms that indicate the need to take initiative and devote energy to what we're going after. To *pursue* means, "to try to find or discover; search for." (In other words, we need to go after love with all our might and focus, and act as though we absolutely cannot live without it.)

There are degrees of desire, and today's verse tells us love requires a high level of desire. We want many things, but there are only a few things God tells us to "seek," and Love is one of them.

If we want to learn about genuine love, we will have to study it and familiarize ourselves with everything God's Word says about it. Notice how a loving person handles difficult or tense situations. Observe how he gives to others. Examine the fruit in his life.

In addition to learning about love, also be diligent to seek and pursue it.

———————————

Love Others Today: "Lord, by Your grace, I am willing to make the effort to seek and pursue love as my great quest."

Passion and Compassion

The Lord is full of compassion and mercy.   JAMES 5:11 NIV

My friend Darlene Zschech is a well-known worship leader; moreover, she is a *worshipper*. Today's devotion comes from her, and I believe it will inspire you to have more passion for God and compassion for others.

"Let's make sure our hearts and lives are fueled for the opportunities that present themselves to us every day. Let's be like the Good Samaritan, who went out of his way to bring help while others simply walked by. This Samaritan was moved with compassion, and not only was he moved, but he responded. Compassion was the emotional 'stop sign' to which Jesus so often responded. Jesus Himself set the benchmark for compassion very high, and then told us to go, fueled by the Spirit, and minister to a hurting world.

"If you are going through a season in which you feel you need to be ministered to rather than being the one to minister, be encouraged. Surround yourself with an environment of worship and praise, fill your home with music that inspires your heart. Get around people who will nourish and encourage you—and allow the Spirit of the Lord to fill you continually from the inside out. Allow yourself to fall into the safe arms of our Lord and our strength, for He will never leave you or forsake you. And remember: Love the Lord your God with all your heart, mind, soul, and strength, and love your neighbor as you love yourself."

———————————

Love Others Today: Have passion for God and compassion for others.

Praise Brings Victory

The Lord is my strength and my shield; my heart trusted in Him, and I am helped; therefore my heart greatly rejoices, and with my song I will praise Him.   PSALM 28:7 NKJV

Do you know that praise is a form of spiritual warfare? It is; it's a means of spiritual warfare that defeats the enemy and his works. Praising God can break the power of fear and help us to get rid of doubt and unbelief. It will drive away spiritual influences that are not of God. We need to say something like, "I praise You, Lord, and I magnify Your name. You're worthy to be praised. Hallelujah. Thank You, Lord. You're awesome! There is nobody like You!" We can use those words of warfare anytime, anywhere. We can defeat Satan much more quickly by praising God than by worrying. That's why the Bible is loaded with examples of praise and instructions for us to sing and praise God. Just look at some of them.

- "Unto You, O my Strength, I will sing praises; for God is my Defense, my Fortress, and High Tower, the God Who shows me mercy and steadfast love" (Ps. 59:17).
- "I will extol You, O Lord, for You have lifted me up, and have not let my foes rejoice over me" (Ps. 30:1).
- "Oh, sing to the Lord a new song! For He has done marvelous things; His right hand and His holy arm have gained Him the victory" (Ps. 98:1 NKJV).

Why does the Bible tell us to sing and praise God? Why did God put songs in our hearts? Because these things are not only a means of expressing our love to Him, but also a way to win the spiritual war.

Love God Today: When you are in a spiritual battle, don't forget to use the weapon of praise.

God Can Make It Happen

*Delight yourself also in the Lord, and He will give you the desires
and secret petitions of your heart. Commit your way to the Lord [roll
and repose each care of your load on Him] and He will bring it to
pass.*   PSALM 37:4, 5

Do you wonder if you will ever have the things you really desire?
According to today's Scripture, if we delight ourselves in the Lord, He
will give us the desires of our hearts. Letting God give us things is so
much better than trying to get them for ourselves. Most of us struggle
greatly in our lives, trying to make happen things that only God can
bring about. He wants us to seek Him, and He promises that He will
add the things we desire when the time is right.

We are to commit our way to Him and let Him bring our desires to
pass. Jesus said all those who labor and are heavy-laden should come
to Him. He promised to ease, relieve, and refresh their souls (see Matt.
11:28, 29). His ways are higher than our ways, and His thoughts are
higher than ours. In other words, God knows much better than we do
what we need to do.

My first Bible was a gift from my mother-in-law, and on the inside
cover she wrote: "Commit your way to the Lord" from Psalm 37:5. Little did I know, when she gave me the Bible years ago, just how long it
would take for me to let go of my ways and submit to God's.

I do not know why we tend to be so stubborn, but we do. I encourage you to let go of your ways and let God be God in your life. He wants
to give you the desires of your heart as you commit your way to Him.

———————————

Love God Today: "Lord, I pray that You will bring my desires
to pass as I delight myself in You."

Stand Firm in God's Plan

Then Peter took Him aside to speak to Him privately and began to reprove and charge Him sharply, saying, God forbid, Lord! This must never happen to You! But Jesus turned away from Peter and said to him, Get behind Me, Satan! You are in My way [an offense and a hindrance and a snare to Me].   MATTHEW 16:22, 23

God has a great plan for your life, and He will help you accomplish it. The enemy always opposes God's will, so he will send people to directly block or hinder what God wants to do in you and through you. That even happened to Jesus. In Matthew 16, Jesus had just told Peter and the other disciples that He would be killed and then raised the third day. Peter, not yet understanding that the full plan of salvation would require Jesus to die on the cross, rebuked Him. Jesus corrected Peter immediately so that God's plan of salvation would be fulfilled and Satan's plans defeated.

The enemy will do his best to use people you love—and people who love you—to keep you from doing God's will. They do not mean to hurt you; they simply do not understand. When you hear God speak or sense a call from Him, remember that the people around you have not always heard or felt what you have. It may not make sense to them, so they try to influence you not to do it.

Satan is afraid of you! He knows that if you are willing to obey God completely, you'll become dangerous to him!

Love Yourself Today: Move forward with confidence in God's plan for your life. Don't let anyone stand in your way!

Take Time to Play

Josiah was eight years old when he began his thirty-one-year reign in Jerusalem.   2 KINGS 22:1

In today's Scripture we see that Josiah became king when he was only eight years old. He was forced to grow up quickly!

Many people feel they were forced to grow up too fast, just as Josiah was. Maybe you feel that way; I certainly did. When people have to grow up too quickly they lose something precious, and that loss often leads to tremendous emotional problems.

As adults we should be able to accomplish things in our lives without feeling burdened. In fact, I believe we should be able to enjoy every single thing we do. Some years ago this fact was brought to my attention because I realized I was at that time forty, and could not say I had ever really enjoyed much of my life.

Not being permitted to play will steal a person's childhood and his enjoyment of adulthood. My problem was thinking I had to deserve every bit of fun, enjoyment, or blessing that came my way.

The good things that come to us in this life are given to us by the Lord (see James 1:17). He wants to give them to us. He wants us to enjoy life to the fullest. If you lost part of your childhood, pray and ask God to restore your joy, your childlike faith, and your ability to celebrate life.

Love Yourself Today: Form a habit of taking time to do something you really enjoy—just for the fun of it!

Bricks or Bulldozers

*The greatest good you can do for another is not just to share your
riches, but to reveal to him his own.*   BENJAMIN DISRAELI

Words create images inside of us, and Proverbs 23:7 says that as a
person thinks in his heart, so is he. The same is true about the words
we speak to others and the words they speak to us. Those words can
shape either a positive or negative self-image in the person who hears
them. Every word we speak to others or to ourselves can be a brick to
build with or a bulldozer to destroy.

Think of these words and then think about how they make you feel:
ugly, stupid, failure, incompetent, slow, clumsy, hopeless. Do they make
you feel uplifted, excited, and happy, as though you can be a success at
anything you attempt? Do they make you feel good about yourself? Do
they make you feel strong and confident? I am sure they don't.

Now consider words like: *attractive, intelligent, hopeful, creative,
blessed, talented, gifted*. I am sure you find that such words affect you in
a much more positive way. If you hear these words spoken about yourself, you will feel encouraged and affirmed. They will create a positive,
confident self-image in you.

The Bible says that encouraging words make the heart glad (see
Prov. 12:25) and that pleasant words are "sweet to the mind and healing to the body" (see Prov. 16:24). Speak life-giving, positive words
to yourself, your family members, your friends, and your co-workers
today. It could not only make their day, but also help them feel good
about themselves.

Love Others Today: Use your words as bricks to build others
up, not as bulldozers to tear them down.

Be a True Believer

"For the oppression of the poor, for the sighing of the needy, now I will arise," says the Lord; "I will set him in the safety for which he yearns."   PSALM 12:5 NKJV

Since the Bible contains more than two thousand scriptures about our duty to the poor and needy, He must be trying to get a message across to us: It's very important for us to be involved in some way in helping widows, orphans, and people who are poor, needy, oppressed, or afflicted.

When people are oppressed, they have a burden that is unreasonable; it overwhelms, overpowers, and depresses them. Their burdens often cause them to lose hope. God is a Father to the fatherless and a defender of widows (see Ps. 68:5). He seems to have a special place in His heart for people who are lonely and have no one to take care of them.

James 1:27 says that true religion that is expressed in outward acts is to "visit, help, and care for the widows and orphans in their affliction." This means, if our religion is real, we will get involved in helping those who are oppressed by life's circumstances.

I have learned that everyone who sits in a church on Sunday may not be a real Christian, according to James 1:27. Following rules, regulations, and doctrines does not make one a true believer in Jesus Christ. I believe that because when we receive Christ as Savior, we receive the heart of God and His Spirit comes to dwell in us. This means we have to learn to care about what God cares about—and He cares about helping hurting people.

———————————

Love Others Today: What are you personally doing for the poor, the needy, and the oppressed in your community?

Power Source

*And what is the exceeding greatness of His power toward us who
believe, according to the working of His mighty power.*

EPHESIANS 1:19 NKJV

In today's Scripture Paul prayed that we would know the exceeding
greatness of God's power toward us. God is powerful, and anyone who
believes in God surely believes that, but the question is: Do we believe
His power is available to us and that it exists for us? Being able to live
power-filled lives starts when we believe that power is available for us.

God's power is greater than any other power in the universe, and it
is limitless. This power, which is "toward us," has *already* been given.
In Luke, Jesus said, "Behold I have given you power…" We do not need
to strive for power or hope to have power someday; we have power
now! The same power that raised Christ from the dead lives in us (see
Rom. 8:11) and we can be quickened (filled with life) by that power.
This is not a one-time filling that slowly drains out of us as the days go
by, but we can be filled day by day and even moment by moment. We
can constantly and continually experience God's presence and power
in our lives. When we belong to Him, there is never a time when His
power is not accessible to us.

Just think: If your local power company called and said you were
chosen to receive free power for the rest of your life, you would probably get so excited! This is the way life is when we are connected by
faith to God's power. You have to pay for the power that comes into
your home, but your power for life has been paid for by Jesus Christ.

———————

Love God Today: Think about this: You are never, ever in a
powerless position, because God makes His power available
to you at all times.

Souvenirs from God

I will remember the works of the Lord; surely I will remember Your wonders of old.   PSALM 77:11 NKJV

Have you ever felt that you forget what you should remember and you remember what you should forget? I certainly have! Jesus chastised the disciples on one of their journeys because they had forgotten about a miracle He had done. They started out on a trip and suddenly realized they didn't have enough bread with them. They only had one loaf, and that would not be nearly sufficient. He then began to chastise them, asking if they had forgotten when He fed five thousand people with five loaves of bread and two fish. Had they forgotten another amazing miracle when He fed four thousand people with seven loaves? Had they remembered, they would not have been worried about going hungry because they didn't have enough bread with them.

If we would remember the miracles God has done in our pasts, we would not so easily fall into worry and fear when we face new challenges. When David faced Goliath and no one encouraged him in the fight, he remembered a lion and a bear he had slain with God's help. Because he remembered that past accomplishment, he had no fear of his current situation against Goliath.

Are you facing something right now that looms like a giant in your life? Remember: nothing is impossible with God.

Love God Today: Take time right now to recall some of the great things God did for you in the past, and courage will fill your heart.

I Know This for Sure

I know that my Redeemer lives, and He shall stand at last on the earth.   JOB 19:25

Let me tell you what I know" would normally be an arrogant statement to make, but today, I want to tell you what I know about you and me as Christians. I believe this will be good news that will encourage you all day long and every time you remember it.

I know that we are children of God, and that we are called, anointed, and appointed by Him for greatness. We are destined to bring God glory and be molded into the image of Jesus Christ. We have—right now—righteousness, peace, and joy in the Holy Spirit. We are forgiven for all our sins and our names are written in the Lamb's Book of Life. Jesus has gone before us to prepare a place for us that where He is we may be also.

I know God loves us with an everlasting, unconditional love and that His mercy endures forever. I know that we can do all things through Christ who is our Strength. I know that God never allows more to come on us than we can bear, but He always provides a way out, a safe place to land. I know that all things work together for good for those who love God and are called according to His purpose.

Because you have trusted Jesus as your Lord and Savior, the words on this page are true for you. I want to encourage you to study and memorize God's Word so you will be able to open your mouth and strengthen yourself with these truths and others anytime you want to do so.

Love God Today: Begin to recite your very own "I know…" statements. Build a good supply of them in your heart.

God Commands a Party

Then [Ezra] told them, Go your way, eat the fat, drink the sweet
drink, and send portions to him for whom nothing is prepared; for
this day is holy to our Lord. And be not grieved and depressed;
for the joy of the Lord is your strength and stronghold.

NEHEMIAH 8:10

Nehemiah and his kinsmen (the Jews) who had escaped exile lived in pitiful conditions. The wall of their city was broken down, and that was a dangerous situation for a city in those days. Their wall was their protection from the surrounding enemies who seemed to be everywhere.

Nehemiah went to the king and asked for permission and timber to rebuild the temple gate, the city wall, and a house for himself. I think it is interesting that he asked to help the people and was willing to work hard, but he also asked for a house for himself. Perhaps he realized that by the time he finished the project he would need a nice place in which to live and relax.

The project was a huge one, and it took a long time and a lot of determination. One of the first things they did after reaching their goal was to celebrate. Ezra the priest spoke the words of today's Scripture, telling them to rejoice and to eat the fat and drink sweet drink!

This celebration was the right thing to do spiritually. God Himself commanded this party. He knew the people needed to celebrate a job well done. I want you to understand that celebration revives and restores us. Rewarding ourselves and celebrating the completion of an assignment is part of God's plan for our well-being.

Love Yourself Today: Next time you work hard and finish a big job, take time to celebrate!

Counted Perfect

Those whom I [dearly and tenderly] love, I tell their faults and convict and convince and reprove and chasten [I discipline and instruct them]. So be enthusiastic and in earnest and burning with zeal and repent [changing your mind and attitude].

REVELATION 3:19

I believe that as long as we are cooperating with the Holy Spirit to the best of our ability, and sincerely want to change, God counts us as perfect in Christ while we make the journey through life. Conviction is the tool the Holy Spirit uses to let us know we are doing something wrong; we sense that our actions, words, or attitudes are wrong. I think today's Scripture makes clear that our attitude toward this conviction needs to be joyful.

God views conviction, correction, and discipline as something to be celebrated rather than something to make us sad or frustrated. Why should we celebrate when God shows us something that is wrong with us? Enthusiasm sounds like a strange response, but in reality the fact that we can see something we were once blind to is good news. For many years of my life I was able to be rude, insensitive, and selfish, and not even know it. That is a sad condition to be in, but people who have no relationship with Jesus are spiritually blind and deaf.

When our hearts are hard, we are not sensitive to the touch of God. When He convicts us, we don't feel it. Therefore, when we make enough progress in our relationship with God that we begin to sense when we are doing something wrong, it is a sign of progress and should be celebrated joyfully.

Love Yourself Today: Rejoice when God corrects you because it is an opportunity to make progress.

Steps in the Right Direction

Let each one of us make it a practice to please (make happy) his neighbor for his good and for his true welfare, to edify him [to strengthen him and build him up spiritually].   ROMANS 15:2

Today's Scripture gives us great advice, but we usually do the opposite of what it advises us to do. We want others to live to make us happy and do what pleases us.

The ways of the world, which are focused on "self," do not work. In general people are more selfish than ever; they are also more dissatisfied. God's ways do work, and His way is to genuinely love other people. If we do as He instructs, we may make some sacrifices, but we will have a kind of joy that cannot be found anywhere except in the center of God's will.

Will you be honest and ask yourself some questions that may be difficult to answer? How much do you do for others? Are you trying to find out what people want and need so you can provide it for them? How well do you really even know the people in your own family? Take a step in love today and another one tomorrow. As you press on, you'll be happier all the time.

Love Others Today: How are you doing on your love walk? Take a few extra steps today.

It's Not Always Convenient

Felix became alarmed and terrified and said, Go away for the
present; when I have a convenient opportunity, I will send for you.
ACTS 24:25

Today's Scripture is part of a Bible story about a man who did not follow God, because doing so would have been inconvenient. Felix asked
Paul to come and preach the gospel to him. But when Paul started talking to him about right living and controlling his passions, Felix became
alarmed and frightened. He told Paul to go away, that he would call
him at a more convenient time. This story clearly depicts the way we
are. We don't mind hearing about how much God loves us and about
the good plans He has for our lives, but when He begins to correct us,
we try to tell Him that "now" is just not a good time. I doubt He ever
chooses a time we would consider "good," and I think He does that on
purpose!

When the Israelites traveled through the wilderness, God gave them
a cloud to follow during the day and a pillar of fire to lead them at
night. When the cloud or pillar moved, they had to move, and when it
hovered, they stayed where they were. When God decides it is time for
us to move to the next level of our journey in Him, we should never say,
"This is just not a good time!"

God knows best, and His timing is always exactly right.

Love Others Today: Next time God asks you to do something
for others and you think you don't have time, remember that
His timing is always perfect.

Living with Uncertainty

For My thoughts are not your thoughts, neither are your ways My ways. For as the heavens are higher than the earth, so are My ways higher than your ways and My thoughts than your thoughts.

ISAIAH 55:8, 9

One of the great mysteries about our walk with God is that we rarely understand everything He is doing in our lives. If we always understood, we would have no need to trust Him. As believers we often catch ourselves questioning God: "What does my future hold?" "Will I ever get married?" "Will I have the provision I need in my old age?"

We have to learn to trust God when we do not understand what is happening in our lives, and we need to become comfortable with unanswered questions. You and I may never have every answer we want when we want it, so we need to relax and get comfortable trusting God, the One who does know.

If you are the kind of person who has to have everything figured out in order to settle down, let me encourage you today to stop demanding explanations and instead to begin practicing trust. When you can only see one step ahead of you, take that one step and trust God to show you the next one.

If His response is delayed, trust Him to answer you in His perfect timing. God's thoughts and ways are not ours; His are higher, better, and wiser. We need to trust Him when we do not understand.

———————————

Love God Today: "Lord, I trust You completely, even when I do not understand."

No Regrets

He who gains Wisdom loves his own life; he who keeps
understanding shall prosper and find good.

PROVERBS 19:8

Regret is one of the primary results of wrong choices; it means "to feel sorry, disappointed, or distressed about something."

The world is full of people who live with regret—and that's a terrible thing for people to do to themselves! Living in an attitude of sorrow and regret simply robs people of the joy they could experience every day and of hope for a better tomorrow. When wrong choices cause regret, we need to deal with it and let it teach us how to make better choices in the future.

I understand firsthand that wrong choices lead to regret. One area where I made a bad choice was in choosing not to exercise most of my life. Dave, on the other hand, has exercised all his life and is healthy, strong, and in good physical shape. When I reached the point where I needed to reap the benefits of exercise, I regretted that I didn't exercise, but I did nothing about it. I finally realized that it is never too late to do the right thing, so I started working out at the gym three times a week in December 2006 and have continued to this day. Now I don't have regret; I have muscles, more energy, and better health.

If there is anything you regret, ask God to forgive you for making wrong choices and do what you can to correct it. If there is nothing you can do, then learn from it and make better choices in the future.

Love Yourself Today: Don't let the regrets of the past ruin today!

First Believe, Then Achieve

Jesus replied, "This is the work (service) that God asks of you: that you believe in the One Whom He has sent [that you cleave to, trust, rely on, and have faith in His Messenger]."   JOHN 6:29

Many dedicated believers who love God have the same question for Him: "Father, what do You want me to do? If You will just show me what to do, I will gladly do it."

For many years, I was excessive when it came to being a "do-er." All anyone had to do was point me in the direction of something that needed to be done, and I did it—and I did my best to do it right. But what frustrated and confused me was when I did something "right" and it still did not work. I had not yet learned that unless the Lord builds the house (unless He initiates and empowers an effort) that "they labor in vain who build it" (Ps. 127:1).

Today's Scripture is Jesus' answer to a group of people who wanted to know what they were supposed to do to please God. They asked Him, "What are we to do, that we may [habitually] be working the works of God?" We can sum up Jesus' response in one word: *believe.*

So many people, including myself and maybe you, too, think we are supposed to be achievers. This is true; we certainly are supposed to achieve and accomplish things. But the way we achieve is to first believe. That frees us from worry and enables us to live victorious lives. We are called "believers," not "achievers," so let's make sure we always believe first and then do what God leads us to do.

Love God Today: "Lord, I believe."

Don't Delay!

All of you must keep awake (give strict attention, be cautious and active) and watch and pray, that you may not come into temptation. The spirit is indeed willing, but the flesh is weak.   MATTHEW 26:41

The secret of Samson's strength was his long hair. God told him not to cut his hair and promised that as long as he obeyed, he would be able to do awesome things. Satan wanted to destroy Samson, so he sent temptation in the form of Delilah, who repeatedly pressured him to reveal the secret of his strength. After Samson eventually told her, she cut his hair while he was sleeping.

When Satan comes to tempt us, he is persistent, hoping to eventually wear us out. This is exactly what happened to Samson. Just as Satan knew Samson's weakness for women and used it against him, he also knows our weaknesses and tries to take advantage of them.

Let me encourage you to be aware of your weaknesses and to pray regularly for God to strengthen you in them. Don't wait until you are in deep trouble and then begin to pray; pray ahead of time. Let your new motto be: "I won't delay; I'll pray right away!"

In today's Scripture Jesus told His disciples to pray not to come into temptation, and He said the spirit is willing, but the flesh is weak. He never said temptation would not come. He said to pray that they would not give in *when* temptation comes. We will be tempted, but God will give us the ability to resist if we are faithful to pray for His strength to recognize and resist whatever attack Satan sends our way, especially when he tries to hit us in our weak spots.

———————

Love Yourself Today: When you're tempted, remember: Don't delay, pray right away!

Live in Your "Zone"

There is nothing better for a man than that he should eat and drink and make himself enjoy good in his labor. Even this, I have seen, is the gift of God.   ECCLESIASTES 2:24

Dave once turned down a nice raise and prestigious promotion at work because he had observed other people in the same position and realized that the job would be extremely stressful. He didn't want to live that way, so he declined, and I think that's one of the wisest things I've ever seen anyone do.

Some people would not have demonstrated Dave's courage and wisdom, because they would have wanted the higher paycheck and the opportunity to be viewed as "successful." But there's surprisingly little long-term satisfaction, and often a lot of pressure, in such a situation. I believe there would be much more happiness and much less stress in the world if people would take time to figure out their "sweet spot" and stay there. If you've found it, don't let it go!

When you have opportunities that will provide a promotion or increase profits for your company, but you know they will not be healthy for you, have the courage to say no.

Your perfect zone is waiting for you out there somewhere. If you aren't in it, get busy looking for it!

———————

Love Yourself Today: Are you in a position that causes you to compromise your health, your family time, or your destiny in God? As fast as you can wisely do so, set yourself free and get into a better situation.

When Love Takes Charge

*You are living the life of the Spirit, if the [Holy] Spirit of God [really]
dwells within you [directs and controls you].*   ROMANS 8:9

When love takes charge of us (which is another way of saying when
God takes charge of us), we cannot think bad things about people. We
don't even want to.

We are not really living the life of the Spirit until we allow the Holy
Spirit to control every area of our lives. He will certainly never get control of our lives until He has control of our thoughts and words.

Being led by the Spirit is central to a victorious Christian life. As
long as we think our own thoughts and speak our own words, we will
never experience victory.

God has a purpose for each of us, and we should learn what it is and
cooperate with it.

Learning God's purpose for us is easy; it is written throughout the
pages of the New Testament. God wants to use each one of us who is
His child to encourage someone else to become His child (to turn his
life over to Jesus by inviting Him to be his Savior). It does no good to
talk to people about Jesus unless we are living a Christian lifestyle to
back up our words. Thoughts have everything to do with this process.

Our lives are a reflection of our thoughts. It is impossible to have a
good life unless we have trained ourselves to have good thoughts. If we
want others to see Jesus reflected in our lives, then His mind must be
reflected in us.

We must be led by the Spirit in our thinking and let love take charge
of our minds; that's where all Spirit-led living begins.

———————————

Love Others Today: "Lord, let love take charge of me today."

Watch What You Say

And let us consider and give attentive, continuous care to watching over one another, studying how we may stir up (stimulate and incite) to love and helpful deeds and noble activities.   HEBREWS 10:24

I have written in this devotional about the importance of loving people with our words. The carnal (lower, sensual) nature points out flaws, weaknesses, and failures. The flesh likes to gossip and say things like, "Did you hear that So-and-So's husband left her for another woman because she nagged him all the time?" The flesh seems to feed on the negatives in life. But the Bible says that we are to overcome evil with good.

Walking in the Spirit (continually following the prompting or leading, guiding, and working of the Holy Spirit through our own spirit instead of being led by our emotions) requires being positive.

It is easy to find something wrong with everyone, but 1 Peter 4:8 says, "love covers a multitude of sins." Love does not expose people's faults and talk about them; it covers them. Believing the best about people and speaking words that build them up is one way of loving them.

All of us need to make a commitment to love people by saying nice things about people in the privacy of our own thoughts and with the words of our mouths. We need to build confidence in others by speaking positively *to* them and *about* them. Use your words to bless others and cover their faults and shortcomings.

Love Others Today: "Lord, help me to choose my words carefully today."

Don't "Get" . . . Receive!

Ask and you will receive, that your joy may be made full.
JOHN 16:24 NKJV

There are certain words in the Bible that I like to refer to as "power words," which simply means that they can be extremely powerful for us if we understand and incorporate them in our lives. One of those power words is *receive*. In our world, we are accustomed to working for everything. We struggle to "get," but God wants us to simply "receive" from Him.

Throughout the Bible, we read about receiving from God. Some of the scriptures that teach us to receive are John 1:12; John 1:16; Acts 1:8; Acts 8:17; Acts 10:43; 2 Corinthians 6:1; Galatians 3:2, Colossians 2:6, Hebrews 4:16. Each of these verses specifies something we are to receive from the Lord and teach us how important it is for us to receive instead of trying to "get."

To *get* is to obtain by struggle and effort, whereas to *receive* is to become a receptacle and simply take in what is being offered.

This distinction between getting and receiving helps us understand why so many Christians struggle in their walk with the Lord. They are trying to get everything from Him when they should simply be asking and receiving.

Today's Scripture is one of my favorites on the subject of receiving. It sounds so simple—and that's the point. Receiving *is* simple! Jesus came to deliver us from striving, not to invite us to struggle continuously. When we cease our efforts to "get" and learn to ask and receive, then truly our joy will be full. Once we have freely received, then we can freely give.

———————————

Love Yourself Today: Have you been striving to "get"? From now on, choose to simply ask and receive.

Who's Will Is It?

I know the power obedience has of making things easy which seem impossible.   TERESA OF AVILA

Many people think they know what they want and need in life, and sometimes they work hard to get it for themselves. This is called self-will. In Isaiah 14:12–15 we read that self-will destroyed Lucifer. In exalting himself, he said, "I will" five times. God had an answer for him: "You will be cast down to hell."

Sooner or later, God will ask us to do something contrary to our will and we will need to remember what Jesus said: "My Father, if it is possible, let this cup pass away from Me; nevertheless, not what I will (not what I desire), but as You will and desire" (Matt. 26:39).

Not getting our own way is one of the most painful things we ever go through in life. We do not like to vote against our own desires! It takes a lot of work, humility and brokenness to bring us to the place where we can say, "Well, God, I'd rather not do this, but I'm willing to do whatever You want."

The lesson here is that we must be willing to obey God and do whatever He says. We need to say, "Your will, God, be done in my life," and really mean it!

We are afraid that we will never get the things we want if we deny ourselves, but God will give us what we desire, and even better, in due time. Do not be afraid to delay gratification, and trust God to give you what you really need.

———————

Love God Today: "Lord, I want *Your* will for my life, not my own."

Don't Be Lukewarm

I know your [record of] works and what you are doing; you are
neither cold nor hot. Would that you were cold or hot! So, because
you are lukewarm and neither cold nor hot, I will spew you out of
My mouth!   REVELATION 3:15, 16

God wants us to serve Him enthusiastically and wholeheartedly. He does not appreciate halfhearted effort. Today's Scripture warns us against being lukewarm and teaches us that being neither hot nor cold is unacceptable to God. His desire is that we be red-hot, on fire, stirred up and excited about Him and His will for our lives.

Actually, God would prefer that we be cold toward Him rather than lukewarm. Why? It seems that lukewarm is better than nothing. But I believe lukewarm people are easily deceived into thinking they are doing what they should be doing when in fact they are not. They are offering sacrifices, not whole-hearted obedience. When a person is totally cold toward God, at least they know it and can be dealt with more easily than someone who is deceived.

I once taught a message entitled, "Get In, Get Out, or Get Run Over." My theory was that God is moving and we can either get on board and move with Him or remain rebellious and obstinate and get left behind. As far as I am concerned, life is not worth living at all if Jesus Christ is not the center of it.

God never does anything halfway and we should not, either. Whatever your task may be, work at it heartily (with all your heart) as something for the Lord (see Col. 3:23).

Love God Today: "Lord, please turn up the heat in my heart."

Keep Yourself Watered!

I give waters in the wilderness and rivers in the desert, to give drink to My people, My chosen.   ISAIAH 43:20

If you have plants in your home, you know they won't live unless you keep them watered. The same is true for the human body. Just as the earth is two-thirds water and one-third dry land, your body is also two-third waters. No wonder we hear so much about the benefits of drinking plenty of water each day!

On a cellular level, water both fills your cells with life-supporting fluid and bathes them in it. Everything you do depends on healthy cell function, so if you want your cells to operate at their best, you need to provide them with enough water to do their job. Without water, energy can't get from your food to your muscles and brain; waste can't get cleansed; kidneys can't function; and your immune system can't circulate. On top of that, without adequate water, your body can't cool itself.

When your body doesn't have enough water, it gets dehydrated. Serious dehydration can lead to death. But even low-grade dehydration can cause your energy level to drop, make you feel grumpy, and hinder your ability to concentrate.

We must also water our spirits with God's word. I think it is interesting that God refers to His Word as water and to Himself as "Living Water." Everything needs water: the earth, our body, our soul, and our spirit. Are you dry? Start with God's Word and spend lots of time in His Presence, then make sure that you drink plenty of water. Then you will be well watered in every area of life.

Love Yourself Today: Make sure you are well watered in every area of your life.

Here's the Verdict

Therefore, [there is] now no condemnation (no adjudging guilty of wrong) for those who are in Christ Jesus, who live [and] walk not after the dictates of the flesh, but after the dictates of the Spirit.

ROMANS 8:1

Most believers know we need to ask forgiveness right away when we sin. We also know God forgives us, but we often continue to feel guilty.

Let me state clearly: *Jesus has already paid for everything you will ever do wrong.* You do not need to add your misery to His sacrifice. When you do something wrong, if you repent *sincerely,* then in that instant, God forgives it and forgets it—completely. Claim your forgiveness, forget your sins, and go on and enjoy your life.

Guilt tormented me for many years. If I didn't feel wrong, I didn't feel right! But the good news of the Gospel is that sin no longer has any power over us. *We do not have to bear the guilt of our sins.*

Today's Scripture makes it clear that you don't have to live under condemnation. God wants to forgive your sin; to cleanse you from everything you have ever done wrong; He wants to remove the burden you carry. This is why Jesus died.

Every time you do something wrong, repent quickly and ask God to forgive you. When the devil tries to make you feel guilty, open your mouth and shout: "I am forgiven! God loves me, and I will not live under this burden of guilt!" Don't let something God has forgotten about waste your time, rob your peace, and steal your joy.

Love Yourself Today: Agree with God that you are forgiven, and extend forgiveness to yourself.

Give Until It Hurts

I have found the paradox that if I love until it hurts, then there is no hurt, but only more love.   MOTHER TERESA OF CALCUTTA

There are levels of giving; some are less painful than others. Giving away things we don't want or no longer use is good, but we should also be ready to give away things we would rather keep. Make everything you own available to God if He requires it.

If you know someone who has been through a difficult time, go shopping for that person; look for that special gift that you feel just right about. Get out of the comfort zone with your giving.

If God leads you to give away a favorite possession, then do it in obedience to Him; I can promise it will be painful. Why is it good to give until it hurts? Jesus did when He was willing to die on the cross for our sins, and I want to be like Him, don't you?

If our motive when we give is to be a blessing, even if it's hard for us, it proves God can trust us with money and things. If He knows we love Him and love others more than we love our possessions and our bank accounts, He will respond to that love with blessings for us.

However, we should avoid giving with the singular motive of getting. Blessing others should be our primary motive for giving.

Don't waste your life just making money and collecting things. Be a giver.

———————

Love Others Today: "Lord, I am willing to give even when it hurts."

Who Is Your Confidence In?

For we … glory and pride ourselves in Jesus Christ, and put
no confidence or dependence [on what we are] in the flesh and
on outward privileges and physical advantages and external
appearances.   PHILIPPIANS 3:3

Today's Scripture destroys any reason to believe we can put confidence in anything we can do or have done. It clearly tells us that our confidence cannot be in "the flesh," but instead must be "in Christ Jesus."

It is freeing to finally see that our worth and value are not based on what we do, but on who we are in Christ. God has assigned value to us by allowing Jesus to die for us. By that very act, God the Father is saying to each one of us, "You are very valuable to Me, and I will pay any price to see that you have the good life I originally intended for you."

Once we recognize who we are in Christ, then and only then can we effectively begin to pray about the things we do for Him, but He wants us to do them *in response* to what He has done for us and in us. He wants our good works to flow out of our love for Him, not out of a sense of mere duty or obligation.

Meditate on what God has done for you in Christ and the value He has placed on you by sending His Son to die for you. It will help you fall more deeply in love with Him daily and enable you to serve Him from a position of love rather than duty or obligation.

Love Yourself Today: Confess that God loves you and you are valuable. Appreciate what God has done for you, and serve Him because you love and adore Him.

Use Your Words to Heal

*There are those who speak rashly, like the piercing of a sword, but
the tongue of the wise brings healing.*   PROVERBS 12:18

Words have a tremendous impact on all our lives. I know people who
have lived lives of crippling insecurity because their parents spoke
words of judgment, criticism, and failure to them on a regular basis.
These people can be healed only by receiving God's unconditional love.
They have been wounded in their souls (their inner selves, mind, will,
and emotions), a place to which only God has total access. Jesus came
to bind up and heal the brokenhearted. He is the lover of our souls, and
through Him we can be secure and successful.

However, once people are wounded by the words of others, it takes
time to overcome the wrong image they have of themselves. That is why
it is important that we learn to use our words for blessing, healing, and
building up and not for cursing, wounding, and tearing down. Ephesians 4:29 says: "Let no foul or polluting language; nor evil word nor
unwholesome or worthless talk [ever] come out of your mouth, but only
such [speech] as is good and beneficial to the spiritual progress of others, as is fitting to the need and the occasion, that it may be a blessing
and give grace (God's favor) to those who hear it."

Generally speaking, if we believe in people, they will make a huge
effort to live up to our confidence in them. They work harder to become
what we have told them we believe they can be.

Multitudes of people need someone to believe in them. They have
been wounded by wrong words, but the right words can bring healing
into their lives. You can change someone's life today by encouraging
them to be all they can be.

Love Others Today: "Lord, let me share healing love with
others through my words."

Strength to Change

And when He comes, He will convict and convince the world...
about sin and about righteousness.   JOHN 16:8

Throughout our journey here on earth, God's Spirit works with and in us, helping us change for the better. God wants us to see truth (reality) so we can agree with Him that change is needed, not so we can punish ourselves or feel condemned.

When Jesus ascended to heaven, He sent the Holy Spirit to help us. The Holy Spirit works holiness in us. He not only shows us what needs to change, He also gives us the strength to change. His goal is to help us be what God wants us to be so we can enjoy what God wants us to enjoy. That requires an attitude that says, "Change me and make me what You want me to be."

Condemnation weakens us; it makes us feel guilty and miserable, but conviction is intended to lift us out of a fault. The Holy Spirit shows us our fault and then helps us overcome it. Before I learned the truth of this principle, I did not understand that conviction was intended to set me free. The devil was able to take the things God meant for my good and turn them into torment. Don't let that happen to you. When you feel the conviction of the Holy Spirit, thank God that He loves you enough to work with you and help you change for the better.

————————————

Love God Today: When the Holy Spirit convicts you, do you feel guilty, or do you realize that the very fact that you can feel God's conviction is good news?

One Knot at a Time

And I am convinced and sure of this very thing, that He Who began
a good work in you will continue until the day of Jesus Christ [right
up to the time of His return], developing [that good work] and
perfecting and bringing it to full completion in you.

PHILIPPIANS 1:6-7

When I speak on the healing of emotional wounds, I like to hold several different-colored shoestrings tied together in a knot. I tell the audience, "This is you when you first start the process of transformation with God. You're all knotted up. Each knot represents a different problem in your life. Untangling those knots and straightening out those problems is going to take a bit of time and effort, so don't get discouraged if it doesn't happen all at once."

If you want to receive emotional healing and come into an area of wholeness, you must realize that healing is a process. Allow the Lord to deal with you and your problems in His way and in His time. Your part is to cooperate with Him in whatever area He chooses to start dealing with you first.

In our modern, instantaneous society, we expect everything to be quick and easy. The Lord never gets in a hurry, and He never quits. Sometimes it may seem that you are not making any progress. That's because the Lord is untying your knots one at a time. The process may be hard and take time, but if you will 'stick with the program,' sooner or later you will see the victory and experience the freedom you have wanted for so long.

Love God Today: Thank you, Lord, that you are more patient than I am!

Who's in Charge?

A fool vents all his feelings, but a wise man holds them back.
PROVERBS 29:11 NKJV

We all have emotions, and we must learn to manage them. Emotions can be positive or negative. They can make us feel wonderful or awful. They can make us excited and enthusiastic or sad and depressed. They can give us courage or they can cause us to shrink in fear.

Feelings and emotions are a central part of being human, and that is fine. Unfortunately, most people live according to the way they feel. They do what they *feel* like doing, say what they *feel* like saying, buy what they *feel* like buying. And that is not fine, because human feelings are not the same as godly wisdom.

Feelings are fickle; they change frequently and without notice. Since feelings are unreliable, we must not allow them to direct our lives. You can be aware of your feelings and acknowledge their legitimacy without necessarily acting on them. God has given us wisdom, and we should walk in that, not in emotions. Wisdom includes common sense; it involves making choices now that we will be satisfied with later to the best of our knowledge. Wisdom also entails discernment, prudence, and discretion. Emotions, on the other hand, often cause us to overlook common sense and prudence.

Emotions are important, and learning to express them in appropriate ways is also important. Good emotional health is vital for a good life. But a good life also means being able to manage our emotions and not let them manage us.

Love Yourself Today: In what areas do you need to exercise greater wisdom and less emotion? Ask God to help you do this.

Eliminate Stress!

Peace I leave with you; My (own) peace I now give and bequeath to you. Do not let your hearts be troubled, neither let them be afraid. (Stop allowing yourselves to be agitated and disturbed; and do not permit yourselves to be fearful and intimidated and cowardly and unsettled.)   JOHN 14:27

According to our Scripture for today we can choose to be upset or choose not to be. Not getting upset about the things in life that don't go our way or that we cannot control is one way of eliminating stress. Why try to do something about something we can't do anything about? We should pray without delay and cast our burden and concern on God, asking Him to take care of it.

Another way to eliminate stress is to not overload your schedule. Learning to say, "I can't do that," is not a sign of weakness. Everyone has limits, and knowing what yours are, and staying within them, indicates that you are a wise person. Don't feel that you need to be able to do what someone else does.

Doing things that you enjoy will help relieve stress, so be sure you include them in your to-do list. Laugh often; it is good for the soul as well as the body. If you really want to eliminate stress and enjoy a more peaceful life, I suggest that you start jotting down when you get upset and what it was that upset you. Such a list is a good place to begin; it makes you aware of how often you're letting yourself get upset and what the things are that you're permitting to steal your peace. After you see the problem, then start making healthy lifestyle changes that will give you the end result you desire.

Love Yourself Today: Eliminate at least one thing from your life today that is causing stress, and continue the process until you are enjoying peace.

Repaying Kindness for Evil

Then he said: "I am Joseph your brother, whom you sold into Egypt.
But now, do not be grieved or angry with yourselves because you
sold me here; for God sent me before you to preserve life."

GENESIS 45:4, 5 NKJV

A lot of cruel, unfair things happened to Joseph and he had many opportunities to become bitter. Do you ever have opportunities for bitterness? It will not do you one bit of good. You may feel like your life has been stolen by people who have mistreated you, and now you're bitter! If you stay bitter, what people did to you will steal your future.

God promoted Joseph, and he ended up in charge of all the food supply in Egypt. That is a good place to be when there's a famine in the land! The brothers had to go to Joseph, and when they saw him, they recognized him and fell down before him. They thought he was going to kill them.

They knew that if Joseph mistreated them, they deserved it. But Joseph said to them, Fear not; for am I in the place of God? [Vengeance is His, not mine.] You thought evil against me, but God meant it for good. . . . Now therefore, do not be afraid. I will provide for and support you. And he comforted them and spoke to their hearts [kindly]."

What an amazing example for us to follow. Don't waste your life being bitter about something in the past, but instead trust God to give you double blessings for your former trouble.

Loving Others Today: Make a decision to love and show mercy to people who have mistreated you.

Thoughts Minister Death or Life

For to be carnally minded is death, but to be spiritually minded is life and peace.   ROMANS 8:6 NKJV

Our thoughts are very powerful and they make a huge difference in the quality of our life. Because this is true, we should "think about what we are thinking about," and make sure we are helping ourselves and others, not bringing harm.

Today's Scripture tells us that the mind of the flesh is death, but the mind of the Spirit is life. Negative, ugly thoughts minister death to us and also to others, whereas positive, loving thoughts minister life.

Here is an example of how much our thoughts affect the people around us. I was shopping with my younger daughter one day when she was a teenager. On that particular day, her hair was very messy and her face was broken out. She had on too much makeup, and it did not look good.

Every time I looked at her I thought, *You really don't look very good today.* After some time went by, I noticed she was looking depressed, and I asked her what was wrong.

"I feel really ugly today," she replied.

When she said that, God whispered in my heart, "See what your thoughts have done to her?"

I was immediately convicted that my thoughts were very displeasing to the Lord, and they brought pain to my daughter when what she needed was acceptance and encouragement.

Often, we think things about people that we would never say to them, but even our thoughts can affect others. Remember that God knows all our thoughts, so let's think on things that will please Him.

Love Others Today: "Lord, help me to minister life to others and to myself with my thoughts."

Are You Empty?

Then he said, Go around and borrow vessels from all your
neighbors, empty vessels, and not a few.   2 KINGS 4:3

Today's Scripture mentions "empty vessels." All of us are empty vessels; we don't have anything within ourselves that has any value, except the power of God that can flow out of us. What do we have to offer God? Nothing. God does not need us; He can do His work without us. Being used by God is a great privilege and an honor, not a right.

Certainly, we have value, but only the value the Lord assigns to us because of the blood of His Son, Jesus Christ. We have nothing in and of ourselves. In Christ, we exist and have everything. But in our flesh, there is nothing of any value.

Emptying ourselves is not an easy task, and it does not happen quickly. I spent many years wondering if I would ever manifest humility instead of pride, trusting in the strength of God instead of my own. If you feel the same way, let me encourage you that as long as you don't give up, you are making progress.

If we press on and are sincere about our spiritual maturity, we will eventually be like the vessels in today's Scripture—empty of ourselves and ready to be used by God to fulfill His great purposes for our lives.

———————

Love God Today: "Lord, empty me of myself and fill me with everything that comes from You."

Knowing God

And this is eternal life: to know You, the only true and real God, and
[likewise] to know Him, Jesus [as the] Christ, Whom You have sent.

JOHN 17:3

Today's Scripture emphasizes the importance of knowing God. There is a big difference between knowing *about* God and really *knowing* God. Knowing God is a lifelong pursuit, something that happens throughout our lives, not over the course of a few days or weeks. Attaining the true knowledge of God doesn't come through reasoning or logic or reading books. It must be God-given, and it comes through revelation. It comes as we seek God and gain experience with Him through trusting His promises.

If we have a true knowledge of God, we are not disturbed by things like scientific theories that seek to disprove His existence. We have come to a perfect rest in the fact that God is, and knowing that, we know that nothing else matters. People often want to explain God, but if we truly know Him, then the first thing we give up is trying to understand or explain Him.

Knowing God goes beyond what we think, see, or feel. It is an inner knowledge of God that cannot be taken from us. When we have this inner knowledge, nothing outward can sway us from our belief in God. We no longer need evidence to protect our faith. I encourage you to pray daily for a spirit of wisdom and revelation (see Eph. 1:17). Celebrate the fact that you are an eternal being and that you are coming to know Him better with every passing day.

Love God Today: Hunger for the type of knowledge that can only come from God Himself.

He Is Your Strength

God is my Strong Fortress.   2 SAMUEL 22:33

God wants to give you strength for every situation you face. He doesn't only want to *give* you strength, though; He wants to *be* your strength.

Many men and women of the Bible knew God as their strength, and they are great examples to encourage us to trust in His strength, too. David wrote in Psalm 18:29 that by his God he could run through a troop and leap over a wall. In 1 Kings 19:4–8, an angel of God ministered to Elijah, who was tired and depressed, and Elijah went forty days and nights in the strength he received from that one visit.

How do we receive strength from God? We receive by faith, by believing His promise to strengthen us. That faith will quicken your body, as well as your spirit and your soul. At our conferences, the Holy Spirit has strengthened with fresh determination people who felt they could not go on. His healing power came as we waited in His presence and received it from Him.

By faith you can receive strength to stay in a difficult marriage, raise a difficult child, or stick with a difficult job. You can receive strength to do great things. Don't worry about your natural weaknesses, but remember that Christ's strength is made perfect and shows itself most effective in our weakness (2 Cor. 12:9).

Have you been trying to push through difficulties on your own? If so, make a change right now. Start getting strength from deep within you, where the Holy Spirit dwells.

Love God Today: "Lord, I do not have much strength on my own. I receive the strength you want to give me through Your Holy Spirit. I believe I can do whatever I need to do in life through Jesus Christ."

Pressure to Be Perfect

The Lord will perfect that which concerns me; Your mercy and lovingkindness, O Lord, endure forever ...   PSALM 138:8

The pressure to be perfect will steal your joy! You won't have any time for joy. You won't have any time to just rest in God and enjoy life. You won't even have time to enjoy God. For many years, I was so busy trying to serve God perfectly and worrying about my imperfections that I failed to enjoy Him. When this happens, Christianity becomes a form of labor.

Sometimes we use our "faith" to believe God for things, healing, or success, but we forget to believe Him to perfect us. We take on that job ourselves. Every day, we get up with a list of things we're not going to do, and we forget to get God involved, so we fail.

While Jesus is interceding for us at the Father's right hand, He must be saying, "They still don't have the message! They still don't understand that, apart from Me, they can do nothing!"

Had there been any hope of living a perfect life in our own strength, I don't think Jesus would have taken on the job of being our continual Intercessor. We need Him to do this because there is a breach between God and us unless we come to Him *through Christ*."

As long as we are in our earthly bodies, we will make mistakes. But Jesus, our Intercessor, is always there to make us acceptable to God. He is our righteousness, not our own perfection. So do your best and keep improving, but don't forget to enjoy God in the process.

Love Yourself Today: I encourage you to release yourself from the burden of perfectionism. Lighten up, relax, and enjoy life today—with all its imperfections.

The Power to Choose

I call heaven and earth to witness this day against you that I have
set before you life and death, the blessings and the curses; therefore
choose life, that you and your descendants may live.

DEUTERONOMY 30:19

You and I have the God-given privilege of making choices every day. Over the course of time, the choices we make determine the quality, direction, and results of our lives.

All of us have to make choices on a regular basis. They may be significant choices, such as what career to pursue or whom to marry, or they may be seemingly minor decisions such as what to wear to work and what to eat for lunch. Any time we have a choice, we have to make a decision. Sometimes we can choose between good and bad; other times we have to choose between a good option and a better option. Whatever the case, we need the skills to make good choices because our choices chart the courses of our lives.

Our verse for today is one of the most powerful scriptures in the Word. In it, God tells us what our options are and then He tells us which to choose. He says, basically, "These are your choices: life and blessings or death and curses," and then He clearly instructs us to choose life. This is like taking a test in school and having the teacher write the answer on the blackboard! God wants to make it easy for us to experience the life and blessings He wants to give us, but we must choose them.

Love Yourself Today: Think about some of the choices and decisions you are facing right now. How can you choose life in these situations?

Find a Strategy for Doing Good

The plans of the diligent lead surely to plenty.
PROVERBS 21:5 NKJV

Just imagine how different the world would be if everyone who claims to know Christ would do one kind thing—or two kind things—for someone every day. The results would be astonishing.

You might be tempted to ask, "That will never happen, so why even try?" Don't let yourself be defeated through negative thinking before you even begin. I have already decided that I am going to do my part and pray for other people to do theirs. I will also talk to other people and encourage them to do as much as they possibly can for others.

I have three friends who flow in this amazing lifestyle, and when we get together, we often use our time to talk creative ideas for fresh ways to be a blessing. I believe conversations like this are very pleasing to God. I would like to challenge you to take a lead role in loving others. Enlist the people you know and invite them to plan practical ways to meet needs.

The idea of encouraging others to be aggressive in doing good works is not a new one. The writer of Hebrews talked about it: "And let us consider and give attentive, continuous care to watching over one another, studying how we may stir up (stimulate and incite) to love and helpful deeds and noble activities" (Heb. 10:24).

Share what you are learning in this devotional with them and find someone who needs help; then make a group effort to help that person.

Love Others Today: Who do you know that you could talk to and work with to find ways to bless others? You can start with your own family and branch out from there.

People Are Watching

Live such good lives among the pagans that, though they may accuse
you of doing wrong, they may see your good deeds and glorify God
on the day he visits us.   1 PETER 2:12 NIV

I believe the world is watching Christians and that what they see us do
is very important. In today's Scripture, the apostle Peter said that even
if unbelievers were inclined to slander believers, they would eventually
come to glorify God if they saw their good works and loving deeds.

If your neighbors know you go to church every Sunday, I can assure
you that they also watch your behavior and may form opinions about
your church or Christians in general based on your words and actions.
When I was growing up, our neighbors dutifully went to church, but
they also did lots of things they should not have done. I recall my father
often saying, "They are no better than I am; they get drunk, use bad
language, tell dirty jokes, and have bad tempers, so they are just a
bunch of hypocrites."

I certainly realize that we as Christians don't behave perfectly and
that people who want an excuse to not believe in Jesus will always
watch us and criticize us, but we should do our best to not give them a
reason to judge us.

The apostle Paul instructed Timothy to charge people "to do good,
to be rich in good works, to be liberal and generous of heart, ready to
share [with others]" (1 Tim. 6:18). Do whatever you need to do in order
to make sure you love, which is what is most important to God.

————————————

Love Others Today: Live in such a way that your love and
good deeds make it impossible for people to believe anything
negative about you.

Seek Peace Every Day

Depart from evil and do good; seek, inquire for, and crave peace and pursue (go after it).   PSALM 34:14

Is peace a priority in your life or do you feel frustrated and stressed out most of the time? If so, you may need to cut a few things out of your life so you can do as today's Scripture says and pursue peace.

But I want to do all those things, you may think.

Then the result will be frustration and stress. As I said earlier in this devotional, you are the one who makes your schedule. You are the only one who can change it.

If you want peace in your life, don't exceed your limitations. Start looking at your life, figure out which things in it are not bearing any fruit and start pruning them, just as you would prune dead branches off a tree.

It is so important not to over-commit yourself.

"But my children have to go to baseball practice on Monday night and hockey practice on Wednesday night."

No, your children don't have to do everything they want to do. It's good for them to be involved in some activities, but you can't let their schedule control your entire family.

We need to follow God's leading as to where we—and our children— use our energy. We must learn to say yes when God says yes and no when He says no. Then we will be able to accomplish what He gives us to do and enjoy a peaceful life.

Love Yourself Today: Seek God for the ways He would have you spend your time and the things He would have you do— or not do. Then make the necessary changes.

God Knows

May the God of your hope so fill you with all joy and peace in
believing... that by the power of the Holy Spirit you may abound
and be overflowing (bubbling over) with hope.   ROMANS 15:13

You cannot have true love, joy, hope, or peace without believing in God and His promises. According to today's Scripture, joy and peace are found in believing. So when you lose your peace, check your believing.

Let your timing be in God's hands (see Ps. 31:15). You'll lose your peace if you try to make things happen out of God's timing. Avoid reasoning, and stop trying to figure out what God is doing in your life and trust Him. Stop thinking so much and start simply believing.

Believe God loves you. Believe God has a great plan for your life. Believe God always has your best interest in mind, and that He is working all things together for your good (see Rom. 8:28). You might as well just get in the flow and go with God. Getting frustrated is not going to make God change His mind.

I have been through a lot of difficult things and have come to know through experience that God is faithful and worrying does no good. We don't have to understand everything that occurs in our lives, because God does understand them and He is in control. You can choose to believe in God and His promises, or to continue in worry and reasoning. But if you choose to believe, your joy and peace will be abundant.

Love God Today: "Lord, I believe that you know all things and you are in control, so help me be comfortable, 'not knowing.'"

He Loves You

In this is love: not that we loved God, but that He loved us and sent His Son to be the propitiation (the atoning sacrifice) for our sins. Beloved, if God loves us so [very much], we also ought to love one another.   1 JOHN 4:10, 11

Have you ever gone through a time in your life when you thought something would make you happy, and then when you got it, it didn't make you happy at all? Maybe you were thrilled for a little while, but you soon realized it wouldn't bring deep, lasting happiness to your life? Lots of people think they will be happy if they get a raise, a new house, a new car. They are focused on what they can get, not what they can give. These pursuits never lead to happiness!

The right way to happiness lies in caring for others and giving to them, not in seeing how much we can accumulate for ourselves. I have learned this by personal experience. In fact, becoming a giver has brought me levels of happiness I never knew were possible. Giving is a great joy!

When we love, we must give; giving is the very nature of love. God is love, and He is the ultimate Giver.

When we have God's love in us, we can give it away. We can choose to love others lavishly and unconditionally, as He has loved us. The love of God is the most wonderful gift we are given. It flows to us, and then it should flow through us to others.

Love God Today: "Lord, help me to remember that you give me so much love that there's plenty for me to share!"

The Power of Preparation

Therefore gird up the loins of your mind, be sober, and rest your hope fully upon the grace that is to be brought to you at the revelation of Jesus Christ.   1 PETER 1:13 NKJV

Today's Scripture says we are to "gird up the loins" of our minds, which means to prepare mentally for things. This is a way to love and take care of yourself because it can help you avoid stress and disappointment. We need to have a mental preparation for things.

Colossians 3:2 says: "Set your minds and keep them set." The best time to do that is to set our minds in the morning. Before we get out of bed, we can say, "Okay, Lord, I want to operate in the fruit of the Spirit today. God, I already know that probably everything is not going to go my way today. I may need to deal with something I didn't plan for. Somebody's going to ask me to do something I don't want to do, and yet it will be someone for whom I feel I need to do it! I may get a phone call that will interrupt my whole day. Someone is going to have a problem I need to deal with. Lord, I'm going to set my mind to be patient today no matter what happens. I hope my day is perfect, Lord, but if it isn't I want my behavior to please you."

Set your mind. Gird up the loins of your mind. Tell yourself, "Whatever happens today, I can handle it because God loves me and He is on my side!"

If you set your mind, you're going to have a lot of victories.

Love Yourself Today: Express love to yourself today by being mentally prepared for anything that may come your way.

Complete Confidence

The man who through faith is just and upright shall live and shall live by faith.   ROMANS 1:17

Today's Scripture teaches us that God's people shall live by faith. This means that, as believers, we are to live our whole lives in an attitude of faith. When I speak about faith, I often use the word *confidence,* because faith really is an attitude of complete confidence in God.

I believe God wants us to be confident about who we are and what we can do, and to live with a confident attitude in every area of our lives. We are to be confident in the gifts God has given us and to exercise them boldly. We need to be confident when we pray, confident in our relationships, confident when we make decisions, and confident as we carry out all our various responsibilities.

We need to take a bold stance and say: "I live with complete confidence toward God. I believe I hear His voice. I believe I make good decisions. I believe my prayers are powerful; I believe God gives me favor with people everywhere I go."

This kind of boldness doesn't mean we never make mistakes. It simply means we are doing our best to live in the confident faith that God asks us to have. Years ago, as I tried to get established in confident living, I worried about "missing" God. He spoke to me and said, "Joyce, don't worry about it. If you miss me, I'll find you." This reassurance helped me gain the confidence with which I live today, and I pray it encourages you, too.

Love Yourself Today: Live boldly and confidently, and trust God to let you know if you're going in a wrong direction. If you are, He will get you back on the right track.

Be Kind to Those Who Aren't Kind to You

And be kind to one another...   EPHESIANS 4:32 NKJV

Christmas is the season of good cheer, but it often becomes a season of stress...so much shopping, wrapping, cooking, baking, and visiting. Before you know it, people are losing patience, snapping at one another. It's easy to become unkind.

I'll never forget something my daughter told me a long time ago. She said that her goal was to learn to love or to treat with kindness, goodness, and mercy every single person she encountered who was unkind or ugly to her. She said, "That's my goal. I want to submit to God in my emotions and the way that I handle myself so that when I'm out in public and someone mistreats me, I respond with kindness."

She said, "One of the things that God has shown me that really helps is when someone is grouchy toward me, I can get angry and frustrated or I can think: *I don't know what this person is going through. Maybe right now her back hurts terribly. Maybe this grumpy man is carrying a financial burden that feels too heavy for him. Maybe that woman's husband has just been told he's losing his job at the end of the week.*"

We don't know what's going on in people's lives.

Kindness will cause you to slow down and give people some space and some grace. Life was not meant to be the way it is today. We were not meant to live at the fast pace at which we live, with thousands of things coming at us at once.

I think we've lost sight of some important things in life and that we need to put kindness back on our priority lists!

Love Others Today: "Help me, Lord, to be especially kind to people who are not kind to me."

A More Excellent Way

And when Jesus went out He saw a great multitude; and He was
moved with compassion for them, and healed their sick.

MATTHEW 14:14 NKJV

Many of us pray that God will move powerfully through us to help others, and God wants us to pray this way. He has made available to us special endowments of supernatural energy, which the Bible calls spiritual gifts, to use for that very purpose. But I believe our first priority should be developing the fruit of the Spirit: love, joy, peace, patience, kindness, goodness, faithfulness, gentleness, and self-control.

The gifts of the Spirit and the fruit of the Spirit work together.

One spiritual gift is the gift of healings. In today's Scripture, we see first in Jesus the fruit of the Spirit, love in the form of compassion, before we see Him move in a gift of the Spirit, healings. First we see the fruit; then we see the gift.

Jesus said, "the tree is known and recognized and judged by its fruit." As believers, we are known by our fruit, not by our gifts (see Matt. 7:15–20). We are known to be Jesus' followers by our love for one another (see John 13:35). According to 2 Corinthians 5:20 we are God's ambassadors, and He is making His appeal to all mankind through us as believers in Jesus Christ. Let's make sure we show them love.

Love Others Today: "Lord, help me to be known more because of my love than because of my gifts."

Don't Get Trapped

*...he continued to send for Paul and was in his company and
conversed with him often. But when two years had gone by, Felix left
Paul still a prisoner in chains.*

ACTS 24:26, 27

God has so many good things for you to do, but the enemy does not
want you to do them, and one way he will try to stop you is to get you
entangled in other people's problems. I call this a "Felix trap." Let me
explain.

Felix was a man who wasted a lot of Paul's time. He seemed to be
interested in what Paul was saying; he appeared to want to learn from
Paul. But underneath, he was greedy and wanted money.

There are pretenders who come into our lives and say they want
help, but they never seem to make any progress. I have seen this pattern
more times than I can count! The enemy sends such people to drain us
of everything we have and to wear us out, and they have no intention of
changing. They want to talk about their afflictions, but they don't want
to get over them. After they wear one person out, they will start all over
again with somebody else. But they really don't want help.

Let me encourage you to ask God to give you discernment so that
you will not innocently allow yourself to get involved in other people's
messes without really helping them. Pray that He will help you know
how to handle those relationships and increase your spiritual sensitiv-
ity so that when the enemy sends someone to drain you dry, you do not
merely waste your time.

Love Yourself Today: Be discerning and pour yourself out to
those God truly sends you to help.

Change Your Focus

And this I pray: that your love may abound yet more and more and extend to its fullest development in knowledge and all keen insight, so that you may surely learn to sense what is vital, and approve and prize what is excellent and of real value.   PHILIPPIANS 1:9, 10

Do you need to readjust your priorities or change your focus? In today's Scripture, Paul prayed that the church at Philippi would abound in love and that their love would display itself in a greater way. He prayed that they would learn to choose what was excellent and of real value. In 1 Corinthians 12:31, he wrote that love is the more excellent way.

Paul was praying that these believers would focus on love. We cannot have powerful, victorious lives unless we love people.

Are you willing and ready to become a student of the love walk? If so, you need to know that it requires education and commitment.

We must have our minds renewed to know what love really is. It is not a feeling we have; it is a decision we make—a decision to treat people the way Jesus would treat them. When we make a true commitment to walk in love, it usually causes a shift in our lifestyle. Many of our ways—our thoughts, our conversation, and our habits—have to change.

Love is tangible; it is not just an emotional feeling, or something that cannot be seen or touched. It is evident to everyone who comes in contact with it. A love walk does not come easily or without personal sacrifice. You may even have to sacrifice some self-focus and begin to focus more on others. But that's a sacrifice well worth making!

Love Others Today: "Lord, change my focus in every area of my life where it needs to move away from me and onto others."

When You Celebrate, Don't Forget Others

As the days on which the Jews got rest from their enemies, and as
the month which was turned for them from sorrow to gladness and
from mourning into a holiday—that they should make them days
of feasting and gladness, days of sending choice portions to one
another and gifts to the poor.   ESTHER 9:22

Esther, the young Jewish maiden who eventually became a queen, commanded that gifts be sent to the poor when she and her countrymen celebrated their freedom (Esther 9:22). Part of our celebrating the good things God has done for us should be to remember to reach out to those who are still in need. A friend of mine is on a church committee that reaches out to homeless shelters at Christmas. The church gets a list of all the children living at a particular shelter, complete with the children's ages and clothing sizes. Church members who are able to do so choose a child's name and purchase a Christmas gift for him or her. In December, they hold a Christmas party at the shelter, with lots of food, Christmas music, stories about Jesus' birth and His love for each child, and, of course, all the children receive their gifts.

After the party, many church members have said that when they return home after the party, they're more grateful for their own homes and blessings than they were before the party.

Seeing and experiencing the needs of others firsthand brings us a fresh awareness of how blessed we are. People tend to be more generous at Christmastime, but we need to realize that the poor and marginalized are needy all the time. We should help them all year long and be extra generous during the holidays.

Love Others Today: In the midst of your holiday celebrations, what can you do to make someone else's holidays happier?

An Overcoming Attitude in an Imperfect World

In the world you will have tribulation; but be of good cheer, I have
overcome the world.   JOHN 16:33 NKJV

I'm sure you've noticed that the world is not perfect. You don't have to live long to figure that out, but something within us as human beings still seems to want to experience perfection in our lives. We want the perfect family celebration, the perfect marriage, the perfect friends, the perfect job, the perfect neighborhood, the perfect salary, the perfect vacation, and the perfect church. Or at least we want what we think would be perfect. But the truth is: perfection is a completely unrealistic expectation. It simply doesn't exist on earth. As long as we live, we will deal with imperfection. We can be miserable about that, or we can be gracious toward ourselves, others, and our circumstances and respond with faith and flexibility.

The enemy often uses unrealistic expectations concerning our circumstances as a tool to bring discouragement and despair into our lives. For example, he knows that if he can get us to focus on the imperfections in our spouse, our marriage will be filled with frustration and disappointment instead of peace and joy.

I urge you to expect good things to happen in your life. But I also urge you to be realistic and realize that we all have to deal with difficult things. Our attitudes will make the difference between whether we live with continual frustration and disappointment or whether we can accept imperfections and enjoy life in spite of them.

———————————

Love Yourself Today: Be determined to never again allow yourself to be discouraged or disappointed by the normal imperfections of life.

See It, Believe It

Where there is no vision [no redemptive revelation of God], the
people perish; but he who keeps the law [of God, which includes that
of man]—blessed (happy, fortunate, and enviable) is he.

PROVERBS 29:18

God has satisfaction, fullness, and completeness in mind for us. I never felt satisfied or complete in my life until I was doing what God had ordained for me to do. Fullness only comes through being in the center of God's will.

We all need and want to believe that the future will be better than the past for us. If we can't believe that, we will be miserable; in fact, in a sense we will perish if we are without hope and not feeling blessed. Today's Scripture encourages us to have vision.

A vision is something we see in our minds, "a mental sight." It may be something God plants in us supernaturally or something we see on purpose. It involves the hopes and dreams we have for the future. And one of the best things about it is that we simply have to believe in it.

Some people are afraid to believe. They think believing will set them up for disappointment. They need to realize that they will be perpetually disappointed if they *don't* believe. I feel that if I believe for a lot and even get half of it, I am better off than I would be to believe for nothing and get all of it.

I challenge you today to start believing for good things in your life. Believe you can do whatever you need to do through Christ. Dream big dreams and believe they can come true—because nothing is impossible with God!

Love Yourself Today: "Lord, plant in my heart Your dreams and visions for my life."

Thoughts, Attitudes, and Relationships

*[Let your] love be sincere (a real thing); hate what is evil [loathe
all ungodliness, turn in horror from wickedness], but hold fast to
that which is good. Love one another with brotherly affection [as
members of one family], giving precedence and showing honor to one
another.*   ROMANS 12:9, 10

We make a mistake when we think that our thoughts don't affect
people. We can often feel the thoughts of others, and they can feel our
thoughts. If we allow our thoughts about a person to be negative, our
attitude toward that individual will also be negative and a relationship with that person will ultimately be negative. If we want to love
people, we must decide to think good thoughts about them.

God's Word encourages us in today's Scripture to love others with
brotherly affection. This is what Jesus did. I cannot imagine Jesus being
nice to someone while thinking bad thoughts about him. We shouldn't
do that, either. Our love must be sincere, and a right attitude begins
with right thinking.

When I notice my attitude going in a wrong direction, I always find
the problem began with wrong thinking. I have learned that in order
to avoid thinking negatively, I must keep my thoughts and attitudes
renewed daily (see Eph. 4:23).

If you have not been working with the Holy Spirit to break old
thought patterns and form new ones, it's time to get started. Think
good thoughts about people on purpose, and as your attitude starts to
change, watch your relationships start to improve.

Love Others Today: "Lord, help me to have the right
thoughts and attitudes toward people so I will have the right
relationships with them."

Right Thinking

Casting down imaginations, and every high thing that exalteth itself against the knowledge of God, and bringing into captivity every thought to the obedience of Christ.   2 CORINTHIANS 10:4–5

Many people have been controlled by wrong thinking for their entire lives. They think all their problems are caused by the devil, other people, the way they were raised, or something else. But the truth is that in many cases the problem is simply a lack of knowledge; people simply don't know how to be led by the Spirit in their thinking.

Thinking right thoughts will often resemble warfare. The mind is the battlefield on which Satan tries to defeat us. Second Corinthians 10:4–5 teaches us to "cast down" wrong thoughts; once wrong thoughts present themselves to us, we are to refuse to receive them or dwell on them.

The real key to victory is not only to cast down wrong thoughts, but to replace them with right ones. It is virtually impossible to think two things at the same time. When a new thought comes in, the old one must leave. Go ahead; try it!

We get rid of the darkness by turning on the light, and we rid ourselves of wrong thoughts by deliberately turning our attention to the right thoughts.

 This is the only road to true happiness.

Love God Today: "Lord, help me to cast down wrong thoughts and replace them with right ones."

Look How Far You've Come!

The Lord is my Strength and my Song, and He has become my
Salvation.   EXODUS 15:2

It is easy for us to get caught up in looking at how far we have to go in reaching our goals instead of celebrating how far we've come. Think about it. How far have you come since you became a Christian? How much have you changed? How much happier are you? Are you more peaceful? Do you have hope? There is always plenty to celebrate if we look for it.

Biblical men and women God used mightily made a habit of celebrating what God had done. They did not take His goodness for granted, but they openly showed appreciation for what He did.

Have you ever had a time when you felt that your back was against the wall? You had a big problem and no solution, and then suddenly God did something amazing? Most of us can think of a time like that. When Moses led the Israelites out of Egypt, the Red Sea was in front of them and the Egyptian army was behind them. They had no place to go; they were trapped! God had promised their deliverance, and He actually parted the Red Sea and the Israelites walked across on dry ground, but as the Egyptian army followed, the sea closed up over them and they drowned.

When the Israelites reached the other side, the first thing they did was celebrate. They sang a song that came from their hearts (Exodus 15:1–19). After the song, they danced and sang some more. The entire song talked of what God had done, how great He was, how He had redeemed them and dealt with their enemies. We will probably experience more victory in life if we take time to celebrate the ones we have already had.

Love Yourself Today: Be grateful for what you have! God is good.

Love Out Loud

...you shall love the Lord your God with all your heart and with all your soul and with all your mind (intellect). This is the great (most important, principal) and first commandment. And a second is like it; you shall love your neighbor as (you do) yourself.

MATTHEW 22:37–39

Loving God, yourself, and other people should be our focus in life. We should be "love-focused" individuals. Receive God's amazing, unconditional love, then you can love yourself and live to give the love away that God has given to you. It is God's number one priority, and it should be ours also.

Today is the last day of the year and one in which we often look back and look forward. Take time to survey what your life has been like compared to what you want it to be, and work with God to make whatever changes need to be made. I urge you to end this year with a commitment to abide in love, for when we abide in love we abide in God. Jesus said, "I give you a new commandment that you should love one another, just as I have loved you, so you too should love one another. By this shall all (men) know that you are My disciples, if you love one another."

Every one chooses to live for something! What will your choice be? I implore you not to live for yourself, but to choose to live striving to obey the the "new Commandment" that Jesus gave. Now faith, hope, and love abide, but the greatest of these is love (see 1 Cor. 13:13).

Today and Every Day . . . Love God, Love Yourself, and Love Others. And don't forget to love out loud!

About the Author

JOYCE MEYER is one of the world's leading practical Bible teachers. A #1 *New York Times* bestselling author, she has written nearly ninety inspirational books, including *Living Beyond Your feelings, Power Thoughts,* the entire Battlefield of the Mind family of books, and two novels, *The Penny* and *Any Minute*, as well as many others. She has also released thousands of audio teachings, as well as a complete video library. Joyce's *Enjoying Everyday Life*® radio and television programs are broadcast around the world, and she travels extensively conducting conferences. Joyce and her husband, Dave, are the parents of four grown children and make their home in St. Louis, Missouri.

Joyce Meyer Ministries
U.S. & Foreign Office Addresses

Joyce Meyer Ministries
P.O. Box 655
Fenton, MO 63026
USA
(636) 349-0303
www.joycemeyer.org

Joyce Meyer Ministries—Canada
P.O. Box 7700
Vancouver, BC V6B 4E2
Canada
(800) 868-1002

Joyce Meyer Ministries—Australia
Locked Bag 77
Mansfield Delivery Centre
Queensland 4122
Australia
(07) 3349 1200

Joyce Meyer Ministries—England
P.O. Box 1549
Windsor SL4 1GT
United Kingdom
01753 831102

Joyce Meyer Ministries—South Africa
P.O. Box 5
Cape Town 8000
South Africa
(27) 21-701-1056

Other Books by Joyce Meyer

New Day, New You Devotional
I Dare You
The Penny
The Power of Simple Prayer
The Everyday Life Bible
The Confident Woman
Look Great, Feel Great
*Battlefield of the Mind**
Battlefield of the Mind Devotional
Battlefield of the Mind for Teens
Battlefield of the Mind for Kids
Approval Addiction
Ending Your Day Right
21 Ways to Finding Peace and Happiness
The Secret Power of Speaking God's Word
Seven Things That Steal Your Joy
Starting Your Day Right
Beauty for Ashes (revised edition)
*How to Hear from God**
Knowing God Intimately
The Power of Forgiveness
The Power of Determination
The Power of Being Positive
The Secrets of Spiritual Power
The Battle Belongs to the Lord
The Secrets to Exceptional Living
Eight Ways to Keep the Devil Under Your Feet
Teenagers Are People Too!
Filled with the Spirit

*Study Guide available for this title

Joyce Meyer Spanish Language Titles

Las Siete Cosas Que Te Roban el Gozo
(Seven Things That Steal Your Joy)
Empezando Tu Dia Bien (Starting Your Day Right)
La Revolución de Amor (Love Revolution)
Come la Galleta . . . Compra los Zapatos
(Eat the Cookie . . . Buy the Shoes)
Pensamientos de Poder (Power Thoughts)

By Dave Meyer

Life Lines